# TRAUMATIC RUPTURES

For much of its history, psychoanalysis has been strangely silent about sudden ruptures in the analytic relationship and their immediate and far-reaching effects for those involved. Such issues of betrayal and abandonment—the death of an analyst, a patient's suicide, an ethical violation—disrupt the stability and cohesion of the analytic framework and leave indelible marks on both individuals and institutions alike.

In *Traumatic Ruptures*, an international range of contributors present first-person, highly personal and sometimes painful accounts of their experiences and the occasionally difficult yet redeeming lessons they have taken from them. Presented in four parts, the book explores multiple meanings and consequences of the break in the analytic relationship. Part I, Ruptured Subjectivity: Lost and Found, presents accounts of clinical encounters with death. Part II, Rupture: The Clinical Process, addresses the sudden loss of an analyst, the trauma of patient suicide, and the issue of countertransference when working with patients who have suffered the unexpected loss of their first analyst. Part III, The Long Shadow of Rupture, examines the effects of ethical violations in the short and long term. Finally, Part IV, Ruptures' Impact on Organizations, looks at the wider impact of ethical and sexual boundary violations in the context of an organization and the effect of trauma on a psychoanalytic institute. By giving voice to issues that are usually silenced, the authors here open the door to understanding the complex nature of traumatic rupture within the analytic field.

This intimate exploration of psychoanalytic treatments and communities is ideal for psychoanalysts, psychologists, clinical social workers, psychiatrists, and family therapists. It is an important text for clinicians working with individuals who have experienced traumatic ruptures and for members of organizations dealing with their effects.

**Robin A. Deutsch** is Member and Faculty of the San Francisco Center for Psychoanalysis, where she currently serves as President of the Center. She maintains a private practice of psychoanalysis, psychotherapy, and consultation in Oakland, California, and is particularly interested in the development of analytic identity, therapist subjectivity, and the effects of the sudden loss of an analyst.

Relational Perspectives Book Series
Lewis Aron & Adrienne Harris
*Series Co-Editors*

Steven Kuchuck & Eyal Rozmarin
Associate Editors

The Relational Perspectives Book Series (RPBS) publishes books that grow out of or contribute to the relational tradition in contemporary psychoanalysis. The term *relational psychoanalysis* was first used by Greenberg and Mitchell (1983) to bridge the traditions of interpersonal relations, as developed within interpersonal psychoanalysis and object relations, as developed within contemporary British theory. But, under the seminal work of the late Stephen Mitchell, the term *relational psychoanalysis* grew and began to accrue to itself many other influences and developments. Various tributaries—interpersonal psychoanalysis, object relations theory, self-psychology, empirical infancy research, and elements of contemporary Freudian and Kleinian thought—flow into this tradition, which understands relational configurations between self and others, both real and fantasied, as the primary subject of psychoanalytic investigation.

We refer to the relational tradition, rather than to a relational school, to highlight that we are identifying a trend, a tendency within contemporary psychoanalysis, not a more formally organized or coherent school or system of beliefs. Our use of the term *relational* signifies a dimension of theory and practice that has become salient across the wide spectrum of contemporary psychoanalysis. Now under the editorial supervision of Lewis Aron and Adrienne Harris, with the assistance of Associate Editors Steven Kuchuck and Eyal Rozmarin, the Relational Perspectives Book Series originated in 1990 under the editorial eye of the late Stephen A. Mitchell. Mitchell was the most prolific and influential of the originators of the relational tradition. He was committed to dialogue among psychoanalysts and he abhorred the authoritarianism that dictated adherence to a rigid set of beliefs or technical restrictions. He championed open discussion, comparative and integrative approaches, and he promoted new voices across the generations.

Included in the Relational Perspectives Book Series are authors and works that come from within the relational tradition, extend and develop the tradition, as well as works that critique relational approaches or compare and contrast it with alternative points of view. The series includes our most distinguished senior psychoanalysts, along with younger contributors who bring fresh vision.

Vol. 1
CONVERSING WITH UNCERTAINTY
Practicing Psychotherapy in a Hospital Setting
*Rita Wiley McCleary*

Vol. 2
AFFECT IN PSYCHOANALYSIS
A Clinical Synthesis
*Charles Spezzano*

Vol. 3
THE ANALYST IN THE INNER CITY
Race, Class, and Culture
through a Psychoanalytic Lens
*Neil Altman*

Vol. 4
A MEETING OF MINDS
Mutuality in Psychoanalysis
*Lewis Aron*

Vol. 5
HOLDING AND PSYCHOANALYSIS
A Relational Perspective
*Joyce A. Slochower*

Vol. 6
THE THERAPIST AS A PERSON
Life Crises, Life Choices, Life Experiences,
and Their Effects on Treatment
*Barbara Gerson (ed.)*

Vol. 7
SOUL ON THE COUCH
Spirituality, Religion, and Morality
in Contemporary Psychoanalysis
*Charles Spezzano & Gerald J. Gargiulo (eds.)*

Vol. 8
UNFORMULATED EXPERIENCE
From Dissociation to Imagination
in Psychoanalysis
*Donnel B. Stern*

Vol. 9
INFLUENCE AND AUTONOMY IN
PSYCHOANALYSIS
*Stephen A. Mitchell*

Vol. 10
FAIRBAIRN, THEN AND NOW
*Neil J. Skolnick & David E. Scharff (eds.)*

Vol. 11
BUILDING BRIDGES
Negotiation of Paradox in Psychoanalysis
*Stuart A. Pizer*

Vol. 12
RELATIONAL PERSPECTIVES
ON THE BODY
*Lewis Aron & Frances Sommer Anderson (eds.)*

Vol. 13
SEDUCTION, SURRENDER,
AND TRANSFORMATION
Emotional Engagement in the Analytic Process
*Karen Maroda*

Vol. 14
RELATIONAL PSYCHOANALYSIS
The Emergence of a Tradition
*Stephen A. Mitchell & Lewis Aron (eds.)*

Vol. 15
THE COLLAPSE OF THE SELF AND
ITS THERAPEUTIC RESTORATION
*Rochelle G. K. Kainer*

Vol. 16
PSYCHOANALYTIC PARTICIPATION
Action, Interaction, and Integration
*Kenneth A. Frank*

Vol. 17
THE REPRODUCTION OF EVIL
A Clinical and Cultural Perspective
*Sue Grand*

Vol. 18
OBJECTS OF HOPE
Exploring Possibility and Limit in
Psychoanalysis
*Steven H. Cooper*

Vol. 19
WHO IS THE DREAMER, WHO
DREAMS THE DREAM?
A Study of Psychic Presences
*James S. Grotstein*

Vol. 20
RELATIONALITY
From Attachment to Intersubjectivity
*Stephen A. Mitchell*

Vol. 21
LOOKING FOR GROUND
Countertransference and the
Problem of Value in Psychoanalysis
*Peter G. M. Carnochan*

Vol. 22
SEXUALITY, INTIMACY, POWER
*Muriel Dimen*

**Vol. 23**
SEPTEMBER 11
Trauma and Human Bonds
*Susan W. Coates, Jane L. Rosenthal,
& Daniel S. Schechter (eds.)*

**Vol. 24**
MINDING SPIRITUALITY
*Randall Lehman Sorenson*

**Vol. 25**
GENDER AS SOFT ASSEMBLY
*Adrienne Harris*

**Vol. 26**
IMPOSSIBLE TRAINING
A Relational View of Psychoanalytic Education
*Emanuel Berman*

**Vol. 27**
THE DESIGNED SELF
Psychoanalysis and Contemporary Identities
*Carlo Strenger*

**Vol. 28**
RELATIONAL PSYCHOANALYSIS, VOL. II
Innovation and Expansion
*Lewis Aron & Adrienne Harris (eds.)*

**Vol. 29**
CHILD THERAPY IN THE GREAT OUTDOORS
A Relational View
*Sebastiano Santostefano*

**Vol. 30**
THE HEALER'S BENT
Solitude and Dialogue in the ClinicalEncounter
*James T. McLaughlin*

**Vol. 31**
UNCONSCIOUS FANTASIES AND
THE RELATIONAL WORLD
*Danielle Knafo & Kenneth Feiner*

**Vol. 32**
GETTING FROM HERE TO THERE
Analytic Love, Analytic Process
*Sheldon Bach*

**Vol. 33**
CREATING BODIES
Eating Disorders as Self-Destructive Survival
*Katie Gentile*

**Vol. 34**
RELATIONAL PSYCHOANALYSIS, VOL. III
New Voices
*Melanie Suchet, Adrienne Harris,
& Lewis Aron (eds.)*

**Vol. 35**
COMPARATIVE-INTEGRATIVE
PSYCHOANALYSIS
A Relational Perspective for the
Discipline's Second Century
*Brent Willock*

**Vol. 36**
BODIES IN TREATMENT
The Unspoken Dimension
*Frances Sommer Anderson (ed.)*

**Vol. 37**
ADOLESCENT IDENTITIES
A Collection of Readings
*Deborah Browning (ed.)*

**Vol. 38**
REPAIR OF THE SOUL
Metaphors of Transformation
in Jewish Mysticism and Psychoanalysis
*Karen E. Starr*

**Vol. 39**
DARE TO BE HUMAN
A Contemporary Psychoanalytic Journey
*Michael Shoshani Rosenbaum*

**Vol. 40**
THE ANALYST IN THE INNER
CITY, SECOND EDITION
Race, Class, and Culture
through a Psychoanalytic Lens
*Neil Altman*

**Vol. 41**
THE HERO IN THE MIRROR
From Fear to Fortitude
*Sue Grand*

**Vol. 42**
SABERT BASESCU
Selected Papers on Human
Nature and Psychoanalysis
*George Goldstein & Helen Golden (eds.)*

**Vol. 43**
INVASIVE OBJECTS
Minds under Siege
*Paul Williams*

**Vol. 44**
GOOD ENOUGH ENDINGS
Breaks, Interruptions, and Terminations from
Contemporary Relational Perspectives
*Jill Salberg (ed.)*

Vol. 45
FIRST DO NO HARM
The Paradoxical Encounters
of Psychoanalysis, Warmaking, and Resistance
*Adrienne Harris & Steven Botticelli (eds.)*

Vol. 46
A DISTURBANCE IN THE FIELD
Essays in Transference-Countertransference Engagement
*Steven H. Cooper*

Vol. 47
UPROOTED MINDS
Surviving the Politics of Terror in the Americas
*Nancy Caro Hollander*

Vol. 48
TOWARD MUTUAL RECOGNITION
Relational Psychoanalysis and the Christian Narrative
*Marie T. Hoffman*

Vol. 49
UNDERSTANDING AND TREATING DISSOCIATIVE IDENTITY DISORDER
A Relational Approach
*Elizabeth F. Howell*

Vol. 50
WITH CULTURE IN MIND
Psychoanalytic Stories
*Muriel Dimen (ed.)*

Vol. 51
RELATIONAL PSYCHOANALYSIS, VOL. IV
Expansion of Theory
*Lewis Aron & Adrienne Harris (eds.)*

Vol. 52
RELATIONAL PSYCHOANALYSIS, VOL. V
Evolution of Process
*Lewis Aron & Adrienne Harris (eds.)*

Vol. 53
INDIVIDUALIZING GENDER AND SEXUALITY
Theory and Practice
*Nancy Chodorow*

Vol. 54
THE SILENT PAST AND THE INVISIBLE PRESENT
Memory, Trauma, and Representation in Psychotherapy
*Paul Renn*

Vol. 55
A PSYCHOTHERAPY FOR THE PEOPLE
Toward a Progressive Psychoanalysis
*Lewis Aron & Karen Starr*

Vol. 56
HOLDING AND PSYCHOANALYSIS
A Relational Perspective
*Joyce Slochower*

Vol. 57
THE PLAY WITHIN THE PLAY
The Enacted Dimension of Psychoanalytic Process
*Gil Katz*

Vol. 58
TRAUMATIC NARCISSISM
Relational Systems of Subjugation
*Daniel Shaw*

Vol. 59
CLINICAL IMPLICATIONS OF THE PSYCHOANALYST'S LIFE EXPERIENCE
When the Personal Becomes Professional
*Steven Kuchuck (ed.)*

Vol. 60
THE ORIGINS OF ATTACHMENT
Infant Research and Adult Treatment
*Beatrice Beebe & Frank M. Lachmann*

Vol. 61
THE EMBODIED ANALYST
From Freud and Reich to Relationality
*Jon Sletvold*

Vol. 62
A RELATIONAL PSYCHOANALYTIC APPROACH TO COUPLES PSYCHOTHERAPY
*Philip A. Ringstrom*

Vol. 63
CYCLICAL PSYCHODYNAMICS AND THE CONTEXTUAL SELF
The Inner World, the Intimate World, and the World of Culture and Society
*Paul L. Wachtel*

Vol. 64
TRAUMATIC RUPTURES
Abandonment and Betrayal in the Analytic Relationship
*Robin A. Deutsch (ed.)*

# TRAUMATIC RUPTURES

## Abandonment and Betrayal in the Analytic Relationship

*Edited by Robin A. Deutsch*

NEW YORK AND LONDON

First published 2014
711 Third Avenue, New York, NY 10017

and by Routledge
27 Church Road, Hove, East Sussex BN3 2FA

*Routledge is an imprint of the Taylor & Francis Group, an informa business*

© 2014 Robin A. Deutsch

The right of the editor to be identified as the author of the editorial material, and of the authors for their individual chapters, has been asserted in accordance with sections 77 and 78 of the Copyright, Designs and Patents Act 1988.

All rights reserved. No part of this book may be reprinted or reproduced or utilised in any form or by any electronic, mechanical, or other means, now known or hereafter invented, including photocopying and recording, or in any information storage or retrieval system, without permission in writing from the publishers.

*Trademark notice*: Product or corporate names may be trademarks or registered trademarks, and are used only for identification and explanation without intent to infringe.

*British Library Cataloguing in Publication Data*
A catalogue record for this book is available from the British Library

*Library of Congress Cataloging in Publication Data*
Traumatic ruptures: abandonment and betrayal in the analytic relationship/
edited by Robin A. Deutsch.
    pages cm.—(Relational perspectives book series)
 1. Psychotherapist and patient.  2. Diseases—Relapse.  3. Transference (Psychology)  4. Psychoanalysis.  I. Deutsch, Robin A., editor of compilation.
 RC480.8.T75 2014
 616.89'17—dc23                                            2013044455

ISBN: 978-0-415-53929-6 (hbk)
ISBN: 978-0-415-53931-9 (pbk)
ISBN: 978-1-315-77975-1 (ebk)

Typeset in Times New Roman
by RefineCatch Ltd, Bungay, Suffolk

# CONTENTS

|   |   |   |
|---|---|---|
| *List of Contributors* | | xii |
| *Foreword: Traumatic Ruptures: Abandonment and Betrayal in the Analytic Relationship* | | xv |
| MURIEL DIMEN | | |
| *Acknowledgments* | | xvii |
| **1** | **Introduction** | 1 |
| | ROBIN A. DEUTSCH | |

**PART I**
**Ruptured Subjectivity: Lost and Found**     11

| **2** | **Psychoanalytic Process in the Shadow of Rupture: Clinical Encounters with Death, Dead Mothers, and Deadly Mothers** | 13 |
|---|---|---|
| | ADRIENNE HARRIS | |
| **3** | **A Voice Lost, a Voice Found: After the Death of the Analyst** | 32 |
| | ROBIN A. DEUTSCH | |

**PART II**
**Rupture: The Clinical Process**     47

| **4** | **Abandoned Without Warning: Resonance of the Shame of Early Loss When an Analyst Dies** | 49 |
|---|---|---|
| | JENNY RANDLES AND FRANCES THOMSON-SALO | |

CONTENTS

5  The Trauma of Patient Suicide    66
JANE TILLMAN AND ANNE CARTER

6  On Being the Second Analyst: Two Patients Who Suffered Unexpected Loss of Their First Analyst and the Issue of Countertransference    79
MADELEINE BACHNER

## PART III
## The Long Shadow of Rupture    91

7  Losing a Training Analyst for Ethical Violations: Short-Term and Long-Term Effects    93
ELIZABETH WALLACE

8  Collateral Damage: The Fallout from Analyst Loss Due to Ethical Violations    109
CANDACE YOUNG

9  A Chorus of Difference: Evolving from Moral Outrage to Complexity and Pluralism    126
JANE BURKA

## PART IV
## Ruptures' Impact on Organizations    145

10  Silencing: When a Community Loses an Analyst to Ethical Violations    147
KATHY SINSHEIMER

11  Trouble in the Family: The Impact of Sexual Boundary Violations in Analytic Institute Life    163
DONNA FROMBERG

12  Trauma as a Way of Life in a Psychoanalytic Institute    176
CHARLES LEVIN

**PART V**
**Endpaper** 197

13 **Saying Goodbye: Traumatic Reverberations in
 the Subjective Sense of Time** 199
 DIANNE ELISE

 *Index* 216

# LIST OF CONTRIBUTORS

**Madeleine Bachner, MS**, a Training and Supervising Analyst, is the past President and current Director of the Training Institute of the Swedish Psychoanalytical Society. She is past European representative to the IPA Board and to the Executive Committee of the IPA. She is a psychoanalyst in full-time private practice.

**Jane Burka, PhD**, is a Personal and Supervising Analyst at the Psychoanalytic Institute of Northern California in San Francisco and a member of the International Psychoanalytic Association. She has published and presented on the subject of breach of confidentiality. Dr. Burka has a private practice in North Oakland, CA.

**Anne Carter, MD**, is a graduate of the Austen Riggs Psychiatry Fellowship Program and worked for several years at Austen Riggs as a staff psychiatrist. She currently works at the Providence Hospital and has a private practice in Brookline, MA.

**Robin A. Deutsch, PhD**, is Member and faculty of the San Francisco Center for Psychoanalysis, where she currently serves as President of the Center. She has presented on the subject of analytic identity, therapist subjectivity, and analyst death. Dr. Deutsch has a private practice in Oakland, CA.

**Muriel Dimen, PhD**, is Adjunct Clinical Professor of Psychology, New York University Postdoctoral Program in Psychotherapy and Psychoanalysis, and Editor-in-Chief of *Studies in Gender and Sexuality*. Her most recent edited book is *With Culture in Mind: Psychoanalytic Stories* (2011). Her *Sexuality, Intimacy, Power* (2003) received the Goethe Award from Canadian Psychological Association. She is in private practice in Manhattan.

**Dianne Elise, PhD**, is Personal and Supervising Analyst and faculty, Psychoanalytic Institute of Northern California, and Training Analyst, International Psychoanalytic Association. She is Associate Editor of *Studies in Gender and Sexuality*, and has served on the Editorial Board of the

## LIST OF CONTRIBUTORS

*Journal of the American Psychoanalytic Association.* She is in private practice in Oakland, CA.

**Donna Fromberg, PsyD**, is a member and faculty of the Boston Psychoanalytic Society and Institute and faculty in the Advanced Psychotherapy Training Program. She is also Director of the College Counseling Program at the Boston Institute of Psychotherapy, School of Museum of Fine Arts, Boston. She is in private practice in Newton Center, MA.

**Adrienne Harris, PhD**, is faculty and Supervisor at New York University Postdoctoral Program in Psychotherapy and Psychoanalysis. She is on the faculty and is a supervisor at the Psychoanalytic Institute of Northern California. She is an Editor at *Psychoanalytic Dialogues* and *Studies in Gender and Sexuality*. In 2009, she, Lewis Aron, and Jeremy Safran established the Sándor Ferenczi Center at the New School University.

**Charles Levin, PhD**, is currently Director of the Canadian Institute of Psychoanalysis and Editor-in-Chief of the *Canadian Journal of Psychoanalysis*. He writes on clinical, cultural, and ethical dimensions of psychoanalysis. He maintains a private practice in Quebec, CA.

**Jenny Randles, MBBS, FRANZCP**, Cert Child Psych, Honorary Fellow, Department of Psychiatry, University of Melbourne is a Consultant Psychiatrist and Psychoanalytic Psychotherapist working in private practice. Dr. Randles has a special interest in treating patients who have been traumatized following the sudden termination of their therapies.

**Frances Thomson-Salo, PhD**, trained with the British Psychoanalytical Society, and is IPA Committee of Women and Psychoanalysis Chair, *International Journal of Psychoanalysis* Board member, immediate past President of the Australian Society, Honorary Principal Fellow, Department of Psychiatry, University of Melbourne, and affiliate researcher of the Murdoch Children's Research Institute.

**Kathy Sinsheimer, MFT**, is a Personal and Supervising Analyst and a faculty member affiliated with the Psychoanalytic Institute of Northern California. She has a private practice in the San Francisco Bay Area.

**Jane G. Tillman, PhD, ABPP**, is the Evelyn Stefansson Nef Director of the Erikson Institute at the Austen Riggs Center in Stockbridge, MA. She frequently presents on the topic of suicide and consults to clinicians and organizations experiencing the loss of a patient by suicide.

**Elizabeth Wallace, MD, FRCPC**, is a Clinical Assistant Professor in the Department of Psychiatry, University of Calgary, and Clinical Medical Director of the Outpatient Mental Health Program. She teaches at the

Toronto Institute of Psychoanalysis, and practices psychiatry and psychoanalysis in Calgary.

**Candace Young, PhD** is Training Analyst and Faculty Member at the Institute for Contemporary Psychoanalysis in Los Angeles and is also a faculty member at the Oregon Psychoanalytic Institute. She is a psychoanalyst in private practice in Portland, OR.

# FOREWORD: TRAUMATIC RUPTURES
## Abandonment and Betrayal in the Analytic Relationship

*Muriel Dimen*

Consider this a book of witnessing and testimony. If it is analysts who usually witness and patients who testify, here, in this anthology, the two acts fold into one: the authors, most of them analysts, testify to personal experiences of rupture that, in a new form of witnessing, they go on to illuminate with psychoanalytic insight. Their testimony, in turn, serves to witness psychoanalysis as collective experience made public via its common language.

Emergent in this project is a new sort of psychoanalytic writing that makes us aware of a need we did not know we had. In the usual research report, the analyst's impassioned personal voice defers to the neutral tones of the scientist. The standard case study, for its part, always features two figures—analyst and patient—but rarely two voices: The analyst tends to speak for the patient. These chapters, in contrast, employ a multilayered form of speech. The authors not only utter but also address their own experiences of loss, fracture, and disillusionment. Like Tibetan monks who chant chords, do they sing two notes at once? Do their voices fuse the ego that experiences with the ego that observes? Or do they occupy the space between rupture and reflection?

This book's layering is heteroglossic, too. Like any authors, these analysts write with their readers in mind. They testify to us, their colleagues and community; they take us into their confidence; they engage us in witnessing the crucial but quotidian dilemmas of psychoanalysis. Reciprocally, we read vicariously; we witness the troubles they have seen and thereby create new experience, new public testimony from our private resonance with their struggles.

Be prepared for the delight of the new. Here is analytic subjectivity speaking of itself. Temporarily freed from the disciplined work of receiving and containing patients' experience, it is given room to breathe, to know itself, a self-care necessary to maintain our responsible, holding clinical presence. Contained by this chorus of voices, we are freed to contemplate and marvel at the depths and rigors of our work. At liberty to sift through the shades of self and other represented here, our reflective capacity is enriched; our capacity to know the other in ourselves enhanced.

Watch out, too, for the shock of the new. Authors here write in myriad voices. They are analysts, patients, second analysts after the death of the first, candidates, analysts bereft of a mate or a sibling. Unafraid to reveal their dismay and disappointment—or, if afraid, they do so anyway—they remind us of the fractures in psychoanalysis that we come across from time to time. Analysts have been known to die suddenly, mid-treatment. Analysts, knowing they are mortally ill, fail to prepare patients for the oncoming loss. Eros carries analysts across the river into sexual misconduct. Analysts deny their weak spots, go silent. Analytic discipline cannot bear the weight of personal disorders and treatments are spoiled. Analysts do not seek supervision or further treatment when to do so would help, not harm. Cover-ups beckon, and analysts do not say no, participating instead in the systemic silencing of sexual boundary violations. Institutes and training programs turn a blind eye to individual and organizational limitations and infractions.

This book helps launch an essential voyage. We need to travel to a land beyond the idealization and demonization of psychoanalysis. We are made of gaps and disappointments; we are our scars. The mind's heart is a rupture that does not heal. Death comes for us all. And rupture, these works tell us, is as common in psychoanalysis as in life. Do not, say these authors, believe your fantasies of total healing, of complete repair, of restoration to a seamless state, whether in personal history or in psychoanalysis.

Daring to disturb, this unavoidably melancholy volume ruptures complacency. It demands we remember how difficult it is to be an analyst, how ordinary our insufficiency, how ubiquitous the shame. This book calls on our agentic capacity to learn from our mistakes. It interpellates us as not only subject to rupture, but subjects of it: Rupture happens to us, and we do it, too. Just as each analyst has once been a patient, so each of us has failed as well as succeeded, met our ideals as well as fallen abjectly short. We are divided and damaged beings, striving for and occasionally achieving repair.

Depressive position: Welcome to our ethical repertoire.

# ACKNOWLEDGMENTS

I am deeply grateful to the authors who contributed to this volume. I value their willingness to publicly share the impact of their own experiences with traumatic ruptures. Each author has illuminated her or his own unique experience in well-written and deeply engaging chapters.

I want to thank Adrienne Harris and Lewis Aron, co-editors of the Relational Perspectives Book Series, for including my book in such an impressive series. I am especially grateful to Adrienne Harris as a mentor and colleague, encouraging my professional growth and helping me learn the editorial skills I needed to bring this book to a successful conclusion.

It really does take a village: from the book proposal to the finished manuscript, my friends and colleagues, willingly and with enthusiasm, read proposal drafts, reviewed chapters, gave feedback, and made suggestions. They provided the kind of support that enabled me to work on the book with confidence. Special thanks to Sharon Bass, Elizabeth Biggart, Barbara Cohen, Dianne Elise, Gary Grossman, Jeanne Harasemovitch, Marilynne Kanter, Eileen Keller, Patty Marra, Milton Schaefer, Dena Sorbo, and Abby Wolfson. I am thankful to them. I want to express my appreciation to Elise Miller for her encouragement and editing skill; Kristopher Spring for turning the manuscript into a book; and Kate Hawes and Kirsten Buchanan at Routledge for patiently answering myriad questions from a first-time editor.

My husband, Ed Levin, is my greatest support. For over 24 years, he has listened to me and nourished my efforts.

Chapter 3 was originally published in *Psychoanalytic Inquiry* 31: 6 (pp. 526–535, 2011) and is reprinted here by permission.

Much of Chapter 7 was originally published in the *International Journal of Psychoanalysis* 88 as "Losing a training analyst for ethical violations: A candidate's perspective" (pp. 1275–1288, 2007) and also appeared in the *Canadian Journal of Psychoanalysis* 18 (pp. 248–254, 2010) and is reprinted here by permission.

Parts of Chapter 13 were originally published in *Psychoanalytic Inquiry* 31: 6 as "Time to say goodbye: On time, trauma, and termination (pp. 591–600, 2011) and is reprinted here by permission.

# 1
# INTRODUCTION

*Robin A. Deutsch*

Within the last century, certain traumatic events have essentially altered how many people think about themselves and their world. Each of these catastrophes (e.g., Pearl Harbor, Kennedy's assassination, Oklahoma City Federal building bombing, World Trade Center, Newtown) shattered what we thought we fundamentally knew, revising the familiar field in which we live. In a moment, these traumas tear the social fabric, rupturing what we essentially believed about the stability and cohesion of our culture, our society, and ourselves. Not all ruptures are as horrific as these are, but each splits experience into what was once spoken and understood and what is now unspeakable and incomprehensible. This book is about the effects of sudden traumatic rupture within the psychoanalytic world in which we live. It is an intimate exploration of psychoanalytic treatments and communities where betrayal and abandonment have left their mark.

Morrison (1996) posits that environmental trauma "exerts a destabilizing impact on the self-state" (p. 44). Self-state, as he means it, is a personal sense of "stability, tranquility and equilibrium" (p. 43). In this sense, he is emphasizing the relationship between an external event and the fracturing, for however long, of a secure internal sense of self. In this description, I suspect Morrison means something akin to Winnicott's concept of "going-on-being." Strictly speaking, a baby's sense of going-on-being is established within the facilitating environment of the mother's primary maternal preoccupation, a time when the mother promotes her baby's development, "to be and to grow" (Abram, 2007, p. 262). Subsequently, in the literature, the concept of going-on-being has evolved into broader use, such as a personal sense of self as the result of confident reliance on one's internal environment, taken in through good early care (Winnicott, 1958). Seligman's (in press) evocative descriptions of responsive and non-responsive parent-infant interactions make these concepts tangible.

Psychoanalysis offers such a place, and as such has extraordinary power and meaning when the work succeeds. Psychoanalysis centers on an engagement with the unbearable, whether wish, affect, or experience (Gerson, 2009). In this enterprise, two people come together to witness, digest, and make speakable the internal world of one. Britton (1992), in a case description, describes analysis as providing a sanctuary, a place for the patient to be "inside something good" (p. 103). In order to provide something good and ensure the protection of the patient and the analyst, the analyst establishes a framework in an effort to assure the safety of such a difficult, challenging, and rewarding enterprise. Frequency of meeting, session length, beginning and ending on time, payment, confidentiality, and prohibition against sexual contact are all elements that create the necessary environment of safety, support, and containment. Embedded in the analytic relationship is the indissociable relationship between seeming opposites: love and hate; creativity and destructiveness; hope and dread (Klein, 1929; Mitchell, 1993; Winnicott, 1969). Rather than dichotomous, these pairs are intertwined, generating and preserving clinical potential.

However, in the intensity of an analysis, the intermingling of these progressive and regressive tendencies for both the analyst and the patient can capsize the treatment. This collection of chapters explores what happens when creativity and destructiveness tilt and the analysis itself becomes the conveyor of the unbearable. For each author, a traumatic event has occurred in the analysis affecting the patient, the analyst, the community, or subsequent treatments. Something that was, is no longer, both inside and out. Left in the wake of promise and process is an inchoate sense of fright, helplessness, shame, anger, and dislocation, destroying the necessary sense of sanctuary and goodness as articulated by Britton.

Typically, in the process of an analysis, we develop a collaborative way of working with each patient. As analysts, we have frequent experience with those moments when empathic attunement to our patient is lost. These types of rupture and subsequent repair, however jarring, inevitably occur throughout a treatment, bringing an opportunity to move the analysis forward. Sometimes these ruptures are momentary, lasting a second, a session, a month. This book, however, addresses a different, more traumatic kind of rupture (Anonymous, 2001; Barron, 2011; Charles, 1997; Elkind, 1996). Within the analytic dyad, a traumatic rupture questions and threatens the analytic life created by patient and analyst, leading to an abrupt loss of continuity and connectedness. A rupture of this kind is an intersubjective crisis, with intimate and far-reaching repercussions: a sudden, traumatic break after which things are not the same. But, as this book demonstrates, the repercussions go far beyond the dyad, eventually taking up residence within the analytic community and its history.

Judith Butler (2003) addresses the sense of personal dislocation and fracture that occurs as a result of the type of rupture I am describing. She states:

> It is not as if an "I" exists independently over here and then simply loses a "you" over there, especially if the attachment to "you" is part

of what composes who "I" am. If I lose you, under these conditions, then I not only mourn the loss, but I become inscrutable to myself. Who "am" I, without you? When we lose some of those ties by which we are constituted, we do not know who we are or what to do. On one level, I think I have lost "you" only to discover that "I" have gone missing as well.

(p. 12)

In this quote, Butler eloquently describes the undermining impact of profound and sudden loss on an individual's sense of self: an impermanent loss of cohesion and equilibrium. With rupture, meaning is demyelinated at the individual, institutional, and social level.

In this book, it is my intention to offer the reader a first-hand experience of issues that have been off-limits and yet need to be articulated. Sweetnam (2007), writing about psychoanalytic writing, describes how Ogden "has been demonstrating how the form of our writing helps to create an experience for the reader rather than simply offering a discussion 'about' an experience" (p. 9). What I am addressing is the way many of the authors find themselves reaching for evocative metaphors to convey these life-altering events. For each author, writing is one medium for involving the community in the process of repair. By breaking the silence and taboos about speaking personally about the effects of traumatic rupture in psychoanalysis, these writers invite the reader to bear witness to the unspoken and incomprehensible as it enters the realm of the knowable.

Some traumatic ruptures—such as analyst death, patient suicide, and ethical violations—are seemingly easy and tempting to categorize. However, trauma is inherently outside language, leaving people unable to think or talk about it. When we are unable to think about trauma, it remains unmetabolized and unregulated. Within the community, reports of these events are often responded to in polarizing, confusing ways, or spoken about in false, sanitized ways or sometimes not at all. Part of the challenge in writing this introduction has been locating words that express the kinds of traumatic rupture described by the contributors to this book. Each author has painstakingly crafted a chapter that details an external event and its internal echo. When I sought a label that would adequately connect the reported, external event with its internal reverberations, I sometimes experienced the same loss of language that I believe is at the heart of these ruptures: a rupture of what is known and taken for granted.

My own engagement with this topic began when my analyst suddenly died midway through a productive analysis (see Chapter 3). To borrow from Winnicott, my sense of going-on-being was fractured. Feeling my internal world turned upside down, I turned to our literature. Finding scant first-person reports on traumatic rupture in the analytic dyad, I became increasingly intrigued about the effects of analyst death on individual identity and sense of self (Adams, 1995; Rendely, 1999; Traesdal, 2013). I immersed myself in Gerson's (1996) edited volume that included many chapters describing first-person experiences of loss, death, and grief in the therapist's life, and the impact on the clinical encounter. Reading words that articulated my grief and sense of disorientation and fracture was a relief. The authors did not mince words; they eloquently recounted the loss that had befallen them and expressed their grief. It was as if these chapters had been written to capture my internal experience. Reading them helped me think and rediscover my sense of self. The author's descriptions of their return to work, voicing their uneven capacity to be available to their patients, became a holding environment for me as I relocated my analyst identity. Later, professional literature began to include more first-person narratives about the trauma caused by ethical violations (Burka, 2008; Wallace, 2007). These papers began to name what had been previously unnamable. Each of these writings added more individual voices to our professional literature.

However, attention to how indigestible these types of trauma and rupture are for the individual, group, and community has been missing from this conversation. Each chapter in this book is the author's attempt to digest and illuminate how each individual wrestled with her or his experience. A trauma that is devastating to an individual may impact the community minimally or not at all. But whether it is the individual or clinical couple that is affected, or the institute and community, the rupture reverberates deeply within the unconscious, continuing to impact because the rupture remains unmetabolized. Previously, the literature has treated these ruptures separately. This volume brings together different types of rupture, offering perspectives on the commonalities of the internal echoes of an external event.

This book demonstrates that writing can help name and relocate what's been lost. My voice, for example, evolved after the death of my analyst, from a mourner's voice to an authorial voice. Later, as I began to present publicly about my experience, other analysts began to tell me their stories out of their desire to be heard: stories of sudden death; a return to a beloved analyst, now demented, able to interpret but unable to remember their patient's name; an analyst and analysis lost to a boundary violation. I began to be interested in what all these breaches had in common. I started to think about rupture not only in terms of the now disappeared analytic relationship, but also in terms of what has been lost and what has to be brought back into time and into thinking.

Psychoanalysis is embedded in previous generations of analysts, an unconscious lineage of which we are previous members. The individual and the community carry the history of trauma: previous deaths, previous boundary crossings, and other events that should not have happened but did. Within the analytic community, a rupture, known first-hand or by rumor, disrupts what we think and know. Aftershocks from abandonment and betrayal undermine the analytic undertaking and destroy the essential illusion that analysis should be able to withstand human frailties. Like earthquakes, dyadic disruptions are not limited to the epicenter. Traumatic fact and rumor color and influence our psychoanalytic world. Rippling through the community, gossiped about, quarantined, these events can remain undigested for future analytic generations (Gabbard & Peltz, 2001; Levine, 2010; Pinsky, 2010, 2012; Ruskin, 2011). These deeply felt events continue to contaminate and affect functioning specifically because they remain unmetabolized, isolated, and unwitnessed. None of the authors in this volume could have known the effect of the trauma on themselves, after one month, six months, one year, 10 years. Each thoughtful and heartfelt essay is a snapshot of the author's internal experience as he or she actively uses writing as a way to metabolize trauma.

But as Ogden (2005) reminds us:

> [I]t is important not to know the shape of the story from the start, but to allow it to take form in the process of writing it. Not knowing the end of the story while at the beginning preserves for the writer as well as for the reader a sense of the utter unpredictability of every life experience: we never know what is going to happen before it happens.
> (p. 18)

So, too, with each author's effort to make sense of events that seem beyond understanding, as well as with this volume's development.

I began the search for authors with something specific in mind, what I now recognize as a formulaic attempt to describe a particular, yet unarticulated, experience of rupture. Gabbard and Ogden's (2009) emphasis on the discovery and creation of what one thinks in the process of writing came to life as I was influenced by each author's abstract. I continued to wrestle with how to define and describe what I meant by rupture. "Watching ideas develop in unplanned ways" (p. 320) took on personal meaning for me as some of the authors began changing topics as they started writing. I started to find descriptors for the types of rupture that could be exemplified in the book: ruptured subjectivities, ruptured personal and professional identities, ruptured relationships, ruptured senses of self, ruptured and traumatized organizations.

In the process of writing this introduction, I discovered that the word *reader* comes from the Old English *rǣdere*, meaning interpreter of dreams (*New Oxford American Dictionary*, online, 2/17/13). This surprising revelation immediately immersed me in thoughts about the relationship between the writer and the reader. Ogden (1997) and Gabbard and Ogden (2009) emphasize the interdigitating relationship of writer and reader. Like mother-baby or patient-analyst, one does not exist without the other. While creating, the writer has an imaginary reader in mind with the hope of evoking a response in that reader. On completion, the writer must trust the reader to animate the author's

INTRODUCTION

work, generating a personal meaning for the reader: an interpreter of the author's message as it reverberates within the reader. The authors in this volume have revealed their subjectivity by writing their experience and sharing it with the reader. In the process, each written-about experience, no matter how similar, is different because of each writer and each reader. Each author, by evoking an experience, makes the reader a joint collaborator in the book, joining with me, as editor, and the authors. This volume invites the reader to become the *rædere* in transforming these experiences of traumatic rupture.

## The Chapters

This book is divided into four parts, each taking up a different aspect of rupture. These parts are: Ruptured Subjectivity: Lost and Found; Rupture: The Clinical Process; The Long Shadow of Rupture; and Ruptures' Impact on Organizations.

Ruptured subjectivity is taken up in Adrienne Harris' chapter (Chapter 2). She asks, "What kind of analyst am I now?" when her identity as an analyst is ruptured at the time of her husband's sudden death. Her chapter poignantly describes the impact of her grief on her analytic identity as she returns to her professional life in the shadow of this significant loss. In Chapter 3, I raise the question of the fate of the analytic life created by patient and analyst after the analyst's death. Aware of double loss, of my analyst and of my own voice, I describe a process of retaining and cementing the relationship with my now dead analyst through mourning. This in turn facilitated the return of my own voice.

Shame is an overarching theme in several chapters. Jenny Randles and Frances Thomson-Salo (Chapter 4) poignantly describe the shame that patients experience when a successful therapy is ruptured by the abrupt death of the therapist. They illustrate how shame threatens to engulf the subsequent treatment with the new analyst with humiliation and failure. Jane Tillman and Anne Carter (Chapter 5) frame for the reader the impact of patient suicide on the therapist. The bereft clinician is left to manage overwhelming feelings in isolation. They detail how the traumatic rupture of patient suicide can lead to personal and professional identity becoming contaminated with shame. In Chapter 6, Madeleine Bachner offers an emotionally rich illustration of subsequent clinical work with patients whose analysts have suddenly and unexpectedly died. In the aftermath of such a traumatic rupture, Bachner finds both herself and her patient dislocated: the patient, in mourning, and Bachner, contending with being the analyst she is.

Elizabeth Wallace, Candace Young, and Jane Burka all take up the challenges involved in being candidate analysts losing their own analysts to ethical violations. Wallace (Chapter 7) describes being sworn to secrecy after her institute informs her of her analyst's sexual violation. Having only her analyst—the analyst under investigation—to speak with about her dislocation, Wallace describes her experience as a future analyst who worries that she will be infected by her analyst's violation. In Chapter 8, Young's touching chapter uses the metaphor of nuclear fallout to describe the impact on her of her analyst's sexual boundary violation with another of his patients. Emphasizing fracture points, where faith in psychoanalysis is compromised, Young highlights the impact of ever-expanding rings of de-idealization on her as patient and analyst and on her analytic community. Burka (Chapter 9) also lost her analyst and analysis to a sexual boundary violation. In a revealing chapter, she describes reexperiencing her own traumatic rupture when she found herself wrestling with ethical transgressions within her institute.

In their chapters, Donna Fromberg, Charles Levin, and Kathy Sinsheimer focus predominantly on their experience of traumatic rupture within their organizations. Intriguingly, each author identifies the candidate group as a locus for significant disruption subsequent to organizational trauma. Sinsheimer (Chapter 10) describes the institutional effect of silencing on her and her analytic community after a member's ethical violation. As the ethical violation becomes known, through formal, official as well as informal, social channels, she details how she grapples with strong institutional pressures to keep silent. As a candidate and early career analyst, Fromberg (Chapter 11) describes the impact of institutional disorganization as a result of sexual boundary violations by senior analysts on her and her nascent analytic identity. In a heartfelt chapter, she recounts her confusion and disorientation in the shadow of institute rumors, member resignations, and organizational silence. Levin (Chapter 12) uses his own experiences as candidate, graduate analyst, and training analyst to highlight the displacement of organizational dysfunction and longstanding institutional trauma onto candidates and early career analysts. In an intriguing chapter, he highlights the intersection of what he refers to as "institutional illness," trauma, and sexual boundary violations.

Dianne Elise's contribution (Chapter 13) brings the book to a close. In her chapter, Elise takes up the question of time: external, real time and internal, psychic time. Emphasizing the complex relationship that each of us has with temporality, the author underlines the deep sorrow involved in saying goodbye.

For the authors in this book, time has special meaning: There has not been enough. The promised ending, a good enough termination for patients and analysts, a community that functions effectively in the best interest of its members, has been denied. Time is needed to repair traumatic ruptures and their unmetabolized internal echoes. For patients who have lost analysts, for analysts who have lost patients, for analysts who have lost part of themselves, it takes time. Writing has facilitated these authors finding their way.

## References

Abram, J. (2007). *The language of Winnicott: A dictionary of Winnicott's use of words* (2nd ed.). London: Karnac.

Adams, B. (1995). Ulysses and I: A brief memoir of a long analysis. *Psychoanalytic Review, 82*, 727–740.

Anonymous. (2001). Killing me softly: An analysand's perspective on the ethical problems of relocating a psychoanalytic practice. *Psychoanalytic Social Work, 8*, 41–55.

Barron, G. C. (2011). Depressive rumination in an analysand after a traumatic treatment. *Psychoanalytic Quarterly, 80*, 287–304.

Britton, R. (1992). Keeping things in mind. In R. Anderson (Ed.), *Clinical lectures on Klein and Bion* (pp. 102–113). London: Routledge.

Burka, J. B. (2008). Psychic fallout from breach of confidentiality: A patient/analyst's perspective. *Contemporary Psychoanalysis, 44*, 177–198.

Butler, J. (2003). Violence, mourning, politics. *Studies in Gender and Sexuality, 4*, 9–37.

Charles, M. (1997). Betrayal. *Contemporary Psychoanalysis, 33*, 109–122.

Elkind, S. N. (1996). The impact of negative experiences as a patient on my work as a therapist. In B. Gerson (Ed.), *The therapist as a person: Life crises, life choices, life experiences and their effects on treatment* (pp. 159–174). Hillsdale, NJ: Analytic Press.

Gabbard, G. O., & Ogden, T. H. (2009). On becoming a psychoanalyst. *International Journal of Psychoanalysis, 90*, 311–327.

Gabbard, G. O., & Peltz, M. L. (2001). Speaking the unspeakable: Institutional reactions to boundary violations by training analysts. *Journal of the American Psychoanalytic Association, 49*, 659–673.

Gerson, B. (Ed). (1996). *The therapist as a person: Life crises, life choices, life experiences and their effects on treatment*. Hillsdale, NJ: Analytic Press.

Gerson, S. (2009). When the third is dead: Memory, mourning, and witnessing in the aftermath of the Holocaust. *International Journal of Psychoanalysis, 90*, 1341–1357.

Klein, M. (1929). Infantile anxiety-situations reflected in a work of art and in the creative impulse. *International Journal of Psychoanalysis, 10*, 436–443.

Levine, H. (2010). Sexual boundary violations: Psychoanalytic perspective. *British Journal of Psychotherapy, 26*, 50–63.

Mitchell, S. (1993). *Hope and dread in psychoanalysis*. New York: Basic Books

Morrison, A. P. (1996). Trauma and disruption in the life of the analyst: Enforced disclosure and disequilibrium in the "analytic instrument." In B. Gerson (Ed.), *The therapist as person: Life crises, life choices, life experiences and their effects on treatment* (pp. 41–54). Hillsdale, NJ: Analytic Press.

*New Oxford American Dictionary* (US English). Available at oxforddictionaries.com/us/definition/american_english/reader (accessed February 16, 2013).

Ogden, T. H. (1997). Some thoughts on the use of language in psychoanalysis. *Psychoanalytic Dialogues, 7*, 1–21.

Ogden, T. H. (2005). On psychoanalytic writing. *International Journal of Psychoanalysis, 86*, 15–29.

Pinsky, E. (2010). The Olympian delusion. *Journal of the American Psychoanalytic Association, 59*, 351–375.

Pinsky, E. (2012). Physic himself must fade: A view of the therapeutic offering through the lens of mortality. *American Imago, 69*, 29–56.

Rendely, J. (1999). The death of an analyst: The loss of a real relationship. *Contemporary Psychoanalysis, 35*, 131–152.

Ruskin, R. (2011). Sexual boundary violations in a senior training analyst: Impact on the individual and psychoanalytic society. *Canadian Journal of Psychoanalysis/ Revue Canadienne de Psychanalyse, 19*, 87–106.

Seligman, S. (in press). The subjective experience of time: Unresponsive objects and the vacuity of the future. *Psychoanalytic Dialogues*.

Sweetnam, A. (2007). "When I was a fish": An experiment in different ways of reading. *fort da, 13B*, 9–21.

Traesdal, T. (2013). Analysis lost and re-gained. In G. Junkers (Ed.), *The empty couch: The taboo of ageing and retirement in psychoanalysis* (pp. 82–90). London: Routledge.

Wallace, E. M. (2007). Losing a training analyst for ethical violations: A candidate's perspective. *International Journal of Psychoanalysis, 88*, 1275–1288.

Winnicott, D. W. (1958). The capacity to be alone. *International Journal of Psychoanalysis, 39*, 416–420.

Winnicott, D. W. (1969). The use of an object. *International Journal of Psychoanalysis, 50*, 711–716.

# Part I

# RUPTURED SUBJECTIVITY: LOST AND FOUND

# 2

# PSYCHOANALYTIC PROCESS IN THE SHADOW OF RUPTURE

## Clinical Encounters with Death, Dead Mothers, and Deadly Mothers

*Adrienne Harris*

Everyone said, in one way or another, work will be good for you because work would be a distraction. Even at the beginning that did not seem right, in at least two directions. To work to be distracted seemed wrong and a misuse of work and of patients. It also seemed, frankly, impossible.

Two and a half months after the sudden death of my husband, I went back into my office. In the interim, I had consultations, worked a little on the phone, and processed a lot with several close colleagues who had served as consultants for me and for people in my practice, in the immediate aftermath of my husband's death and during the several months I was away.

While away from work, I read, apparently somewhat randomly, in my psychoanalytic library. I think I needed to discover if I was still an analyst. I needed to reconnect to what kind of an analyst I was, or could be, in the recognition that the whole span of my marriage had also spanned the arc of my professional analytic career as clinician, teacher, and writer. What had been lost, what eclipsed, what altered by what had happened? What does it mean to even ask such questions, to have so much of identity in question?

In this chapter, I am saying something particular about the experience of mourning for the *analyst*, when the central instrument of his or her work is deeply charged with another more private task. I want to open up a complex reality, which I hope will have very general utility. Inevitably, at one time or other in the experience of all analysts, there will arise the parallel processing of trauma and trouble in one's own life arced along a clinical day, with often a variety of clinical and personal interruptions to the meditative focused elements in analytic work.

In thinking about the analyst's modes of work and functioning under conditions of normal and abnormal circumstances, I have found myself drawn to the myth of Philoctetes, the archer. That core myth—the exquisite accuracy of Philoctetes' bow linked to the chronic and agonizing and suppurating wound of his snake-bitten foot—can be usefully deployed to think about our own professional practices, both generally and in crises. We are always curing with contaminated tools (Harris, 2009), our skill and our anguish deeply interwoven. So, in circumstances both usual and extreme, wound is at the center of creativity and transformation. This chapter is written in the spirit of that idea.

What I am writing about—the clinical impact of an experience of rupture on the analyst's subjectivity, a dramatic fissure in the analyst's sense of going on being—lies along a spectrum. Along two spectra, actually. First, we all will have or have already had experiences of loss, but not all the same, and not all in the same way. So there is something generic here and something that is also specific and local. There is diversity in modes and circumstances of mourning and it shapes the clinical situation. I return to this later in the chapter in more detail.

The second spectrum to consider is simply the general and wide range of ways in which analysts conduct clinical work. In thinking about how I have been working these past two years, there are several key strands to pull out and examine. It was both extreme work and it was usual work. There were enactments, intense preoccupations with countertransference by both people in the dyad, there was attunement to the bi-personal field, the many circuits of unconscious communication. There was more of everything: reverie, disclosure, particularly of affect states and more dialogue internally, with colleagues, and on paper.

## Theory: From Mourning and Melancholia to the Dead Mother

One book I read and treasured was a collection of essays, edited by Gregorio Kohon (1999), written in homage to Andre Green's paper, "The Dead Mother Complex" (Green, 1983). A prescient choice, as it turned out, but not one I was making consciously. Green's paper has always been important to me, particularly its key idea that children living in relation to a parent caught up in a bereavement (not dead actually but dead to the child) struggled with a loss that could not be borne, a loss that left gaps and holes in the psyche, a loss suffered before there was internal structure to represent loss. Published in English in 1983, Green's work links to many current ideas of unconscious registration of very early trauma (Coates, 2010) and experiences unremembered in narrative form but haunting, nonetheless (Davoine, 2007; Faimberg, 2004; and Harris, 2009).

Loss of love, Green notes, was followed closely by loss of meaning. Patients with such histories, Green argued, were afraid both of closeness and of abandonment, and above all of any reminder of goodness lost. Good objects had often to be destroyed—in treatments and in adult life. Objects remain neither fully housed within nor outside the psyche and under all vicissitudes and affect storms there is one key secret: The patient's love is "mortgaged to the dead mother." The child with a "dead mother" could turn neither to rage nor depression but only tumble into the abyss of "no-thing." My practice included a number of people burdened with such early sudden and disregulating losses and this dynamic was a dominant force in many treatments.

But over the past two years, I have expanded how I think of and use Green. I see his idea of unassimilable mourning as more than a developmental matter. Above all, the magisterial words of Freud (1917) kept entering and reentering my field of vision and action. Freud's great insight is that all else pales against the task of accepting death's finality, and he was masterful in outlining the desperate psychic battle we all wage to evade that experience. That project unifies all the tasks of mourning. And as I read Green over the months of my return to work, I came to feel that for everyone, there are limits and faultlines to the internal structures we have to bear loss. "*Psychose blanche*," Green's term for the catastrophic abyss into which early loss may fall, is a condition of all mourning. It is the place where representation fails. It is the condition we work hardest to avoid, because we know it is the gateway to death.

The dead mother has also the potential to be deadly. The potential for aggression goes in both directions. It may be that bereavement relieves the aggressor of certain aspects of guilt and shame. Every possible extreme of feeling is surely warranted. Bereavement may disinhibit mourner and witness, analyst and analysand. Utility and destructiveness are alive in both.

Rooted very deeply in the relational landscape, with its very generative ideas about two-person psychologies and social construction in the analytic dyad, I had become highly conscious of the implications of co-construction, intersubjectivity, and the interdependence of brains, minds and bodies (Aron, 1996; Anzieu, 1994; Corbett, 2008, 2013; Hofer, 1984, 1996; Knoblauch, 2000; and Stern, 2010). Contemporary writing about transference and countertransference focuses on the porousness of clinical dyads, the immersion of self in other, and the many implications of noting that self and mind are deeply and dyadically embodied (Corbett, 2008; Gallese, 2009; Gallese and Sinigaglia, 2011; Harris, 2005; Merleau Ponty, 2012; Schilder, 1930; 1935; Salamon, 2010; Seligman, in press; and Reis, 2009).

One of my guides here was the work of Myron Hofer (1984; 1996) on hidden regulators and the biology of loss and separation. His research charts the powerful visceral, sensory-motor, unconscious, even metabolic interweavings through which people (and animals) carry ruptures and bereavement in their social or intimate worlds. The interdependence of these processes is one crucial element in understanding how loss is held and held with others. Hilary Berlin's (2011) review of the research on unconscious communication and process also opens a stunning vista into the ways we are dyadically and socially, as well as intra-psychically, expressing and receiving information about each other's complex psychic states, affects, motives, memories. Crucially, she argues, these transmissions occur at astonishingly, shockingly high speeds. Berlin's work is, for me, a contemporary anchor to Ferenczi's abiding interest in unconscious communication across clinical dyads.

To work with this knowledge of our entrainment with patients in clinical work requires resilience in the best of times. In the past two years, in a state of heightened vulnerability, I have had to be vigilantly mindful. It's a contradiction, of course, to be vigilantly mindful of the manifold states of not knowing and uncertainty. Hardly a day without the unsettling questions: Whose mind was this? Whose affects were these, and very often, whose tears were these?

What this has meant for me over this past year is to have conducted clinical work in moments of intense acuity and movement and moments of utter blindness. In a memorable paper, Goldberger (1993) reminds us to pay attention to blind spots and bright spots. Bright spots are points of apparent deep contact which also mask difference and blind spots are moments of evacuated meanings and a kind of scotoma in relation to the other. For me, both kinds of experience, moments of linking and unlinking, scatter across the year.

We might think of analytic work as lived and practiced in certain kinds of reveries (Ogden, 1998), acoustic envelopes (Harris, 2009; Anzieu, 1994), or conversation (Cooper, 2010; Corbett, 2013), and also in the context of a web of life events (ours, families', colleagues', history, intergenerational, and culture) and these are part of the fabric of our interactional, interpersonal processes (Ferenczi, 1933; Ferro, 2005). We are often in analytic sessions held in webs of narrative, dialogue, and shared consciousness (Harris, 2005). And, in certain moments, we are and need to be frighteningly alone while with a patient. Bromberg (2006) has a phrase for this: "Safe but not too safe." This idea was only sometimes consoling to me. And although it is in my character to feel challenges as bracing, moments in this past year had often the dual character of devastating and instructive.

## *Bandwidth*

This term "bandwidth" occurred to me quite often. In technological terms, it indicates the range and frequencies in which some instrument can function and, in more metaphoric terms, it is intended to convey what resources, internal or external, one has to undertake some task. Thinking of the analytic instrument as entailing bandwidth was useful to me, considering the wide range of bodily affective and mental resonances and frequencies in which we undertake this work. It is perhaps a necessary narcissism to diminish the burden on the patient, if the analyst is working in conditions of self-protection and self-preservation. Perhaps this is a useful paradox: self-care in the service of patient care.

I also had occasion to re-read my own papers on impasse, self-care, and the subjectivity of the analyst, and to wonder if I could possibly follow any of my own advice. As a relational analyst who has written about impasse (Harris, 2009) and the analyst's mourning, about the uncertainty in the mix of self and other, about intersubjectivity and unconscious communication, and about self-care as part of patient care (Harris & Sinsheimer, 2008) I was forced to face and examine my own ideas and proscriptive views about treatment. What was self-care in my current life context? And what would I have to do to ensure movement in patients mired often in their own stifled or stunted mournings? How would my mourning be tied up as stimulus or impediment to the work of and with patients? What practices would be useful to expand and perhaps ventilate my bandwidth, my analytic instrument?

## *Circles of Containment*

I was returning to practice after a shocking event. I was rightly worried about my dissociative states. But I was functioning within an amazing web of people holding me in mind: immediate friends, family, a wider community of mine and my husband's whose students and colleagues wrote blogs, letters, emails all carrying the person, his life, our life, his meaningfulness as a scholar and teacher. Holding in mind in this way was both public and private. The constructive capacity of such holdings was invaluable, our lesson from Bion (1959). Containment in and from many quarters does its work in the consulting room, in institutions, in collectivities. Gerson's (2009) work on witnessing seemed deeply relevant to me and the steadiness of collective and collaborative witnessing was extraordinarily helpful.

A colleague, whose husband had been killed on 9/11, said to me: "Right after that time I did my best work and my worst work." I held that idea in mind as well. I noticed that my office increasingly became, over the first six months of being back there, an island of safety. I found I was much better there than in larger groups. Perhaps normalcy, to some degree, returned first there, a space not so deeply or obviously inhabited by my husband before his death. Before his death, he had usually been evoked as "your husband"; now, interestingly, he entered the room and the discourse much more usually as "Bob." In that light, I will call him Bob going forward in this essay, reflecting the no doubt joint project of analyst and patient to hold him in mind. Fantasy and imagining of "Bob" as presence (or more accurately present absence), as a being, an object to be loved and hated, cherished, and destroyed, became much more potent in this year. Again, I consider this phenomenon of the evocation of Bob in many analytic sessions and narratives, to be sometimes a care of me and good use of a circumstance of great power and meaning, and sometimes angry and destructive, with all the mixed motives that aggression can bring to the surface. As the more detailed clinical work that follows attests,

Bob's death was used to help me, to come close to me, to hurt and unsettle me, and to find me. The potential for constructive and destructive use was always present.

## *Mourning and Diversity*

I believe I can only speak about the particular experience of my bereavement and its impact on patients if I can speak first of the significant differences in kinds of loss the analyst may suffer, with significantly different impacts on our participation in treatments. Losses and mournings are, in crucial ways, very different from each other even as they also share certain indelible deep common features. There are differences in the degree of visibility, in the type of loss, its impact (sudden or continuous) and the depth or extent of disruptions to the analyst, disruptions of many kinds.

Losses may be explicitly known, semi-transparent or off-radar. Loss and rupture in the analyst may be borne silently or invisibly both in the larger community and in the clinical dyad. And there will be losses and gains for the analyst, and the analysand, in this regard. Loss will be metabolized differently when the bereavement is public and visible and when it is held collectively and therefore witnessed. This crucial matter of witnessing and containment is something we are newly sensitized to (Davoine, 2007; Gerson, 2009).

Loss comes for some with shocking unexpected immediacy, and in other circumstances, loss is a slow, ongoing and dread-filled accompaniment to every other waking activity. Even in protracted long declines, emergency probably never becomes fully expectable or fully dissociated. Death comes as nightmare or as relief, and continues to be terrible even when also relieving. And unquestionably the processing of the loss of an ambiguously loved or hated object has powerful differences from the loss of someone experienced by self and others as hugely precious.

Each of these manifestations will leave a particular mark on the analyst and those marks are, of course, made and experienced within the context of his or her character. And, as we have countless clinical moments to confirm, buried experience, encrypted and unknown perhaps even to the analyst, appears in inchoate or explicit terms in a patient's material. Clinical knowing, on either side of the couch, slides and dips in uncanny and also obvious directions.

It has occurred to me often this year how invisible the losses in divorce and break-up may be. No one sends condolence notes when a couple separate. The loneliness of mourning is both necessary and yet often too terrible and invisibility may not be as protective as we sometimes think. I am mindful of Jane Tillman's very evocative writing about the impact of patient suicide on the analyst, the huge and often unremitting isolation of that experience for the analyst. I feel convinced that my own capacities to keep analysands in mind has been deeply tied to the great and ongoing gifts of my communities' capacities to hold me. In the context of isolating private practices and so much shrouding of analytic anonymity, this is something to think about.

## *Patient as Supervisor*

As many of my consultants reminded me, people would be wanting to take care of me. How to find the measured way through the patient's wish to be human and empathic and yet not pervert treatment too exclusively to take care of the analyst. Work under conditions of ruptures in one's subjectivity will be deep and difficult. It made me feel sturdy to work. And it made me feel alive. I think, in retrospect, that being helpful and involved in the expansion of self and others was a form of identification with Bob, a site of our mutual identifications. But this insight could not be, should not be, stable, or settled or outside interrogation.

There are many questions to attend to. When was frankness or apology a bid for sympathy? When was my vulnerability truly available for love and hatred and when was it a shield? Again, I stress these are questions always potentially applicable, here found in extreme form. Quite consciously, I felt that I needed to consider that questions and communications from patients about my state of mind and functioning had the potential to operate as a form of supervision. Bass (2009) would argue that this is always potentially true but it seemed particularly so in this time. If someone said she felt fearful to enter the suite, afraid I might be gone, I needed to take time, with myself and the patient, to wonder what was being noticed. Sometimes worries seemed to surface along with shifts in temporality or season. The return to summery weather (Bob had died in early July) revived many fears and worries in a number of patients. But was this patient concern also registering a shift in some internal psychic weather in me? I was committed to honoring the patient's inquiry as relevant and worth exploration. We were often in the zone of radical uncertainty of boundaries and insights. And what was insight and what projection? These kinds of question reverberated on any moments of potential anniversary reactions (the fall marking a year since my return to work was particularly tumultuous).

The question of the analysand's "knowledge" of the analyst has been centrally in play in relational work. I could cite many contemporary authors (Davies, 1996; Bass, 2009; and Aron, 1996) but I am going to draw on an essay that conjures the analytic field and the bi-directional intersubjectivity that stretches beyond the dyad yet immersed in it. The Barangers' highly influential 1961 essay, newly retranslated (2005), drew on Lewinian field theory, on phenomenology, on the ideas of Gestalt and pattern, and other wide-ranging theories emerging in Europe in the 1930s.

All these perspectives claimed a complex bi-directional field for social and psychic life. Experiences of temporality and of social and physical space are, for the Barangers, animated with psychic life and affect and meaning. The analytic situation contained a bi-personal unconscious field, a stream of narratives and conscious projects emanating and crossing between and within both participants. (See Ferro, 2005, for a modern variant of this technical project.)

In thinking of the analytic situations as a field, complexities of temporality, the aliveness and potency of objects, spatial configurations, and personal histories of all participants are all operative. In work I had been doing on ghosts, I had become sensitized to the perturbations of space and time that arise with the appearance of present absences, uncanny resonances arising within patient and analyst. In this first year of mourning, I was particularly susceptible to odd distortions of time. I gave a patient a bill that we both realized reflected her fee in the year before Bob's death. "But I am so much better," she said, laughing perhaps to lessen the sting of criticism or worry, "you can charge me the current rate." But also we both noted what trick of the mind had wound back the clock. Even as rupture and repair are normative in dyadic interactions (Beebe & Lachmann, 1994) and these ruptures in functioning hold out the possibility of repair and analysis, at the same time there is no escape from action's consequences and there is no certainty. It was with this understanding that I was listening to patients, or, as Faimberg (2004) notes, listening to listening.

Bass describes his clinical strategy in the light of Ferenczi's ideas about mutuality, as often engaging the patient in an inquiry of what the patient imagines the analyst is feeling or contributing to a clinical moment. This inquiry may be to stimulate fantasy in the patient, it may be to confirm the patient's reality judgment, and the interaction may include disclosures or not. Often an inquiry into the patient's observations was sufficient although sometimes people wanted to know what my sense of my own state was. Sometimes even the acknowledgment that something was being apprehended and worried over was relieving. I could feel, throughout my practice, that many people worried that I might disappear again, that loss was often or perhaps always imminent. I felt that I needed to keep open, in my own mind, and between myself and the patient, the question of whether this was transference, countertransference, or some complex intersubjective new formation. And, in the spirit of a Bionian answer to that question, I was not always the best judge of where feeling and affect and image was really emanating from.

As the first anniversary approached I tracked the days on which patients seem unsettled, worried about me, often in inchoate ways. There are fantasies of collapse, of aging, of flight and again of loss as I prepared to take a first trip back to Europe to a conference. My face and body were scanned for signs of distress or deadness (and which would be worse) and I felt bound to consider that the patient was reading me better than I might be reading myself. I know even in moments where I did not feel I had very direct access to my own process that this clinical scene is a two-person system and that patients are reading me as well as living their own experience. I believe that I was trying to follow Ferenczi and others' (Gerson, 2009) idea of the centrality of meaning and witnessing as a mode for processing something traumatic. Whether in dialogue with a patient or in my own self-analysis, I had to be willing to take up patients' judgments and perceptions as always about both them and me. One might say this is potentially always a project in analytic work. It seemed crucial for me in this year. In this regard, Bion (1959) is sometimes a consolation and sometimes a scourge. I felt I had to monitor efforts to take care of me and efforts to attack me and sometimes to have difficulty telling the difference. (See Ghent, 1990, on sadism as object finding.)

### *Aggression and Disavowal*

From every serious writer treating loss and mourning, we know the potent role played by aggression and the often accompanying tendency or wish to disavow the depth of violent and destructive feeling that attend on love and loss (Torok & Abraham, 1994; Spielrein, 1995; see also Freud, 1917).

Looking back I can see there have been moments of bravery and moments of cowardice, and that mostly these cowardly moments came about in the presence of aggression and destructiveness in different forms and variously in the transference and the countertransference. When several people wrote to say they were not returning to treatment, I noticed that, in certain situations, I did not discourage them from that decision. In two cases, I felt that there was in the treatments more disavowed aggression than I felt I had bandwidth for.

One person had been too much a caretaker in her family and the thought of taking care of a crippled analyst seemed too terrible. While in our last session I could see that she was actually wanting me to dissuade her from leaving, I did not follow that line. One person, in explaining her departure, mentioned that she had read the notices about my husband, commenting on a "sumptuous" obituary. Now "sumptuous" is an odd word to use about an obituary. Poetic, surely. But I believe I caught, in that phrase, the mix of triumph and envy, psychic phenomena I knew to be deeply in this person's character.

In teaching about technique over the years, I have often used the analogy of the stewardess' instructions to airplane passengers. If you need oxygen, a parent puts on her mask first and then helps the child. You have to be able to breathe if you are going to be able to help someone else. I tried to follow that instruction. What I knew was that it was disavowed aggression, aggression wound around hidden but palpable feelings of triumph that felt, at least initially, beyond my capacities.

I found that direct anger and aggression were not actually so problematic. People could express anger for a variety of reasons that they could see were right and wrong, transferential and countertransferential. Over the first weeks and months of my return, I needed to be able to field a number of difficult questions. Had I been careless? Why had I gone away on vacation at all? Now they were left with a damaged analyst. Direct states of rage and disappointment seemed engaging and important for some patients immediately; for almost all others this anger emerged over time. Disavowed aggression proved to be the most difficult affect I was drawn to handle. I was often feeling decidedly not up to that task. As I have worked on my experiences over this period, I have come to be more curious about my antipathy to disavowed aggression and consider now that the problem arises in my disavowal. My own aggressive reactions to the loss of my husband have been very attenuated. I notice how much I am still caught up in the romance of mourning, the romance in mourning, the melancholy preoccupation Abraham and Torok (1994) write about as the fantasy of the exquisite corpse, the refusal of reality. These splits in my own functioning seem so palpably to have shaped and affected what I could process in patients' material.

I turn now to a series of clinical vignettes. In these treatments powerful problems of identity, shame, aggression, loss, and transference countertransference shakeups taught me a great deal about working in a state of crisis.

## Clinical Vignettes

### *I. Falling*

Because there was some visibility in Bob's death, an obituary in the *NY Times*, students blogging, many people in my analytic community aware of what had occurred, and because a return to work had to be delayed and eventually explained and extended, many patients and supervisees were struggling with difficult fantasies and realities, with too much information or too little.

One patient, B, felt she had to begin talking to her couples therapist (to whom I had referred her) about the "accident". As we processed this later in our sessions, she felt very ashamed at having had fantasies that there had been a violent accident. She felt too terrified of losing me to resume our work while so consumed and shamed with those ideas and worries/wishes. In this instance, we spent time processing her shame and the impossibility of bearing the violence of her fantasies. It is likely that we were also struggling to bear the violence in death itself. This was a patient who had grown up in a household with handguns in every bedroom except her own and a home in which violence was imaginatively and actually always just about to happen.

She wanted to know what I might be willing to tell her about the accident and I told her a simple yet inevitably obfuscated story, aware that the difference between reality and fantasy might again shame her but also had the potential to be calming. The accident had actually been a seemingly minor fall from a bicycle. Complications had come later and with no conscious sense of impending trouble on our part.

The patient and I talked about the meaning of a quiet and easy death, a bike ride on a sunny morning in Spain, a fall, and later sleep. That Bob was spared the fear and shock that came later for me, was clearly consoling for me. I think the patient saw that and also saw that such a feeling could only be part of the experience. I was certainly aware that something was being mystified as well as narrated, that a perspective was being selected. When I reflect on that construction of the experience I feel the truth and the denial, the romance of melancholic images, again my focus on mourning as romance. That account covered over the truth that of course regardless of the chain of events, the violent finality of death itself had marked everything and everyone.

In this way I did not, at that moment, help the patient with her violent fantasies and aggression. And as always in such matters, the cost of leaving aggression unprocessed has been significant. For reasons not solely linked to my experience of loss, the patient's violent angers, long swallowed and evacuated now live much more fully in B's conscious mind and experience although the hardest spot to allow this is in the transference. I suspect, at some unconscious but increasingly preconscious level, the shared fiction of easy death is an evocative repetition of the patient's way of joining her mother. Disavowed aggression, in each of us and in the shared story, awaited our attention and work.

In this case, I felt sometimes successful in the work and sometimes, failed and blocked. We were to return again and again to that first experience of reconnection and avoidance. I was, with difficulty, keeping the question of violence and rage alive. I felt that I used experiences of omnipotence and guilt, which I believe the patient and I shared (in her response to her mother's death and in my response to Bob's) as a way to open up the patient's resistances to mourning, resistances that had been hugely problematic for this patient for over a decade. Perhaps as a form of caretaking this patient (and others) often felt the internal push to make progress, to take up difficult matters, to feel the immediacy of change. I think this was complex. A determination to get better was a way to help me, also to identify with me, to absorb and share with me one of death's lessons about the preciousness of life. The work also loosened my resistances, at least to some extent.

The patient and I remembered together the suddenness of her mother's death – a fall also, a stroke while getting out of bed, a death which at the time for the patient got all tangled in the falls and deaths of 9/11, which she, living downtown, had witnessed. I can see that we were holding death in mind and holding death in suspension and at a distance. The reverie of a sunny morning and a man falling asleep buffers shock, aggression, re-traumatizing images which might come to both of us and perhaps this allowed me to help her work on the recall of images and her mother's death around 9/11. This material, over a number of sessions, held for both of us much traumatic recall alongside peaceful thoughts, suffering suspended. And it became the occasion to work on the patient's longstanding guilt about her mother's death. Inevitably, I think that this was helpful to me in regard to my guilt over Bob's death. We talked about omnipotence and its relieving defense against powerlessness, a process I had been thinking about a lot in my own situation, a potent lesson about the defensiveness in guilt.

There was in this work a strong aspect of parallel process, both of us struggling with guilt and omnipotence. If I am responsible, I could make the story come out differently, if I am in the chain of events, I can alter them. Susan Coates, (personal communication), was helpful in developing this idea for me. If the circumstances of a death are ones in which the bereaved person was actually present and somehow implicated in what happened, omnipotence has a particular virulence. I made it happen. I will unmake it. And I think this potent and mad thought is braided in many experiences of mourning, in which I would include my own experience and B's. Melancholy suspensions of reality come in many forms.

It is one of the ironies of thinking about my reactions to patients and to grieving that, omnipotence, is both a defense against mourning and a core aspect of many analysts' formation and functioning . My analysis of the therapist's difficulties in self care included the link of analytic vocations to histories as caretaking precocious children turning into caretakers of others, turning the ordeals of disorganized attachment into professional functioning (Harris, 2009). Our very central organizing fantasies, productive of our best work and often best selves, also work defensively against absorbing powerlessness. Opportunities are taken, some are missed, some present themselves again and another chance for growth opens. I think of the disequilibrium and chaos at the edge of change, the movement to and away from the emergence of something new, this time in me and the patient.

I continue to learn this with B. To both our surprise – and yet how odd to be surprised – during the time of the first anniversary of Bob's death, the falling bodies reappeared. The patient began a session with the somewhat shakily delivered sentence "You look worried." And we began to work with who was worried. What was she noticing that I was not? How was worry circulating in this week? We spent much of the rest of the session after this very intersubjective beginning, looking at the way she was handling family and relational crises and in that speaking of her great difficulty in finding the right space for memory: not fetish, not erased, metabolized. Speaking tearfully about a beautiful film about the history of the city, she found herself cycled back to 9/11, and I was able to open up this moment as one about memory and anniversary, including the falling bodies in and around 9/11 and the man falling off his bicycle in Barcelona. The patient could say that what she most feared was losing me and from that point could get back to the crisis at hand in her relational life. For me, this session illuminates the complex but useful cycle in which moments of mutuality release the patient to his/her own internal and unconscious process. The intersubjective feeds the intrapsychic and vice versa.

## *II. The Big Death and the Little Death*

P. is tearful and unsettled. Weeping, she tells me that she does not know how to bring me her concerns that seem so minor, so little. And in the early sessions in the fall, she is one of the patients whose tears do leave me questioning who is crying: she or I? Or are we both flooded and flooding? An analytic patient, deeply intellectual and capacious, P. balances family and ambition and work in a way I find easy to support. With P., there are many bright spots of identification. But, by her own estimation, she struggles a lot with dissociation, with living as if not mattering.

Yet P. has come back after my absence with a family death on her mind as well. She has, in my absence, had to process a confusing and enigmatic death, of a confusing and enigmatically constituted grandparent. A little death, P. says ruefully, and often a little scornfully. And so we try to hold a space for the big death and the little death and inquire into this apparently insignificant loss. P.'s own mother has no way to speak of this death or of her identifications with this parent. Alienated from this mother since her childhood, she has had to scrabble for a life without an abiding maternal presence. The grandmother lived into extreme old age, stripped in everyone's mind of presence, meaning, attachments, and practically of citizenship. As P. and I talk, I keep hearing the declarative voice of P. ringing in my ears: "my grandmother has no mind." And mind in this extended, highly intellectualized, family is everything.

It is so stark, this antiphony of the big and the little death. I am clearly mourning the most unimaginable loss in my life. My face and P.'s can be tearfilled. But we both know that something is radically wrong with this proposed asymmetry. What is it about this death that is "little"? This woman with a few family members fled Europe in the 1930s. P. and I have many reference points of intergenerational transmission but nothing can be spoken within P.'s family and real acknowledgment of the traumatized grandmother remains utterly off-radar. Damaged, unable to mother well or even adequately, this émigrée stripped of her European citizenship and humanity, eerily takes up that same space of exile and disavowal in a new country. P. reports a dream of her mother who is visiting. "My mother tells me she had a dream that her boss [actually a man deceased for some years] calls her on the phone and says, 'Why have you not visited me?'" And her mother recounts, "I say to him, I can't come and see you, I am visiting America." P. gently but firmly suggests to her mother that this is actually a dream about her recently dead mother. This is a parallel process to analysis; P. and I have these conversations all the time. No, assures her mother, it was a dream about my boss. I ask P. her associations to the element of visiting America, the fact that seems to explain no visits or connection. America, P. says softly, and now weeping, the place where meaning can become shallow, thinned out, where there is no history. Now, for the first time, since I have returned to work, I feel P.'s tears are hers, for the migrant exile who left so much in Europe, and was unfound, unnamed, and un-minded in the new world. I feel this as a turning point in my return to being P.'s analyst.

But this return is not always stable. Months later, P. deep in a difficult and embattled scene with family and overwhelmed in a way that seemed oddly out of character, came to session. And for the first time in a long time, she opened her session with the worried thought that she must not burden me. I wondered if something in the sunnier weather, a reminder of the previous summer, or was something in me spurring this worry. She thought not and I decided to think of this as transference, as a fear that I could not hold her. And shared an idea I was having about her current difficulties that I was aware that, oddly, I had never had, consciously about P. She is a woman of great independence and potent determination in a life full of projects and accomplishments, so I found myself wondering if P.'s current agitation was actually about separation anxieties, about her fear of abandonment. I was practically shy about making such a suggestion. But the more I thought of her precocious independence, her early autonomy and early strivings for independence and control, the more I began to wonder about what fearfulness might lie behind this.

Omnipotence and its defensiveness have been much on my mind this year, the way both guilt and control mask the powerless in grieving. Something perhaps in my making this suggestion in the spirit of my identifications with her made it possible for us to think. And very early experiences of feeling swamped and overwhelmed began to appear, linked to the current crisis in her family life. I say this to P. and then she remembered she had had a dream, in which an older woman appears, someone in her current life, who is very impaired. She is communicating with people, there is a large group talking with her, and although she cannot speak, she can take in everything. An older woman without a functioning communicating mind, or with mind locked into silence. We think of her grandmother, the flow of this lack of maternal holding intergenerationally and we think of me, the fear that my mind, too, is in lockdown, that I cannot hold and contain P. A mother with a hole in her mind. "*Psychose blanche*" is Green's term for the experience of the child in the presence of bereavements in the mother that the child has insufficient structure to hold and experience. Perhaps the abyss in me can be of use, reveal the historic roots of P.'s omnipotence and her fears of mattering.

### III. "Maybe Widowhood is Contagious"

J. said this, in passing. A remark tossed off with a signature little chuckling laugh that she and I, over the years, have learned to pay close attention to. The laugh allowed me to inquire. J. wanted to distance herself from this inquiry.

J.'s rage erupted at any signs of incompetence, neglect, or vulnerability in another person. Now, in this period, perhaps one could say at last, my circumstances matched the family story. We had often been struck by the repetition in J.'s adult relationships of the maternal scene in which a mother caught in her own bereavement cannot hold, find, carry, and mirror her child.

Working on her idea, and its communication to me that widowhood might be contagious, opened up some work on aggression and a wish to hurt the weakened and saddened (m)other. But this work went slowly and with much resistance. It was shortly after the "widowhood as contagious" comment that another comment finally opened a process for us. J. was angrily recounting a familiar and disappointing scene in her marriage and suddenly and angrily said that often she envied me widowhood, being able to live alone, not bothered by disappointment and overwork for others. I had two almost simultaneous reactions: first, that this spoke to such loneliness in J. and, second, that this was a communication of great hostility. I was simultaneously stunned and sad. As we unpacked this, J. and I found ourselves in a very familiar spot. She can speak of her desperation for connection and yet also her equally intense assumption that she would be abandoned and rejected if she needed something. And in her communication to me she had ensured that her need would be expressed in a way that might/would/did prevent a fully empathic response by the listener. I could say to her both that I had heard the terrible loneliness and heard it in a way that made me careful and attentive as to what might come next, wary of her intent to hurt. J. found this idea of a wariness in me impossible to bear and yet saw deeply that this was all too accurate. She spent several sessions trying to deflect and transform the experience. Others were angry with her. She was the victim. She needed forgiveness but could never offer it to the neglectful hurtful others of her childhood.

Here, I felt that the mix of object finding and object murder tipped more on the destructive end of that spectrum. In a later session, J. was able to notice that she had "contempt" for mourning, a reaction to feeling excluded from the other's mourning. That idea opened the links between me, J.'s mother, and figures in her current life. She could probe the question, which I think is genuinely difficult to answer: Is forgiveness possible? What should happen in the presence of a parent's significant failures and destructiveness? What should our attitude be? What could be transformative? I conjure up Derrida's (2001) wonderful idea that you can only forgive the unforgiveable. J. sits with the worrying understanding that the anger she feels she needs to survive in safety is spoiling precious links and possibilities. But as J. pushes into new ways of relating, she worries that without the carapace of contempt and anger, she is reduced and unsafe.

## Conclusions

Looking back at this year and at this chapter, I feel how complex and unstable the experiences with patients' aggression have been. It has been the source of profound and psyche-altering, experiences of J. and for the patient B. struggling with falling bodies. With P, somewhat differently, the process had involved awareness of her vulnerability, perhaps seen through my own. I can penetrate both our defensive uses of omnipotence. But I see both my strengths and my limits in how that work has gone.

For J. the magnitude of early loss feels much clearer but still very formidable. Interestingly, J., whose resistance to being able to take account of her anger and destructiveness had *seemed* so impenetrable and off-line, has moved into a much more expansive form of a depressive position. She is more loving because more able to notice the impact of her hate.

Not all clinical challenges have been about hatred and aggression. Loving and appreciative affects bring their own challenges. Some patients felt excited at what they sensed was a new vulnerability, intrigued at the possibilities of a newly and differently available analyst. Fantasies of rescue and healing love appeared both guiltily and triumphantly. Also, it is useful to be reminded that rescue fantasies can be laced with sabotage and with an aggression-filled wish to control the more vulnerable analyst. Love, hate, and my vulnerability often moved us to the edge of chaos, a site both productive and dangerous.

A patient found herself talking about what Bob's death might mean and what role Bob was playing in the treatment. I had never exactly thought of this, but I found myself saying that I thought that knowing about my process gave her access to my interior spaces, my mind and that this was profoundly new for her. She has begun to experience a therapist with a mind. And I said that I thought that Bob was crucial in this. That he was a Third, and we worked on all that that might mean. She agreed and then ruminating on Bob's death and what it stirred for all of us, she spoke excitedly. "Should I be talking in this crazy way about your dead husband?" I said, "but maybe he is not dead". Laughter. Sadness. Thirdness. We stay in the safer spaces of melancholy, slowly approaching the darker spaces of mourning.

In this context, I was aware that (except for my gender) I now met the demographic criteria for analysts at risk for boundary violations. Was my bereavement a dangerous vulnerability? How would I know this? For several years, I and a number of colleagues have been considering and processing a number of significant boundary violations, inevitably entertaining the important discussion of how such breaches so relentlessly stain and enter our communities and institutions and, at the same time, remain so silenced and unthinkable.

I had, mid-year, gone back to see my old analyst, who was himself weathering some illness and disability. As he was talking about the question of aging and debility, he raised the concept that was widely accepted in institutions, 20 years ago, that beyond a certain age an analyst should not begin new analyses. Why not, I asked? He used an old-fashioned expression, "Object hunger," and it struck a chord. What does one do about "object hunger," however it has arisen in normal or challenged aging?

In an earlier version of this chapter, read by colleagues, someone giving me feedback read my concern about boundary violations and said, summarily, that I should take that section out. I did so, without much thought until I sat in a committee meeting for a conference on sexual boundary violations and, listening to colleagues talking about silence and disavowal, suddenly remembered my quite dissociated obedience to censoring those thoughts. So I put them back into the chapter now, in this version, with a wish to keep open the question of the analyst's vulnerability, her object hunger. My hope is to know and live with wounds, and with the question of use and misuse of patients. But that hope is likely to depend on the presence of witnesses, containment, and dialogue. And, as a colleague gently reminded me, writing this chapter has been part of processing unmanageable life and death.

## References

Anzieu, D. (Ed.) (1994). *Acoustic envelopes*. London: Karnac.
Aron, L. (1996). *A meeting of minds: Mutuality in psychoanalysis*. Hillsdale, NJ: Analytic Press.
Baranger, M., & Baranger, W. (2005). The analytic situation as a dynamic field. *International Journal of Psychoanalysis, 89*, 795–826.
Bass, A. (1993). *Learning from the patient*: By Patrick Casement (New York: Guilford Press) *Psychoanalytic Dialogues, 3*, 151–167.
Bass, A. (2009). The mutuality of change and personal growth in analytic relations: Commentary. *Psychoanalytic Dialogues, 19*, 463–467.
Berlin, H. A. (2011). The neural basis of the dynamic unconscious. *Neuropsychoanalysis, 13*, 5–31.
Bion, W. (1959). Attacks on linking. *Internernational Journal of Psychoanalysis, 40*, 308–315.
Bromberg, P. (2006). *Awakening the dreamer: Clinical journeys*. Hillsdale, NJ: Analytic Press.
Coates, S. (2010). How early can babies experience trauma. Paper presented at Columbia Psychoanalytic. Winner of Mahler Prize (unpublished).
Cooper, S. (2010). *A disturbance in the field*. New York: Taylor & Francis.
Corbett, K. (2008). *Boyhoods*. New Haven, CT: Yale University Press.
Corbett, K. (2013). The analyst's private space. Paper presented at the NYU Postdoctoral Program in Psychotherapy and Psychoanalysis.

Davies, J. M. (1996). Linking the "pre-analytic" with the postclassical: Integration, dissociation and the multiplicity of unconscious processes. *Contemporary Psychoanalysis, 32*, 553–576.

Davoine, F. (2007). The character of madness in the talking cure. *Psychoanalytic Dialogues, 17*(5), 627–638.

Derrida, J. (2001). *On cosmopolitanism and forgiveness* (Trans. Mark Dooley & Michael Hughes). London and New York: Routledge.

Faimberg, H. (2004). *The telescoping of generations.* London: Library of Psychoanalysis/Karnac.

Ferenczi, S. (1933). *The confusion of tongues between adults and the child. Final contributions to the problems and methods of psychoanalysis.* London: Hogarth Press.

Ferro, A. (2005). Bion: Theoretical and clinical observations. *International Journal of Psychoanalysis, 86*, 1535–1542.

Freud, S. (1917). Mourning and melancholia. In J. Strachey (Ed. & Trans), *The Standard edition of the complete psychological works of Sigmind Freud.* (vol. 14, pp. 237–258). London: Hogarth Press.

Gallese, V. (2009). Mirror neurons, embodied simulation, and the neural basis of social identification. *Psychoanalytic Dialogues, 19*, 519–536.

Gallese, V., & Sinigaglia, C. (2011). What is so special about embodied simulation. *Trends in Cognitive Sciences, 15*(11), 512–519.

Gerson, S. (2009). When the third is dead: Memory, mourning and witnessing in the aftermath of the Holocaust. *International Journal of Psychoanalysis, 90*(6), 1341–1357.

Ghent, E. (1990). Masochism, submission and surrender. *Contemporary Psychoanalysis, 26*, 108–136.

Goldberger, M. (1993). "Bright spot," a variant of "blind spot." *Psychoanalytic Quarterly, 62*, 270–273.

Green, A. (1983). The dead mother complex. In G. Kohon (Ed.), *The dead mother: The work of Andre Green.* London: Routledge, 1999.

Harris, A. (2005). *Gender as soft assembly.* Hillsdale, NJ: The Analytic Press.

Harris, A. (2009). You must remember this. *Psychoanalytic Dialogues, 19*(1), 2–21.

Harris, A., & Sinsheimer, K. (2008). The analyst's vulnerability: Preserving and fine-tuning analytic bodies. In F. Anderson (Ed.), *Bodies in treatment.* New York; Routledge.

Hofer, M. (1984). Relationships as regulators: A psychobiologic perspective on bereavement. *Psychosomatic Medicine, 46*, 183–197.

Hofer, M. (1996). On the nature and consequence of early loss *Psychosomatic Medicine, 58*, 570–578.

Knoblauch, S. (2000). *The musical edge of therapeutic dialogue.* Hillsdale, NJ: The Analytic Press.

Kohon, G. (Ed.). (1999). *The dead mother; The work of Andre Green.* London: Routledge.

Merleau-Ponty, M. (2012). *Phenomenology of perception* (Trans. Donald A. Landes). New York: Routledge.

Ogden, T. (1996). *Reverie and interpretation.* New York: Jason Aronson.

Reis, B. (2009). Performative and enactive features of psychoanalytic witnessing: The transference as the site of address. *International Journal of Psychoanalysis*, *90*, 1359–1372.

Salamon, G. (2010). *Assuming a body: Transgender and the rhetorics of materiality*. New York: Columbia University Press.

Schilder, P. (1930). The unity of body, sadism and dizziness. *Psychoanalytic Review*, *17*, 114–122.

Schilder, P. (1935). *The image and appearance of the human body*. London: Kogan Paul/Trench, Trubner & Co., Ltd.

Seligman, S. (2003). The developmental perspective in relational psychoanalysis. *Contemporary Psychoanalysis*, *39*, 477–508

Seligman, S. (in press). Temporaality, intersubjectivity and 'going on being'. *Psychoanalytic Dialogues*.

Spielrein, S. (1995). Destruction as cause of becoming. *Psychoanalytic Contemporary Thought*, *18*, 85–118. [First published as Die Destruktion als Ursache des Werdens. *Jahrbuch für psychoanalytische und psychopathologische Forschungen* (*Yearbook of Psychoanalytical and Psycho-pathological Research*), 1912, 4, 465–503].

Stern, D. (2010). *Forms of vitality: exploring dynamic experiences in psychology, the arts, psychotherapy and development*. New York: Oxford University Press.

Tillman, J. (2006), When a patient commits suicide: An empirical study of psychoanalytic clinicians. *Journal of the American Psychoanalytic Association*, *87*, 159–177.

Torok, M., & Abraham, N. (1994). *The shell and the kernel*. Chicago, IL: University of Chicago Press.

# 3

# A VOICE LOST, A VOICE FOUND
## After the Death of the Analyst[1]

*Robin A. Deutsch*

It is getting to be twilight on a late Friday afternoon in winter, the end of my last analytic hour before a 10-day holiday break. Getting up from the couch, I say, "See you a week from Monday," and my analyst, sitting with a blanket around her shoulders, looks at me and smiles, confirming her return. Nine days later, another analyst calls to tell me that my analyst has died during the night.

What is the fate of the analytic life created by the analysand and the analyst when only half the dyad remains? Ogden (1997) writes of the analyst's untimely death:

> The analyst's death forecloses for the analysand the possibility of fully retrieving his mind (a mind that has not been exclusively his own personal possession for some time). The aspect of mind that has (in part) been "lost" is the mind that has been generated and developed intersubjectively. It is a mind that can be appropriated by the analysand only gradually in the course of an uninterrupted analytic experience.
>
> (p. 10)

In this chapter, I describe a process of an alteration in my relationship with the person, transferential and real, of my analyst, during which I took leave of my analyst as we had been. I will focus on a series of dreams I had during this time of transition that illustrate how retaining and cementing my relationship with my lost analyst, through internalizing her, facilitated the return of my analysand voice, and the freedom to take a new object even as I retained the old.

In my experience, everything following the death of my analyst went as it should. I was fortunate not to learn of her death through rumor; another analyst informed me of her death within hours. She was as specific as she could be concerning what was known about the cause of death. She offered me an appointment the next day, and indicated her willingness to work with me during this very acute time as well as offering to help me decide what I wanted to do about ongoing treatment. My supervisors and colleagues were very supportive. I was not excluded from the analytic community's experience of my analyst's death, and when her memorial was held, I attended. There, sitting among many others, I listened to her family and friends describe a woman I knew in the way analysands know their analysts. As I sat at this communal event, I was relieved to notice that these descriptions of my analyst were like my own.

Judith Butler (2003) describes evocatively the loss of a loved other:

> It is not as if an "I" exists independently over here and then simply loses a "you" over there, especially if the attachment to "you" is part of what composes who "I" am. If I lose you, under these conditions, then I not only mourn the loss, but I become inscrutable to myself.... On one level, I think I have lost "you" only to discover that "I" have gone missing as well.
>
> (p. 12)

My analysis included an almost ever present dialogue with my analyst between analytic hours. Upon leaving her office, I would continue our shared conversation of the most recent hour. I came to appreciate that my experience of this imaginary but very active ongoing dialogue between us was part of my analytic process and our shared dialogue. Walking to my car after I left her office on Friday for what turned out to be our last time, this voice—our dialogue—abruptly, disturbingly, and uncannily disappeared. And then, after losing her voice, my own became silent.

Sitting in the office of the new consultant, I mourned my dead analyst, and was simultaneously aware of what more I had lost. I missed not just my analyst, but also my analysis. I had lost contact with that part of me that had come to think in certain ways, to access fleeting thoughts and feelings and share them with another. I sat in the chair and stared at the couch. Yearning for the way I had become accustomed to thinking, mourning the person I thought with, and the language we used together, I tried to speak and found myself silent. I wanted to lie on the couch, but when eventually I did, I found it unfamiliar, and this feeling contributed to my distress and disorientation. The acute loss of my voice fueled my confusion. I could not locate in me my analysand voice, my working voice, or the language I shared with my analyst. Not only had my words been lost, but my pleasure in using them as well. I could not find the way I had been in my analysis. It was inaccessible to me. My pleasure in our fluid exchange was gone. In its place was something that felt dry and unfamiliar. Choking on dialogue that used to be familiar, the tone, cadence, and rhythm of my thought and dialogue felt foreign.

The consulting analyst said she would continue to work with me until I could decide what I wanted to do. As I began to feel I wanted more, I asked to enter treatment with her. I did not realize at the time that I was agreeing to enter a relationship I was not prepared for. And while I think this is often true when a patient enters an analytic process, these special circumstances, the circumstances where I held onto my dead analyst but was asking someone else for help, were fraught. In order to retrieve my voice, I had to move on, but to move on I had to be willing to begin a new relationship and accept help from someone new. At the time, I could not reflect on what I had known. I was fearful that entering this relationship would harm the old.

Ogden (1998) describes the way analyst and analysand come together to create an analytic treatment:

> [A]nalyst and analysand together generate conditions in which each speaks with a voice arising from the unconscious conjunction of the two individuals. The voice of the analyst and the voice of the analysand under these circumstances are not the same voice, but the two voices are spoken, to a significant degree, from a common area of jointly (but asymmetrically) constructed unconscious experience.
>
> (p. 444)

This chapter is about voice: developing, having, losing, and recreating. With my analyst, I learned to enjoy words, to use them to craft a multilayered expression of experience: words to play with, words that evoked, words that provoked, words at play, rich words. I learned to use language to create a voice uniquely my own that described my internal experience and the process of my mind. I learned about using language to affect the other. Words floated in the room between us, a space for joint thinking, and interwoven with my words was our shared, collaborative voice.

In retrospect, it seems my struggle—and perhaps this is true for others as well—was not just to find another analyst with whom to work, but to find a part of myself—my analysand voice, my working voice—that allowed for an engagement with my mind and with another person and her mind in this intimate way. Whether the analysand works briefly with another analyst to deal with the immediate crisis or begins more comprehensive work, the bereft analysand must find the part of her that existed in this interwoven state with the original analyst. I offer my experience as only one of many.

Analysts write more personally about death and loss than one would suppose. We write about the death of patients: through suicide (Chassay, 2006), through sudden death (Buechler, 2000), through protracted illness (Mayer, 1994). We speak about termination as a death (Coltart, 1996). We write about the death and illness of spouses, children, and the loss of pregnancies (Chasen, 1996; Gerson, 1994; Mendelsohn, 1996; Morrison, 1996). Periodically, we write about the process of our own illnesses as well as our impending deaths (Dewald, 1982; Fajardo, 2001; Feinsilver, 1998; Morrison, 1990, 1997; Pizer, 1997). Interestingly, when it comes to the analyst's death, most of what is written is from the viewpoint of the analyst; the analysand's unique and singular voice is not heard.

The few articles in the analytic literature that focus on the death of the analyst from the analysand's vantage point often address the question of what is best done to help the surviving patient if an analyst dies during a treatment. These evocative and heartfelt articles attempt to articulate how best to assist the traumatically bereft analysand. Citing the remarkably small amount of clinically useful thinking about the analyst's death, Traesdal (2005) recommends that the analyst be alert to the patient's worries about the analyst's death from both the reality and transferential vantage points. In her paper, she emphasizes attunement to the analysand's reality needs to discuss what the analysand should do if the analyst should die suddenly during the course of the analysis. Rendely (1999) describes the analysand's privileged position within the analysis as a protected place and relationship. If the analyst dies prematurely, the protected position of analyst and analysand alone isolates the bereaved analysand. Rendely's paper speaks of the need for the analytic community to assist the candidate analysand, and outlines areas where the analytic community can intervene. Both Traesdal and Rendely also review recommendations about what kind of therapeutic help should be offered the bereft analysand. Garcia-Lawson and Lane (1997) focus on practical steps that can be taken at the death of an analyst to lessen the analysand's pain. Ziman-Tobin (1989) suggests dividing the analysand's needed intervention into two functions: the bridging analyst and the treating analyst. The bridging analyst works with the analysand through the immediate crisis, while the treating analyst remains available to initiate an analytic treatment after the crisis passes. By implication, the result of this bifurcation is that the treating analyst remains free to begin a treatment because the bridging analyst has absorbed the emotional impact of the immediate crisis and transition. My experience suggests otherwise. Each of these articles expresses the deep hope that some action could ameliorate the painful effects of this traumatic loss, a practical solution that will somehow undo the analysand's sorrow. The common desire for action in each of these articles reveals a hidden wish for a magical solution that will hold mourning at arm's length.

What about the analysand's voice? With few exceptions (Adams, 1995; Garfield, 1990; Rendely, 1999; Traesdal, 2005), the voice of the analysand is expressed as a composite, homogenized voice in a research project. The earliest, as well as most frequently cited paper, written by Lord, Ritvo, and Solnit (1978), is an exploratory study of 27 analysands, all of whom had lost their analyst to death during the course of the analysis. Eleven bereaved analysands and 16 subsequent treating analysts responded to a questionnaire. This exploratory research focused on the quality, intensity, and length of mourning. No individual voice is heard. In 1989, Barbanel introduced a panel dealing with the experience of working with bereaved analysands. While this panel dealt with the authors' collective experience in treating individuals whose analysts died during their analysis, once again the individual analysand's singular voice is missing. Galatzer-Levy (2004) presented composite data based on his treatment of 10 analysands subsequent to the death of the original treating analyst. In his conclusion, he emphasized collusion between analyst and analysand to avoid the painful topic of the analyst's visible illness and impending death. Firestein (1990) cited composite data gathered from colleagues who were treating 13 patients whose analysts died during their treatment. He concluded that, once the patient infers the analyst's illness or is directly informed, the treatment is ended, no matter how much longer the terminally ill analyst and analysand continue to meet. These data raise a question about the presence of an unseen collaborative process between the dying analyst and analysand to avoid speaking together of the analyst's vulnerability.

The first part of my analysand voice to return was my dream voice. Looking back, I can see that my dreams were organized around themes, where I worked on the loss of my analyst, as well as my voice within that analysis, while I engaged in creating a new voice within a new relationship. My dream images developed and shifted as they were interwoven with my conscious working voice, and foreshadowed changes in my new analysis. While I am certain that each dream I report represents my psychological underpinnings in a broader way, I am restricting my discussion of them to the context in which they were dreamt: the traumatic loss of my analyst and my analysis. My discussion includes the confounding variable of entering another analytic relationship within the context of that traumatic ending. For the purpose of this chapter, I am oversimplifying the discontinuous but interpenetrating dream themes, which integrated my dream voice with the development of a working voice in my new treatment.

From this vantage point, the first dreams I report emphasize my initial attempt to deal with the sudden death of my analyst. Immediately after my analyst's death, my dreams became inchoate, raw emotion in a sea of swirling colors. I would wake from these dreams disrupted and disconsolate. After one month, I began to have dreams linked to my loss. For the first time in my life, I recorded my dreams, which kept me connected to my analyst. In retrospect, I also believe that recording my dreams was a way to reestablish a connection to myself. Three years and some 230 dreams later, I was ready to write about my experience.

*Dream 1*
I am lost and looking for help. I go into a building seeking someone who would tell me where I should go. I wander from empty room to empty room. In the last room, I expect to find someone, but no one is there.

Not surprisingly, a wordless dream is my first cohesive dream after the death of my analyst. This dream underlines my felt experience of emptiness and abandonment precipitated by my analyst's death. The building represents my mind and the empty rooms, the lack of internal objects to rely upon. Lost and aimless, I am unable to find my own course. While I search for help, I am unable to find any, which to me represents the hopelessness I felt at the time. Wordless, I cannot ask for help. Despite actual support from friends, colleagues, and the consulting analyst, I felt profoundly alone.

In the next series of dreams, beginning three months after her death and extending over 24 months, I believe that my dream voice allowed me to do what I had not in fact been able to do: prepare to end my analysis and say goodbye while I try to make some sense of what had happened. These dreams also provided something equally important to me in mourning my loss: I made my analyst alive, I made her tell me what was wrong, I made her say goodbye to me, and I made her cry with sadness at our mutual loss.

*Dream 2*
My analyst tells me she is going to close her practice in two months.

*Dream 3*
My analyst tells me that she is too tired to go on. She says we can talk about it if I want.

*Dream 4*
I am in my analyst's office. When I come in, she tells me she is dying and asks if I want to know what is wrong. I say yes. She is sitting on one end of her couch and I on the other. As she sits on the couch and reads to me about her illness from a book, she begins to cry. I do as well. She asks if I am all right. I say I am fine and reach to hold her hand as we cry together.

With my analyst's sudden death, I now must do the psychological work that my analyst would have helped me with were she still alive. I recreate my analyst and our relationship so that she can begin to help me come to a meaningful termination of my analysis. She invites me to discuss with her the impact of her statement that she is too tired to go on. In the last of these dreams (Dream 4), she tells me what will bring our analytic relationship to a close. We are sitting together on her couch, not in our usual places as analyst and analysand. She cries in my presence and I comfort her. In my dream, I attempt to maintain my past relationship to her as I knew it, but our positions are changed. By comforting her, as she might comfort me, I begin to transform our relationship.

At the same time that I was searching for a way to maintain and transform the relationship with my dead analyst, I was also attempting to permit the relationship with the new analyst. As part of my process of developing a relationship with the new analyst, I painted her as distant and inept. Angry with her for not being my dead analyst, I could not allow myself to deepen the relationship with her because I feared damage to my lost analyst.

In the midst of speaking with sputtering and hesitant language to an unfamiliar person, I surprisingly would find myself revealing material that I had not discussed with my dead analyst. I became aware of how little I had spoken about bodily issues with my chronically ill, overly thin analyst. I worried we had unconsciously agreed to avoid a path that would have led us to her illness. The appearance of never explored material buoyed a feeling in me of recovery of my analysand voice. The reappearance of my capacity to work in an analytic session made me feel more familiar to myself. By using my analysand voice, I felt less disrupted in my inner relationship with my dead analyst. I felt excited about the possibility of exploring the previously unspoken. Through the experience of creating an emerging analytic voice, I felt less distant from my own voice.

Noticing this shift was not without worry—worry that by entering this analytic relationship I would harm my dead analyst. During this time, my dream voice became dominated by themes of intense loyalty conflicts and cheating. I committed multiple unspecified criminal acts and relational cheating for which I was punished. Speaking about bodily matters and reporting my dreams reflected a choice between stagnation in an analysis where no more words could be spoken, and the dynamism and excitement of words waiting to be spoken. This conflict made sustained attention to new material difficult. The mere hint that there was some aspect of my internal life that I did not discuss with my dead analyst, in an analysis that was exceptionally helpful to me, felt like a betrayal. As I began to talk about bodily matters, I wanted to retreat, fearing damage to my dead analyst. The new analyst began to speak of my avoidance of anger at my now lost analyst. How could I suggest to this new analyst, never mind myself, that I wanted more? What if I hinted that I felt let down by my dead analyst? In what way did I know that my avoidance of speaking about bodies protected my analyst and me from what we could not bear to talk about? What had I implicitly known about my analyst's health?

Establishing a relationship with the new analyst, and refusing to give up my relationship with my dead analyst as I knew it, trapped me between mourning and melancholia. Freud wrote compellingly about loss and mourning multiple times during his life. His seminal essay "Mourning and Melancholia" (1917) described the process of mourning as dependent on gradual detachment from and relinquishment of the now lost object. By detaching from the beloved lost object, Freud posited that the mourner finds sufficient libido to invest in a new love object. In this way, successful mourning is defined as the detachment of emotional ties from the internal representation of the lost object. In this system, energy is finite. To have the new, the old must be given up. Detachment from the deceased object is an essential precursor to attachment to a new object. In his early work, Freud believed that the melancholic individual, dependent on identification to maintain the relationship with the lost object, remains mired in ambivalence toward the beloved object. As a result of the fixed quantity of libido, the exchange of objects cannot take place. A new love object cannot be taken. In this work, Freud's concept of identification is central. Identification and its relations, more broadly defined as internalization, were linked with melancholia, a depressive state. Melancholia results from experiencing rage toward the internalized object as rage against the self. As Freud's theory evolved, influenced both by his increasing understanding of the mind and his personal experiences, his view of the function of identification also evolved. Identification, presented in "Mourning and Melancholia" as part of a pathological process, became included as part of a normative process, which furthers development. In "Group psychology and the analysis of the ego," Freud (1921) described identification as "the earliest expression of an emotional tie to another person" (p. 105). In *The ego and the Id*, Freud (1923) recognized that normal identification was a way of titrating overwhelming affects of loss and preserving the object permanently (J. S. Chase, personal communication, May 2008). Later still, Freud (1933) mentioned identification as one of the outcomes in the normal mourning process.

Many authors have taken Freud's early theorizing about loss and mourning to task. Gaines (1997) posits that the task of mourning is twofold: detachment and continuity. Freud's early theory made use of identification for the purposes of detachment from the lost object. According to Gaines, by "creating continuity" (p. 549), the bereft individual develops a nourishing inner relationship with the lost object. He also states that the inner relationship with the lost object needs to be transformed so that it can "continue to be animated without ongoing nourishment from an actual relationship" (p. 555). I propose that by the use of the word *animated*, Gaines means a reworking and reinvesting in the libidinal tie. Baker (2001), citing clinical and empirical findings, views mourning as a transformation of self and object in the inner world of the mourner.

These two articles share a premise, which I understand as emphasizing the significance of the inner representation of the ongoing relationship with the lost object. In this sense, the object tie between the bereft and the beloved lost object needs to be sustained in order to help the mourner with moving forward. Rendely (1999) echoes this idea when she states that mourning is not only a process of separation, but also a way to a secure attachment with the lost, beloved other: "Focusing on past memories and experiences, the bereaved attempts to relocate internally what has been lost externally" (p. 142). In a different but related critique, Butler (2003), with her scholar's sensibility, criticizes Freud's premise of libidinal interchangeability and suggests that full substitutability is not what should be striven for in the course of mourning. She directs the reader's attention to the role of the lost object as the object continues to influence and affect the self. For Butler, acceptance of the transforming effect of loss on the self is an outcome of mourning.

I, as do these writers, I have a disagreement with Freud's early theorizing about the primacy of detachment in mourning: specifically, viewing detachment from the lost object as the primary and most essential task of mourning. I propose that, while the loved object is lost, the libidinal tie to the now lost object needs to be maintained so that the inner relationship with the beloved can be transformed and reclaimed. The re-finding of my working voice as part of mourning was precipitated by a change in my relationship with my dead analyst. My dreams during this period capture the fluidity of these states of being, moving me forward into the future, and then backtracking to a constricted and angry emotional state.

*Dream 5*
My analyst is looking at me. She says, "I can't help you as your analyst anymore. But," she continues, touching my chest over my heart, "I'm still with you, here."

This dream is a termination dream, where I continue working toward a transition with my dead analyst. I am giving up my analyst as an analyst to me. She is helping me develop a new and different relationship with her, no longer analyst/analysand. My dream voice during this time alternated between saying goodbye to my dead analyst, and the inclusion of the new analyst as a partner in my venture, albeit ambivalently.

The new analyst suggests that I do not ask much of her. I think how different the voices of these two women are. The insistent and at times impatient voice of my dead analyst and the soft, modulated tones of the new analyst feel at odds with each other. One pushes, one waits. This difference is represented in a dream where my dead analyst instructs the live analyst how to work with me.

*Dream 6*
I am with two men: one tall, thin, and dark-haired, and the other shorter and round with blond hair. Chased by a missile that is intent on killing us, we run into a building, knowing that the missile will blow up the building and kill us. Peeking out windows at the back of the building, the dark-haired man and I plot out a route to go over the roofs because we know, if we do, the missile will lose our track. When it's time to go, the blond man says he's staying behind and that we must go on. All three of us understand he is choosing to die because he knows and we know he will die from the explosion. I embrace him before I leave.

This dream represents my relationship with my two analysts: former and current. Death is within sight, my analyst is choosing death, and I am actively leaving her. I orchestrate my analyst's death by crafting a death whose timing is now under my control and for which I have planned. By redoing her death, I can say goodbye to her. To accompany me into the future, I orchestrate a companion.

*Dream 7*
I am looking for a new apartment. I wander into a horrible-looking building and allow myself to be persuaded by the woman who owns the building to look at the space. When the door opens, I see a breathtakingly beautiful apartment. It's a large room with smaller rooms off it. It's light and airy.

My relationship with my dead analyst is changed. The search for a new apartment is my search for a new analytic home. The dinginess and lack of appeal of the building is how the new analysis appears: bleak and unwelcoming. With persuasion, I find something exciting, desirable, and worth having: a space in which something new can happen. At the same time, I find that accepting the foreclosed and changed relationship with my dead analyst leads me to be more accepting of the loss of what could have been, and more willing to accept and welcome what can and will be.

In this chapter, I am suggesting that the loss of my analysand voice was the result of the traumatic loss of my analyst coupled with a loss of connection to our shared voice, rendering me unable to use our shared voice analytically. Through my dreams, I terminated my analysis and re-found my voice. In a mutually informing process, by relocating my analysand voice, I began to find a working voice with the new analyst. Reclaiming my analysand voice is a resumption of my relationship with my dead analyst—not a relationship with her as it was, but an evolving relationship where the memory and experience of what we accomplished together is available to me. It is a connection to the relationship we had as well as an internalization of her and our work. For me, part of my transformative process was to allow a relationship with both analysts and have both available in my mind to be worked with. For some time, I could not have the old one because she was dead, and I could not have the new one because to do so felt like betraying the old one. The impediment of entering into a new analytic relationship and recapturing my analysand voice was linked to my guilt of desiring more for myself in the context of losing the person who had helped me come so far. Part of my transformation was to allow a relationship with both analysts and have them available in my mind to be worked with. The following dream symbolizes my beginning ability to represent both my analysts in my mind simultaneously.

Dream 8
I am with two women intensely discussing a play we have seen together.

Joan Didion wrote her book *The Year of Magical Thinking* (2005) after the sudden death of her husband. In this book, the reader follows her, befuddled and confused, as one moment follows the next, back and forth, to the place where melancholy yields to mourning. She describes eloquently the minutes and hours surrounding his death, and the year that follows as she struggles to remember that he is dead, to remind herself that her husband is not returning, and to keep alive their life together. Poignantly, Didion shifts from moments of forgetting her husband is dead, expecting him to walk in the door, to moments of remembering his death. She hopes to hold on to her husband and their life together. She does not want to bring her book to a close because, for her, it finalizes his death. She suddenly finds a frightening new moment—a memory of a day that does not involve a memory of her husband. The writing of her experience of this year is a manifest reworking of her relationship with her husband. She engages with her husband in a different way: a rearrangement of memory that encompasses her future life.

With my analyst's death, my analysand voice is interrupted. The voice I had with my analyst has been replaced by a mourner's voice. As I begin to relocate my analyst within me through the return of my dream voice, I complete my leave-taking. With a new analyst, I come to realize what I had known about my analyst's physical condition that I had preferred not to know. I begin to understand how my desire to move forward felt like an abandonment of my lost analyst. The tension in the conflict between desire to move forward and desire to remain behind blocks me from full engagement in the new analysis. The feeling that I can have both analysts available to me is part of my process of working through.

With this understanding, I use my voice as an analysand, an analyst, and a mourner to create a new voice. Once in conversation with my analyst, my authorial voice evolves from this new dialogue.

I would like to report one final dream, which I had on the eve of beginning to write this chapter. In it, I have a guide to take me into the future, and I am going with enthusiasm and willingness. I am going into a museum I have been to before. There are many galleries filled with pre-Renaissance and Renaissance work, which I pass by quickly. I am not so interested in this art, so I return to the entrance hall to get a map that shows me where the modern art galleries are located. As I turn around and pass the long line of Renaissance galleries again, I think, "Why do I have to attend to all this old art when it is the new art that I wish to see? Why do I have to spend my time here?"

## Note

1 This paper was published previously as Deutsch, R. A. (2011). A voice lost, a voice found: After the death of the analyst. *Psychoanalytic Inquiry*, *31*(6), 526–535. Reprinted with permission.

## References

Adams, B. (1995). Ulysses and I: A brief memoir of a long analysis. *Psychoanalytic Review*, *82*, 727–740.

Baker, J. E. (2001). Mourning and the transformation of object relationships: Evidence for the persistence of internal attachments. *Psychoanalytic Psychology*, *18*, 55–73.

Barbanel, L. (1989). The death of the psychoanalyst (panel presentation)—Introduction. *Contemporary Psychoanalysis*, *25*, 412–418.

Buechler, S. (2000). Necessary and unnecessary losses: The analyst's mourning. *Contemporary Psychoanalysis*, *36*, 77–90.

Butler, J. (2003). Violence, mourning, politics. *Studies in Gender and Sexuality*, *4*, 9–37.

Chasen, B. (1996). Death of a psychoanalyst's child. In B. Gerson (Ed.), *The therapist as a person* (pp. 3–20). Hillsdale, NJ: Analytic Press.

Chassay, S. (2006). Death in the afternoon. *International Journal of Psychoanalysis*, *87*, 203–217.

Coltart, N. (1996). Endings. In L. Rangell & R. Moses-Hrushovski (Eds.), *Psychoanalysis at the political border: Essays in honor of Rafael Moses* (pp. 117–129). Madison, CT: International Universities Press.

Dewald, P. A. (1982). Serious illness in the analyst: Transference, countertransference and reality responses. *Journal of the American Psychoanalytic Association*, *30*, 347–363.

Didion, J. (2005). *The year of magical thinking*. New York: Alfred A. Knopf.

Fajardo, B. (2001). Life-threatening illness in the analyst. *Journal of the American Psychoanalytic Association*, *49*, 569–586.

Feinsilver, D. B. (1998). The therapist as a person facing death: The hardest of external realities and therapeutic action. *International Journal of Psychoanalysis*, *79*, 1131–1150.

Firestein, S. K. (1990). Death of the analyst: Termination, interruption, what? In H. Schwartz & A.-L.S. Silver (Eds.), *Illness in the analyst: Implications for the therapeutic relationship* (pp. 333–339). Madison, CT: International Universities Press.

Freud, S. (1917). Mourning and melancholia. In J. Strachey (Ed. & Trans.), *The standard edition of the complete psychological works of Sigmund Freud* (vol. 14, pp. 243–258). London: Hogarth Press.

Freud, S. (1921). Group psychology and the analysis of the ego. In J. Strachey (Ed. & Trans.), *The standard edition of the complete psychological works of Sigmund Freud* (vol. 18, pp. 67–143). London: Hogarth Press.

Freud, S. (1923). *The ego and the id*. In J. Strachey (Ed. & Trans.), *The standard edition of the complete psychological works of Sigmund Freud* (vol. 19, pp. 12–66). London: Hogarth Press.

Freud, S. (1933). New introductory lectures on psychoanalysis. In J. Strachey (Ed. & Trans.), *The standard edition of the complete psychological works of Sigmund Freud* (vol. 22, pp. 3–182). London: Hogarth Press.

Gaines, R. (1997). Detachment and continuity. The two tasks of mourning. *Contemporary Psychoanalysis, 33*, 549–571.

Galatzer-Levy, R. M. (2004). The death of the analyst: Patients whose previous analysts died while they were in treatment. *Journal of the American Psychoanalytic Association, 52*, 999–1024.

Garcia-Lawson, K. A., & Lane, R. C. (1997). Thoughts on termination: Practical considerations. *Psychoanalytic Psychology, 14*, 239–257.

Garfield, D. A. S. (1990). Manifestations of grief and grievance: A therapist's response to an analyst's death. In H. Schwartz & A.-L.S. Silver (Eds.), *Illness in the analyst: Implications for the treatment relationship* (pp. 253–266). Madison, CT: International Universities Press.

Gerson, B. (1994). An analyst's pregnancy loss and its effects on treatment: Disruption and growth. *Psychoanalytic Dialogues, 4*, 1–17.

Lord, R., Ritvo, S., & Solnit, A. J. (1978). Patients' reactions to the death of the psychoanalyst. *International Journal of Psychoanalysis, 59*, 189–197.

Mayer, E. L. (1994). Some implications for psychoanalytic technique drawn from analysis of a dying patient. *Psychoanalytic Quarterly, 63*, 1–19.

Mendelsohn, E. M. (1996). More human than otherwise: Working through a time of preoccupation and mourning. In B. Gerson (Ed.), *The therapist as a person* (pp. 21–40). Hillsdale, NJ: Analytic Press.

Morrison, A. L. (1990). Doing psychotherapy while living with a life-threatening illness. In H. Schwartz & A.-L.S. Silver (Eds.), *Illness in the analyst: Implications for the treatment relationship* (pp. 227–250). Madison, CT: International Universities Press.

Morrison, A. L. (1997). Ten years of doing psychotherapy while living with a life-threatening illness. *Psychoanalytic Dialogues, 7*, 225–241.

Morrison, A. P. (1996). Trauma and disruption in the life of the analyst: Enforced disclosure and disequilibrium in "the analytic instrument." In B. Gerson (Ed.), *The therapist as a person* (pp. 41–54). Hillsdale, NJ: Analytic Press.

Ogden, T. H. (1997). *Reverie and interpretation: Sensing something human*. Northvale, NJ: Jason Aronson, Inc.

Ogden, T. H. (1998). A question of voice in poetry and psychoanalysis. *Psychoanalytic Quarterly, 67*, 426–448.

Pizer, B. (1997). When the analyst is ill: Dimensions of self-disclosure. *Psychoanalytic Quarterly, 66,* 450–469.

Rendely, J. (1999). The death of an analyst: The loss of a real relationship. *Contemporary Psychoanalysis, 35,* 131–152.

Traesdal, T. (2005). When the analyst dies: Dealing with the aftermath. *Journal of the American Psychoanalytic Association, 53,* 1235–1255.

Ziman-Tobin, P. (1989). Consultation as a bridging function. *Contemporary Psychoanalysis, 25,* 432–438.

# Part II

# RUPTURE: THE CLINICAL PROCESS

# 4

# ABANDONED WITHOUT WARNING

## Resonance of the Shame of Early Loss when an Analyst Dies

*Jenny Randles and Frances Thomson-Salo*

The sudden loss of a therapist can be confusing and damaging for a patient who has been in ongoing psychotherapy. We posit that there is a similarity of affect between patients whose analysts die and children who have experienced a variety of parenting failures, including the actual death of a parent. Children react to the death of a parent with a sense of shame, as though they feel themselves to be defective being unable to keep the parent attached to them. A further link is made with the development in infants of a sense of shame in the face of their parents' unavailability because of depression or withdrawal. Children who need to deal with misattuned or rejecting responses from parents who have been unable to sustain interest in them also feel shame. Such infants learn to look without seeing, listen without hearing. We suggest that these early experiences shape a patient's response in the face of their therapist's untimely death, where the child-patient has been unable to keep their therapists attached to them—especially when there has been prior illness.

In this chapter, we will be exploring, through extensive case material, what happens when something goes awry, when the therapist dies and the patient is abandoned part of the way through a therapy, often without warning. Analytic therapists have to work through their denial of their own death (Deutsch, 2011) to reach a space where they are able to see what the patient who has lost a previous therapist through death needs from them (Casement, 1985). If this particular vulnerability to feeling shamed is not recognized in the subsequent therapy, the patient may be left with a sense of a failed therapy and an inadequately worked-through mourning process.

Patients who have lost a therapist have nowhere to go. Their therapists have disappeared, sunk without a trace. Once the ripples have settled, it can seem as though the therapist had never been. Patients whose therapists have died generally get nothing to mark the loss, no condolence cards, no flowers. Their own families and friends may not appreciate the significance of what has happened, if they even knew about it, because many patients feel too embarrassed to tell them. Often, patients do not hear about the funeral until after it is over—and if they do hear about it, they are either not invited, or may feel awkward about attending, feeling they do not belong, that they are intruders in their therapists' real lives.

What follows is based on contact with a dozen or so patients whose therapies have ended very suddenly for a variety of reasons. In each of these instances, the subsequent therapist was presented with a difficult problem. The patients who arrived in her consulting room had, temporarily or permanently, lost the capacity to think and to present themselves in the way they ordinarily would have done. While there had been a loss or death of the prior analyst/therapist, the importance and significance of this loss was minimized by the patient; sometimes it was mentioned only in passing. These patients had become lost, somehow—and with some limitation in their capacities to describe their experiences. I (JR) found them to be unusually dependent on the subsequent therapist's capacity to understand, reach out and help them, while simultaneously having difficulty accepting the new therapist's efforts.

Some of the themes involved in treating this traumatized group will be explored using a composite case illustration, a case in which there had been a double loss for the patient—whom I will call Stacey. She was a 35-year-old single woman who had been in thrice-weekly psychoanalysis for four years. Her previous psychoanalyst had abruptly terminated her treatment when he became seriously and terminally ill. The patient had not been told of her therapist's illness and said she did not know he was ill. (As I discovered from colleagues, the previous therapist had been ill for at least a year.) I first met with the patient nine months after her therapy had ended; her previous analyst died nine months after we began treatment.

I will be illustrating the most difficult part of the work: getting it started. The aim of the therapy was to free Stacey from the deadly tie with her previous therapist, helping her to become a patient again and, in the process, to open up to the world.

## Stacey

Stacey arrived at her first appointment in a wide-eyed and distressed state. Her speech was halting and vague. She appeared very traumatized, gazing around the room with unseeing eyes, like a child who has lost its mother. She was tearful at times, frightened, and apologized frequently for her inability to explain herself. It took time to piece together what had happened. Stacey mentioned, almost in passing, that she had recently been in therapy, which had ended with a few days' notice. Several times, she said, "I just can't live like this!" I understood she was suicidal, and I was not sure whether Stacey clearly recognized that her current predicament was related to the loss of her therapist—how much do infants understand, after all? I also had the impression that she was frantically trying to reach out to me, desperately imploring me for help.

In this situation, I immediately felt that if I wanted to help Stacey, I needed to reach out to her more than I would ordinarily do with a patient. I felt that my position was like that of a foster mother: someone hardly known to a bereft child who is only interested in her real mother, someone who needed to demonstrate her caring capacities and the genuineness of her interest.

Asking Stacey about the way her last therapy had ended, I obtained these details: her analyst had phoned, leaving a message to say that he needed to cancel all her sessions for the following week. No reason was given. Stacey felt immediately gripped by a fear that something terrible had happened. A week later, her analyst called again, saying only that they could meet at their usual time on Monday. Stacey dreaded this meeting, and, as it turned out, for good reason. During the session, her analyst said they would be finishing up at the end of the week. He did not say why. She sensed her analyst did not welcome any questions from her; indeed, she felt she was being implicitly told that his situation was of no relevance. Stacey said she felt desperate and terrified of hearing the news. She seemed confused about whether her therapy had ended or not. Stacey wondered: If he said they were finishing now, at the end of the week, did that mean now, forever? Or now until . . . whatever it was had settled down . . . so they could resume, perhaps? But this was something she had been unable to ask. When I asked why, she said she did not know, and then added that he had been irritable recently, and she was afraid he might become angry. She said her therapist had given her the name of someone she could see, but she had felt unable to call this person. Months had gone by, and she continued to struggle on her own.

It seemed to me that Stacey had already sensed something had been wrong—but she denied this. I thought she had trouble trusting her own judgment.

Patients whose psychotherapists have retired in a planned way generally transfer to another therapist fairly easily. This is in marked contrast to the beginnings with patients who have been abandoned without warning. Arriving in a traumatized and dissociated state, they did not seem to know who they were. It seemed to me as though there had been a sudden loss of self, as if the disappearing therapist had taken the patients' identities away with them. For most patients, memories of their previous therapy, and what they had learned, seemed to have been lost completely. It seems to me that the patient whose analyst has died is in a similar position to that of a child who has lost her mother. The child feels bereft, as though a rug has been pulled from under her—and yet manages to keep going somehow. But does the child understand that the way she has been left feeling is a direct consequence of that loss? And how is the child to convey this experience to another person who may have no idea about the enormity of what has happened? And what is to be done to help a child who rejects any substitute mothering that is offered because she only wants her own mother?

When I asked Stacey about her childhood, I learned that her mother had been a very disturbed person who tended to deny the obvious, or to maintain, for example, that black was white. Stacey grew up into a child who had great difficulty trusting her own mind; she said her mother frequently told her she was not nice, dangerous, crazy.

Concerned, I suggested Stacey come twice weekly but she refused. After what she had been through, she was clearly reluctant to allow herself to be close to another therapist. In these early sessions, I noticed some echoes of Stacey's recent experiences with her previous therapist. She gave me very little information, just as she had been given very little information by him. I found myself waiting for more details, which never came, just as she had waited for her previous therapist. Like a small child, Stacey seemed to be showing me what she was unable to express in words.

For the first few months, the therapy had the flavor of a rescue operation, as my patient seemed bewildered and distressed. I needed to fill in some gaps for her, resetting the frame—letting her know, for example, that I had made some inquiries and discovered her analyst had been ill for some time, that he had retired through illness, and that he continued to live although he was terminally ill. I explained to her about how therapeutic termination is normally managed; in special instances, when a therapist needs to retire from practice, the patient should be given as much notice as possible. I could sense that my explanations were helpful; her extreme distress and sense of urgency gradually settled.

But then the question emerged: What happens now? Stacey seemed to compliantly accept whatever I said without question—but I was uncertain what she made of it. She appeared to be using the therapy as a refuge. I remained concerned about her passivity. She had completely lost interest in completing her Master's degree and appeared isolated. There seemed to be little going on in her life. She seemed happy to come to her sessions but unconcerned that her life had been put on hold; like a small child, she felt she could not possibly manage. Gradually, a few more details about the ending of her previous treatment emerged.

Stacey said that when they met for their last few sessions, her therapist had told her their work had been completed, and she did not need to see anyone else. Stacey told him she felt she really did need to see someone; while her therapist had agreed, Stacey felt he actually did not want this. Although he had given Stacey a name, she felt unable to call for an appointment. She agreed with me that she felt guilty for opposing his wishes:

> I was in a terrible state when I finished with him. Didn't he anticipate this would happen? I think he may have been trying to keep everything a secret, and stop other analysts from knowing what had been going on. I wanted to finish my therapy on a good note, not like this. My therapy was very helpful but now I can't remember anything about it. It's all gone. What have I learned? I seem to have thrown it all out. I'm left with nothing.

Even though Stacey was sometimes able to express anger and frustration, she would put it aside, and, as she said, we would both be left with nothing but a sense of timelessness. It was as though her anger had never been, for little seemed to come of it. I found this pattern frustrating and hard to tolerate.

She felt a persistent sense of shame for several reasons. Her analyst seemed to have cared more about his reputation than about her. She felt devalued by him. Her own behavior caused her embarrassment and shame: She had angrily wiped out all the work they had done; she was unable to work or study; she had been behaving badly and, like a small child, was unable to do anything about it.

Over the next few months, the sessions continued in this way. Unreachable, she would come to her sessions but fail to bring herself. Occasionally, she slipped into a collegial way of relating, where it seemed as though she and I were fine but some other person had some serious problems. There would be plenty of talk, yet for much of the time I felt that nothing real was being spoken about. Frequently, there was a feeling that we were just going through the motions. The atmosphere in our sessions sometimes had a deadness about it, and I would sometimes find myself becoming bored and sleepy. I felt I needed to communicate constant interest in my patient, to facilitate, to be encouraging—but at times, maintaining an optimistic stance became a strain. I even began to develop an eerie sense of the previous therapist directing the therapy from his sickbed. Sometimes, it felt as though the therapist was actually present in the room with us.

I began to see this as a reenactment. I wondered whether her previous therapy had been like this—frustrating and tantalizing, with an ill analyst who was sometimes present but then despairingly absent. Had Stacey's own mother been like this also? I asked Stacey about this and she said she did not know about her analyst, but as for her mother, definitely! I soon began to discover how much of her energy with me and in her life was spent trying to magically recreate the good relationship she remembered having with her old therapist:

> I can't bear to stay at home, I constantly want to go out, and when I do, I find myself searching for him, all the time. I go to the shops and look around for him, in the supermarket, in the street. I can't help it. It's

> awful, I can't bear it. If I do stay home, I can't bear it either, so I have to go to bed and sleep. I feel constantly exhausted. I phoned him many times after I finished, just to listen to his voice on the answer machine—until the message was changed. I got some medical and nursing friends to look up hospital records to see whether he had been admitted to hospital. I felt like I was stalking him and really, I feel I'm still doing it. I don't feel I have the right to be speaking about him here, and behind his back. I know he wouldn't like it. Whenever I speak about what happened and how angry I feel, I feel really bad afterwards.

I felt her shame was evident. She said, "I've become obsessed by him."

To Stacey, it seemed that even trying to establish what had happened was deemed to be stalking. Accusing herself of stalking her previous therapist reinstated the therapist in an idealized position, and reinforced a sense of herself as the transgressor—a reversal of what had really happened. My patient had been wronged, not the therapist.

It was now obvious that Stacey remained much more invested in her old therapist than with me and our therapy—I was a mere foster mother, and she had a life unlived. The situation was complicated by the fact that the patient's analyst was still alive but neither of us had any up-to-date information. I wondered whether Stacey still hoped to return to work with him again, so that she could reconnect with him, perhaps to finish her therapy properly, but also to nurse him as, it now seemed to me, she had been doing. It appeared that she felt guilty, as though engaging more with our therapy meant abandoning him—as though he was the patient and she the therapist. This repeated what had gone on with her own mother. I was concerned that she had not yet separated from him, or recovered the capacity to listen to herself and put her own concerns first.

At this point in the therapy, the question that seemed most important for us to consider had to do with information. Where was the truth? Did the patient already feel her analyst's words were not to be trusted? How long had she felt this way? Stacey's analyst, like her mother, had denied the obvious, had failed to look out for her and keep her in mind. Did she feel unambiguously loved by him? Or loved by her mother? When I asked her this question, she emphatically replied no.

Six months into the therapy, Stacey brought the following dream, a dream that I felt illustrated the slippage that had occurred so that she and her therapists, old and new, were out of touch with each other:

> In the dream, I was sitting on the bottom of a swimming pool looking up and watching someone who was swimming laps on the surface. It was a very deep pool, and the surface was a long way away. I could see the swimmer, but the swimmer couldn't see me. I didn't recognize

the swimmer but knew it was me. There was an empty feeling in the dream, and everything was dark in color. As the dreamer, I felt worried, seeing myself at the bottom of the pool; it felt strange and dangerous, surely I would drown. I knew I didn't want to continue to mechanically swim laps, up and down . . . I just wasn't interested. I would just stay down here on the bottom of the pool, out of sight and out of the loop, and not engage. Death was everywhere.

It seemed evident to me that the figure on the bottom of the pool represented Stacey's old therapist. Stacey agreed with that, and also that the swimming version of herself had been unaware of the person on the bottom of the pool, who had withdrawn and was no longer interested in being with her—unlike the dreamer, who was very concerned about what was happening.

I suggested that her dream showed Stacey was not interested in mindlessly coming to sessions; the work needed to be relevant and useful to her or there seemed to be no point. Now, she was presented with two hopeless options: mindlessly swimming, coming to her sessions but without engaging, and a dangerous kind of passivity into which she would withdraw from the therapy and marginalize herself. With this encouragement, she began to open up more, telling me about her life. When her previous analysis ended, Stacey felt she became a different person overnight:

> Since my [last] therapy ended, I have been trying to keep myself busy and active. Whenever I stop, I feel someone inside me is screaming. It's unbearable. One weekend, just before I first came to see you, I went for a long drive in the country. On the way home, the screaming was really intense. I noticed how many large trucks were passing me, driving very fast in the other direction. As it got dark, their headlights came on. It occurred to me just how easy it would be to turn the wheel very slightly, and end up underneath one of those trucks. I didn't feel like doing it, but somehow my car seemed to move towards the middle of the road by itself, and I had to really grip the steering wheel and concentrate. It was an awful way to drive home, with the effort to keep my car on my side of the road. I didn't want to have a head-on collision, but I felt exhausted and distracted and terrified of making a mistake. I felt I needed to get home urgently. I'm glad I had my dog with me, sitting beside me. Perhaps she kept me alive. Since then, I've become afraid of driving; short trips are all I can manage now.

My patient had survived a near-death experience, and I felt she had been in great danger.

After telling me her dream, Stacey agreed to come twice a week. She became more present, interested, thoughtful, and more able to hold on to new things that emerged instead of immediately retreating. I discovered that, during her previous therapy, she had indeed formed an impression that something concerning had been going on, but she had felt under pressure to deny it. Now, she spoke with more feeling about the messages left by her analyst when he had phoned her. She had felt chilled by the coldness in his voice and his businesslike delivery. The first message made her feel like a nuisance. She had felt deeply shamed by this reaction. When he called the second time, she had been at home. She froze and had been unable to pick up. Did he really want to see her? Instead, she listened to his words, very carefully, playing the message over and over, struggling to identify what it was in his tone that distressed her so much, and trying to find the person she knew. "It was so impersonal," she said. "It felt like I didn't matter to him at all, that he had become another person." She felt humiliated. Later, Stacey revealed she had kept her analyst's message for many months and had played it over and over to herself. She felt extremely guilty about this and had been too ashamed to tell anyone.

Stacey remembered that the previous winter had been very cold, but her analyst had, uncharacteristically, not turned the heating on in the waiting room. Stacey, puzzled, had asked him about it. The heater had been turned on a couple of times, then they were back to the cold room. It seemed that his mind was elsewhere. Irritated about having to wait in the cold room, Stacey considered asking him about it again, but did not do so. She continued to wonder why her analyst allowed his patients to wait in such a cold room. Even if this was only for a couple of minutes, it seemed mean. Did she matter so little that he would not heat the room for her? Stacey had become distressed and preoccupied by this issue. She did not ask him about the heater because to do so seemed pedantic and small-minded. "Really, it was only for a couple of minutes." I pointed out it had become a huge issue for her, one she thought about every day, so why was she telling herself it was nothing? She became tearful, saying that she was used to doing this, as this is what it was like with her mother.

From that time onward, whenever she mentioned her former analyst, Stacey now presented him as someone who had become more withdrawn, less thoughtful, and more dismissive for the last one, perhaps two years. She allowed herself to wonder whether he had been ill for a long time. She continued to maintain, however, that her therapist's appearance remained normal, yet I now knew, from my own inquiries, this to be untrue. He had been gaunt in appearance and was obviously very ill. Stacey's insistence on his normal appearance was of concern to me. I felt that Stacey's dream, and her dream-like vignette (the drive home), showed the tie to her former therapist had become malignant ("death was everywhere"). She had come into therapy with him seeking help to separate from her maternal object so she could live effectively and form healthy relationships. At some point during the therapy, without any discussion, the therapeutic goal had changed. There could be no help, no sharing, because there were no other people.

I felt that Stacey had, during her previous therapy, come to align herself with the "preferred view" of her therapist, in the process denying what she also knew. During the therapy with me, she was now moving back and forth between two states, one rooted in reality but another that was rooted in denial, dissociation, and trauma. Stacey continued to deny certain realities in the face of the obvious, like her analyst's appearance. To do otherwise left her with a sense of terrible pain. Her failure to give voice to what she witnessed appeared to leave her feeling disappointed in herself, fueling her shame. Anything that reminded her of her previous analyst—including her previous analysis and what she had learned there—needed to be avoided because it linked with her feelings of shame and humiliation. Stacey persistently and consciously believed that she had continued to allow something toxic to drift on. She said that she must have known, in her heart, that he was unwell; she should have spoken up or left the situation and she had done neither. Like a parentified child, she now felt she was entirely to blame and her analyst was absolved.

Christmas and my four-week holiday were approaching. Our therapy had been going for nine months at this point. I was concerned how she would manage the long break, the second since her analysis had finished. I took this up with Stacey, who calmly assured me she would be fine. Curiously, this response had an unsettling effect on me. During the sessions, I was sometimes conscious of feeling despair and helplessness; assuming these were transference communications, I fed them back to the patient, who responded politely, but without taking my remarks on board.

Stacey's analyst died the last weekend before the Christmas break. It was left to me to give her the news. She received it calmly enough, but I was conscious that, again, she was only being given a week to process the information, replicating what had happened with her analyst. I made sure that she understood that I was very concerned about her and wanted her to take special care of herself.

When we resumed after the break, Stacey told me she had gone away for the weekend to stay with friends at their country home. While she was away, she had become ill—she said, "It felt as though I was dying." She had an urgent need to get home. The drive home was a battle; her arms were heavy, it felt as though they were being dragged down by some invisible force. But she managed. Friends rallied around to help, and she felt comforted and recovered over the next few days. Her analyst had died, yet she had lived. Now, Stacey was able to tell me how invested in him she had remained, and how much of her energy had been taken up with secretly wishing she could resume her sessions with him and planning to leave her therapy with me. She said she no longer felt that she wanted to get away from me. She was becoming more interested in the world and in herself.

A couple of weeks later, she dreamed the following dream: she was sitting beside a pool, very quietly, and looking at the water. All was still. The pond was made of stone, it was round and surrounded by a classical stone terrace with balustrades, in the style of the ancient Romans or Greeks. There was no greenery at all, not a blade of grass. Stacey emphasized how beautiful it was. She watched while an unseen person threw a stone into the pond, and wondered about this—who threw the stone, and why? The stone quickly sank and disappeared from view. The penny had dropped. She said, "My analyst wasn't there—he was invisible because he had died; he disappeared like that stone. It looked as though he had never been. As I dreamed the dream, I remember thinking to myself, with great determination, I am *not* going to disappear like that stone. I'm not going to die. I'm going to live." She had found her voice!

In the dream, the absent and now dead analyst, represented by the unseen person who threw the stone, could be clearly acknowledged. Her position had shifted to one that was benign rather than dangerous. Life was equated with movement and thought, but more work was needed.

I mused about how the classical concrete and stonework surrounding the pool might say something about the responsiveness of therapists and organizations in the face of illness and death. Psychotherapists and analysts may become so concerned about maintaining proper boundaries that they can, unwittingly, appear cold. These responses may be faultless, but lacking in humanity and aliveness. In order to work with patients who have endured the traumatic loss of a therapist, the usual classical approach will not be enough—something more is needed.

The two themes—movement and stasis—were echoed in our therapeutic work. I now found myself focusing more on the atmosphere in the sessions, themes of emotional deadness, and aliveness.

During the second year of her therapy, Stacey often greeted me with what I came to refer to as "the death stare"—a hard and unflinching gaze that was very piercing, markedly different from the way she had been in the first year of treatment. It often seemed that she was either looking right through me, as though I was a ghost, or alternatively right inside me. I needed to tolerate my very existence being negated (O'Shaughnessy, 1964). This was unsettling at first, but I soon became used to it. Now, after many months of stasis, something was definitely happening! Soon after the dream of the stone thrown in the pool, the death stare was frequently present, but over time this appeared less and less. I began to understand that it was linked with the presence of her old therapist in the transference, and noticed the atmosphere in the sessions starting to change; the deadness I had seen in her gaze became a part of her that she now knew about. Over time, there was a feeling of something warmer, a new sense of life and spontaneity, which was lighter and hopeful.

As I began to pay more attention to deadness and aliveness in the sessions, I found myself remembering the "dead mother" (Green, 1983) and found it helpful to read on this subject. I began to reformulate my work with Stacey; as Ogden (1999) has described, it seemed most important for me to focus on promoting more aliveness, and connectedness, in my patient.

Around 18 months, memories of her first therapy were coming back. It was a great relief to her that these memories were returning, and Stacey began to feel grateful for the good work that had been done. Instead of a pervasive feeling of stasis, her approach to life was becoming more purposeful. The therapy was moving and felt more ordinary to me. It now became clear to me that the absent therapist may stir up primitive forces which, if not addressed, can take residence in the patient's mind, so that the absent therapist becomes an important transference figure in its own right.

About 22 months into the therapy, Stacey brought another dream showing the presence of a new transference object, represented as a lion. The dream took place in her apartment. She had been standing outside on her balcony and then came back inside into her living room. Her sister was in the living room; she had her baby with her, but Stacey could not see the baby anywhere. No one was holding the baby. Suddenly, she noticed there was a lion in the room. At that point, the lights went out; it was dark and she could see nothing. Her sister began to scream, and Stacey presumed that her sister was being mauled by the lion. Then there was silence. She woke up screaming.

I felt Stacey's dissociation was represented by her being outside on the balcony. People now existed in Stacey's world—and in addition there was her own creative self, represented as a baby, which she needed to learn to take care of. As a result of our therapy, Stacey, now in the living room, reconnected with herself and me in the analysis only to encounter the dangerous lion, representing her dying and now dead analyst, which attacked her (represented in the dream by her sister) and may have done some terrible damage. I felt the balcony represented a place she could easily retreat to and come back from.

I started to notice that memories of the dead therapist began surfacing around breaks and holidays as anniversary phenomena, but were not mentioned by the patient. She seemed not to notice. Several times, I sensed that the dead therapist was present in the room; when I asked her about this, she confirmed that she had been thinking about him. She might then share some new memory of her time with him. While Stacey continued to maintain that his appearance had been normal, she was now becoming curious and intrigued about this and more able to accept that, in reality, he had looked very ill indeed.

Stacey felt that her life was made more difficult by the fact that she knew no other person who had shared this experience with her analyst. She wanted to speak to people who had known him, either first- or second-hand. Not knowing any of her former analyst's other patients, she began to seek people out to try and find some people she could speak to about her experiences. She made a number of attempts and was rebuffed. These experiences made her feel bad and were unhelpful, contributing to more shame. Despite the progress in her ongoing treatment with me, she continued to report feeling shame and distress, more than I would have expected. The shame reaction seemed so persistent I felt it was important to devote space to think about this in its own right.

Feeling small is shameful. So is breaking down. Stacey used to worry that she looked odd to her friends and colleagues. She said people had been concerned about her and asked her how she was—she had been unable to answer, except to say that she did not know. This had been a very disturbing experience for her, to be the only person who was burdened by what she "knew" because she was also burdened by her own self-doubts and inability to trust her own judgment. This led to feelings of confusion and embarrassment, which accounted for some of the shame.

Three years into the treatment, Stacey now realized the dream of the classical pond reminded her of one she had dreamed in the early stages of her first analysis; her dream had given her an important clue, which she had been unable to recognize at the time. She felt quite sad about this but not shamed. She remembered her dead therapist used to say, "Now don't throw the baby out with the bathwater." She said, "And that's just what I did: in the dream I'd put myself out of the bathwater [pond] and onto the sidelines. He would have had something to say about the way I hadn't been looking after myself. But he wasn't there." The therapist had been rediscovered as the benign figure he had originally been for Stacey, before he had fallen ill—and Stacey had rediscovered the capacity to care for herself.

Stacey went on to say,

> My therapist used to be terribly fussy about having me do the right thing for myself, and for the therapy—the importance of my coming on time, the importance of my coming to all sessions. He started sessions exactly on time, and gave me his accounts right at the beginning of the month. Before starting therapy, I used to be a very chaotic person, all over the place. He used to be firm but fair, always giving notice of his breaks. And then suddenly, when we finished up with only a few days' notice—which was really the wrong thing to do—he had done the opposite, by throwing the baby out with the bathwater himself. He had become a different person overnight, just as I had become a different person overnight after my treatment ended, and, like a small child, I couldn't understand it.

Toward the end of our third year of therapy, Stacey spoke about a fleeting image she had seen in a film that had caused her to feel extreme distress and revulsion. The image was of a character from a sadomasochistic world who lived as a prisoner in an underground cell. What horrified her the most was the rubber wetsuit he wore so that even his face was kept invisible. She cried when she spoke about this, but felt some relief afterwards. We came to understand that the black wetsuit stood for a second skin, which had been grafted onto her by her dying analyst and needed to be removed. She felt a great sense of shame about this—shame about having had a defective analyst, and the wetsuit skin which she had found so abhorrent that speaking about this was an achievement for her.

Stacey's treatment with me ended the following year; she had been in therapy for five years and now felt ready to resume her life. A few years after her therapy ended successfully, Stacey called and asked if she could come back and see me for a few sessions. She seemed happy and somewhat exhilarated. She had recently had a chance meeting with someone she knew distantly, who had also known her therapist. This person had spoken frankly with her, saying, "I remember what he was like at the time, and what his state of mind was like—he was in complete denial. It must have been awful for you." She had found this brief conversation amazingly helpful. Stacey said,

> For so many years, I puzzled about his behavior. I was still thinking about him every day. I felt upset about it, every day. But that's settled. I feel a lot better. Just having someone acknowledge his state of mind made such a difference. I used to feel that I was mad, and not him. But now that's stopped. How I wish I could have had such a conversation with someone earlier.

I found myself remembering her story about the scream she used to carry inside herself. When, I asked her about it, she said, "The screaming thing disappeared years ago, during my therapy with you. But . . . it's just occurred to me that the scream may have belonged to my old therapist. I think he was furious that he was dying. He was screaming—in rage and pain. I think he didn't want to go." Stacey felt he had passed on his mourning to her, and that she had been doing it for him.

## Shame of Loss: A Developmental Context

Here we return to the point about how childhood events and experiences shape responses and affect the process when a patient's therapist dies. A sense of shame can develop as an organizer of affects in the earliest months from birth onward (Trevarthen, 2001). Painful shame trails with it other affects, such as betrayal, anger, confusion, and feeling exposed—which, in excess, feel unmanageable for a child. In addition to the usual mourning reactions of grief seen from childhood onwards (Bowlby, 1980; Furman, 1964a), we are highlighting the sense of shame that may ensue. Children often react to the death of a parent with shame, as though they felt themselves to be defective in being unable to keep the parent attached to them. The therapist's death is a repetition of loss that re-evokes the parental transference and the feeling of being unworthy of keeping the analyst alive and connected to the patient. However, not only death evokes a sense of shame. Separation traumas for a parent who is felt to be unavailable, because of depression or withdrawal, may feel too hard for a sensitive infant to bear. Infants can experience shame and feel depressed if their parents are unresponsive, or their behavior is not contingent on their infant's responses, or if the infant does not feel confident about captivating their parents (Broucek, 1979; Mollon, 1984). In losing a parent or a parent's investment, a child feels ashamed and deficient, with a loss of social esteem, and cannot in a developmentally age-appropriate way take pride in their parent.

A child may fear that they are to blame for another's death, as a patient may fear contributing to their therapist's illness and death. As in Stacey's case, shame is compounded by this guilt. Shame may block or mask expression of anger, which is part of the mourning process. If this vulnerability to feeling shamed is not recognized, it may make it difficult in a subsequent therapy to adequately work through mourning the dead therapist (Lichtenberg, 1998). The patient may be left with an infantile transference that has not been explored, contributing to their sense of having had a failed therapy (Chessick, 1998).

Any trauma in childhood is, in an *après coup* effect, magnified by a therapist's death. If the patient has a central presence of absence at their core, a "dead mother" internal object (Green, 1983) as Stacey felt herself to have, this increases the difficulty. Even more important may be the fear of the shame of loss. Some patients repeat childhood experiences of caring for vulnerable parents if their therapist has a period of illness before dying (Galatzer-Levy, 2004), a role reversal in which they again feel trapped in caring for a needy parent figure (G. Junkers, personal communication, July 15, 2012). What a patient may carry for the therapist is similar to the shame and anxiety (and occasional delusional states) that a child may carry for vulnerable parents. A therapist who is ill feels shame (and guilt at some level) if they fail in their capacity to allow observation of themselves as ill, and shame may be evoked when a dying man's glance meets that of someone who will remain alive (Rosenblum, 2009), as if the patient sees the therapist's shame and feels shame themselves. As Schachter (1990) stated, "A personal history of early loss and deprivation appeared to be the most important factors associated with pathological mourning reactions" (p. 478).

Whether or not they reengage in therapy, patients who have been traumatized by the death of a therapist try to protect themselves from retraumatization. When the analyst dies prematurely, childhood ways of coping with loss are revived. For some extremely vulnerable children and patients, any defense used may feel like the death of a part of the psyche. As noted in the case vignette, while there may often be a sense that the dead therapist is in some way present in the consulting room, a patient may often not refer to this unless the current therapist brings it up. This "ghost" is reminiscent of Fraiberg's (1980) concept of ghosts in the nursery, referring to transgenerational loss. Stacey's "death stare" reminds us of the importance for the new mother–infant dyad of an infant's gaze for attachment; this staring gaze may hold the dead therapist's face in mind while minutely checking it against the face and health of the therapist in front of them. Children often respond to a trauma by learning how to look but not see, listen but not hear; patients often try not to see when their therapist is physically unwell but somewhere have a sense that the therapist is terminally ill, that there is something "odd," even when the therapist hides it from them, just as with Stacey. If a patient finds it difficult to be curious about a therapist's health, this is likely to be relived in the transference with the next therapist. Some patients report that they did not know that the analyst was ill or were the last to know: André Green describes his analyst, Maurice Bouvet, dying after his last session, not having known that he was ill (Kohon, 1999). This was also true for Stacey, who took a year to begin to know what she unconsciously knew. Just as some children identify with the lost person as a way of keeping them with them (Furman, 1964b), the shadow of the object falling over the ego as Freud (1915) evocatively described, other children identify with the aggressor (Chessick, 1998). A child who is mourning may invest a dead parent with anger, who thereby becomes a dangerous internal parental object with whom the child has to make peace; this may be as a patient repeated, as with the lion in Stacey's dream.

Some patients who transfer to another therapist behave as though there is an impermanence to the arrangement in a similar way that some foster children do. They may search for the dead therapist, as some children do when bereaved or placed in out-of-home care; they may struggle with intense feelings of loyalty to the previous therapist, which may extend to refusing to engage with interpretations made by the subsequent therapist. It is as though the patient may feel that any progress made would mean being shamefully disloyal to the former therapist. Importantly, when such a rupture of the frame has occurred, and if shame is a prominent feature, the next therapist may need to consider how to be more actively containing (Alvarez, 1985), for example, in how they introduce material about the dead therapist rather than the stance of waiting for the patient to do so. The patient's experience of feeling ashamed, especially of their oral needs in connection with the dead therapist and earlier infantile experiences, may be communicated in the countertransference by projective identification of, for example, horrible images at times when the therapist feels bored, sleepy, superfluous, or revulsed (Beatson, 2001). Paradoxically, the most difficult feelings to experience may be pleasurable feelings, when these are contaminated by and defended against by shame, and these infantile conflicts become known in the therapist by projective identification.

The traumatic element of the therapist's death has to do with the impossibility of remembering (Gutierrez Pelaez, 2009). This links with what was noted in Stacey's case. When a therapist is not straightforwardly honest about being ill, this evokes common developmental sequelae of being lied to. Deception leads to the feeling of "being lost" (Dupont, 1985), and for children trauma occurs when no adult is available to repair the damage of being deceived and feeling lost. One patient, who lost a therapist whom she felt had been emotionally abusive, experienced the abrupt stopping as meaning that she must be very little and not have meant much to him.

A therapist whose own analyst has died during their analysis may find an unconscious resonance in a larger than expected number of patients in their caseload, as though unconsciously signaling to patients and referring colleagues a readiness to work with these trauma experiences in patients, while at the same time processing this in a contained way for themselves.

## Conclusion

There is something haunting about the plight of patients who were previously well enough to undertake therapy. Having a therapist die is a life-changing experience for any patient. The initial emptiness that may fill the sessions can be hard for a new therapist to tolerate. The presence of the dead therapist in the consulting room is daunting, and can fill both the patient and the subsequent therapist with shame: the patient feels she is doing nothing, and the therapist is left to feel she cannot help.

The subsequent therapist may be saddened and traumatized by what they hear from their patient about the behavior of an esteemed colleague. Therapists are human beings, and denial of illness is very common. In this sense, shame seems to abound. It is hard to see the previous therapist as a human being with human frailties. Simultaneously, as with Stacey, colleagues may take sides against the patient because they also cannot bear to know. Helen Garner (2008) has written movingly about the difficulty of dealing with someone close who refuses to acknowledge his or her own illness, even in the face of the obvious. In her novel *The Spare Room*, the central character has terminal cancer, a bright smile, and a tendency to provoke rage in the people who cared for her. Each person felt guilt and shame about the way they felt. It was not until these people were able to join together and share their experiences that the reality of the situation became clear, and a more helpful course of action could be identified.

As therapists, we need to acknowledge that there is no shame in being mortal. If we dodge this, our patients will be left to do it for us.

A 7-year-old patient, who transferred to another analyst after the death of his first analyst, conveyed something of the pain when he told his second analyst, "Life's not worth living. He was magic. You could never be as good as him" (A. Sandell, personal communication, March 3, 2012). The death of a patient's analyst or therapist, for long a subject that was underreported in the literature, is under increasing scrutiny for what we can learn and how to better help patients who have experienced ruptured treatments.

## References

Alvarez, A. (1985). The problem of neutrality: Some reflections on the psychoanalytic attitude in the treatment of borderline and psychotic children. *Journal of Child Psychotherapy, 11*, 87–103.

Beatson, J. (2001). Shame and its precursors in psychotherapy. Paper presented at the Scientific Meeting, Victorian Association of Psychoanalytic Psychotherapy of Australasia, Melbourne.

Bowlby, J. (1980). *Loss, sadness and depression: Attachment and loss*, (vol. 3). New York: Basic Books.

Broucek, F. (1979). Shame and its relationship to early narcissistic developments. *International Journal Psychoanalysis, 63*, 369–378.

Casement, P. (1985). *On learning from the patient*. London: Routledge.

Chessick, R. D. (1998). Richard D. Chessick. *Journal of the American Psychoanalytic Association, 46*, 38–48.

Deutsch, R. (2011). Picking up the pieces: Treatment following the analyst's death. Paper presented at the IPA Congress, Mexico City.

Dupont, J. (Ed.) (1985). *The clinical diary of Sándor Ferenczi* (trans. M. Balint & N. Zarday Jackson). Cambridge, MA: Harvard University Press.

Fraiberg, S. (Ed.). (1980). *Clinical studies in infant mental health: The first year of life*. New York: Basic Books.

Freud, S. (1915). Mourning and melancholia. In J. Strachey (Ed. & Trans.), *The standard edition of the complete psychological works of Sigmund Freud* (vol. 14, pp. 243–258). London: Hogarth Press.

Furman, R. A. (1964a). Death and the young child: Some preliminary considerations. *Psychoanalytic Study of the Child, 19*, 321–333.

Furman, R. A. (1964b). Death of a six-year-old's mother during his analysis. *Psychoanalytic Study of the Child, 19*, 377–397.

Galatzer-Levy, R. M. (2004). The death of the analyst. *Journal of the American Psychoanalytic Association, 52*, 999–1024.

Garner, H. (2008). *The spare room*. Melbourne: Text Publishing Company.

Green, A. (1983). The dead mother. In A. Green, *On private madness* (pp. 142–173). London: Hogarth Press.

Gutierrez Pelaez, M. (2009). Trauma theory in Sándor Ferenczi's writings of 1931 and 1932. *International Journal of Psychoanalysis, 90*, 1217–1233.

Kohon, G. (Ed.) (1999). *The dead mother: The work of André Green*. London: Routledge.

Lichtenberg, J. D. (1998). Experience as a guide to psychoanalytic theory and practice. *Journal of the American Psychoanalytic Association, 46*, 17–36.

Mollon, P. (1984). Narcissistic vulnerability and the fragile self: A failure of mirroring. *British Journal Medical Psychology, 59*, 317–324.

Ogden, T. H. (1999). Analyzing forms of aliveness and deadness in the transference-countertransference. In G. Kohon (Ed.), *The dead mother: The work of André Green* (pp. 128–148). London: Routledge.

O'Shaughnessy, E. (1964). The absent object. *Journal of Child Psychotherapy, 1*, 34–43.

Rosenblum, R. (2009). Postponing trauma: The dangers of telling. *International Journal of Psychoanalysis, 90*, 1319–1340.

Schachter, J. (1990). Post-termination patient-analyst contact: I. Analysts' attitudes and experience; II. Impact on patients. *International Journal of Psychoanalysis, 71*, 475–485.

Trevarthen C. (2001). Intrinsic motives for companionship in understanding: Their origin, development, and significance for infant mental health. *Infant Mental Health Journal, 22*, 95–131.

# 5

# THE TRAUMA OF PATIENT SUICIDE

*Jane Tillman and Anne Carter*

Early in my (JT) training as a psychologist, I worked for a year in a cancer center, and my dissertation involved working with women with Stage III and IV cancers. One patient I treated during that time developed a recurrence of her cancer, and after a period of valiant but unsuccessful oncological treatment efforts and subsequent decline, Ms. A. died. I had the privilege and deep pain of being her psychotherapist during the last stages of her illness. Ms. A. had struggled in her life with substance abuse, was estranged from her children, and had many regrets about the life she had lived—a life that was now coming to an end. It was in this context that she was referred to me for psychotherapy. In Erikson's life stage model, she wavered between ego-integrity and despair, and at the time of her death this crisis was not resolved. I felt very sad and was deeply engaged and moved by Ms. A. during the final months of our work together. Her death left me with much to think about; somehow I wished our work together could have led her to feel less despair about the course of her life. Yet, I know that it was Ms. A.'s commitment to an honest, if not ruthless, self-appraisal that would not let her rest with too much of a sense of satisfaction. Hers was not an easy death, but I felt that our work together had been deeply meaningful to both of us, and she was grateful to me for the work we did together while she was ill. When she died, I was sad—I felt an empty spot in my week—and I grieved for Ms. A., quietly and alone as therapists often do.

There are other kinds of death that patients meet, through the trauma of plane crashes, automobile accidents, sudden infections, or, in our profession, through suicide. Despite the fact that suicide is the third leading cause of death for young people in the United States, and suicides outnumber homicides five to three (CDC), there is a strange silence in our professional community about an experience that many clinicians have already had, or will have, in the course of a professional career. In psychoanalysis, famous suicides include Victor Tausk, Ellen West, Marilyn Monroe, Anne Sexton, Sylvia Plath, and other publicized patients who ended their lives by their own hand. Often, the suicide of a patient is fodder for gossip, speculation, blame, and the projection of fantasies about "what went wrong" in a treatment, a presumed therapeutic error in assessment or treatment that may, or may not, have occurred or been a factor in the suicide of a patient.

In some instances, clinicians do not experience the suicide of their patients as a total treatment failure. Based on research I (JT) have conducted exploring the reactions of therapists losing a patient to suicide and other discussions with colleagues, I have heard clinicians report a range of experiences and reactions to having a patient complete suicide. It is not unusual for clinicians to say, "I thought the treatment was going well," or, "The patient had been through a rough time several weeks/months earlier but seemed to have worked through it." Are these clinicians being defensive? Are they in a naïve denial? Perhaps such reflections reveal the inherent limitations in any clinician to know with absolute certainty the furthest reaches of a patient's mind. When a patient in treatment commits suicide, questions about what clinicians expect of themselves and what families expect of clinicians are raised. This chapter examines the literature on suicide, findings from various research studies of therapists' reactions to suicide, and provides a very intimate vignette (AC) about the experience of losing patients to suicide. We then discuss how clinicians may manage the aftermath of a patient's suicide.

## Studying the Effect of Patient Suicide on Clinicians

Increasingly, the literature on the effect of suicide on clinicians shows the tremendous potential for trauma and disruption in the therapist when a patient commits suicide (Gutin, McGann, & Jordan, 2011; Hendin et al., 2004; Pilkinton & Etkin, 2003; Ruskin et al., 2004; Tillman, 2006; Wurst et al., 2011). Studies show that between 20% and 60% of psychiatrists will lose a patient to suicide over the course of a career, with the figure of 50% being the generally accepted rate (Chemtob et al., 1988; Pilkinton & Etkin, 2003; Ruskin et al., 2004). Despite these numbers, there is often a deep silence in our training programs, our meetings, and our professional discourse about the experience of patient suicide. It seems as though we have been caught in a collective denial about the frequency of the suicide of patients, how to respond to the suicide of a patient, and what to anticipate as therapists following the death of a patient by suicide. Further, how we respond to our professional peers following the suicide of a patient is important in terms of providing collegial support and assistance. In residency training or in hospital or clinic settings, the suicide of a patient often affects an entire professional community in ways that we may not anticipate, and therefore are not prepared to respond to.

The reasons for our discomfort, or at times outright silence, are complicated; lawyers instruct clinicians not to speak to anyone about the suicide of a patient. This may fuel shame dynamics, which often contribute to isolation, depression, and pent-up anger. The clinician may come to feel punished, and in such a circumstance internal persecutory objects may be revived in the context of external threat, leading to internal anguish and impotent rage. The reality of legal action also inhibits clinicians and hospitals from rigorously collecting and analyzing data about the suicide of patients in treatment, and thus we are deprived of the chance to learn from these experiences as they remain shrouded in silence out of fear, shame, various organizational prohibitions, and the reality of the devastation lawsuits have on clinicians and treatment systems.

Several recent studies have examined the effect of suicide on psychiatrists and psychiatric trainees. Wurst et al. (2011) surveyed 123 clinicians who reported having had one or more patients commit suicide, finding that 30% of the sample reported severe emotional distress following the death of the patient. Ruskin et al. (2004) surveyed 239 graduates of a Canadian residency training program, finding that 50% of participants experienced the suicide of at least one patient, and for this group 62% of these occurred during residency. Of this group, 64% of the biologically oriented psychiatrists reported at least one patient suicide, while 40% of psychiatrists without a biological orientation reported such an event. This may reflect differences in numbers of patients seen or differences in the severity of disorders. In their sample, legal action was taken against the attending psychiatrist in 10 (9%) of the cases. Following the first suicide of a patient, psychiatrists in this study reported a range of feelings, including helplessness (71%) and recurrent feelings of horror (55%). For trainees, the suicide of a patient was a source of significant anxiety in almost half of this sample.

Pilkinton and Etkin (2003) report that psychiatric residents exposed to the suicide of a patient or of a colleague reported a dramatic impact on their mental health. In their sample of 197 participants, 61% of trainee respondents reported the suicide of a patient or colleague in the early phases of training. Hendin et al. (2004) studied 34 psychiatrists who had a patient commit suicide and found that 38% reported experiencing severe distress following the suicide of a patient. The four main causes of this distress were identified as:

1  concern or self-doubt about the failure to hospitalize a suicidal patient
2  concern about a specific treatment decision
3  concern about negative reactions by the therapist's institution
4  fear of a lawsuit.

Over 10 years ago, the first author (Tillman, 2006) undertook a research study interviewing psychoanalytic clinicians who had lost a patient to suicide during treatment or shortly after the treatment ended. These interviews were audiotaped and analyzed to extract the themes common to the experience of having a patient commit suicide. Eight themes emerged from the textual analysis of the transcripts:

1. traumatic responses including feelings of numbness, intrusive dreams and images, avoidance, somatic symptoms, and dissociation
2. affective responses such as anger, crying, sadness, anxiety
3. recollection of treatment-specific relationships with the patient or patient's family
4. relationships with colleagues including one's own analyst/therapist, supervisors, and peers
5. risk management concerns including fear of a lawsuit
6. feelings of grandiosity, shame, and guilt (superego concerns)
7. a sense of professional crisis, including questions about professional and personal identity, feeling a loss of competence or interest in continuing to do psychotherapy with difficult patients
8. the ongoing effect of a patient's suicide on the work with one's other patients, particularly a deep fear that the suicide of yet another patient would be simply unbearable.

Other research on the survivors of suicide study the issue of bereavement, asking what is the same and what is different about those bereaved from sudden death due to other traumas from those bereaved from sudden death because of suicide (Jordan, 2001). Increasingly, the literature on bereavement from suicide shows that such bereavement is different. Survivors of suicide often report feeling stigmatized, blamed, experiences of shame, guilt, and other emotions, which are particularly intensified in the context of suicide (Bell et al., 2012). One recent study (Begley & Quayle, 2007) interviewed survivors who were family members of a person completing suicide. In this study, participants did not report that they were able to "move on" from the suicide, feeling that they were living in the long shadow for five or more years after the event. The attachment to the deceased family member was not relinquished over time but "believed their family member continued to have a role in their families' lives" (p. 32).

The long shadow of the dead patient on his/her therapist may be hard for those who have not lost a patient to suicide to accept or understand, and may lead to private projective speculation or judgment by colleagues or family members of the therapist who remains in the grip of this experience for a period of time. The suicide of a patient, for an estimated one-third of therapists, creates a violent rupture in personal and/or professional identity, pulling to the surface unconscious conflicts and long-repressed aspects of personal history. Yet others seem to manage relatively well, finding this experience to be an opportunity for personal and professional growth. By mobilizing various defensive operations or through experiences of good-enough grieving, a subgroup of clinicians report feeling a deeper connection to their professional work.

## Reflections on Losing Patients to Suicide

When I (AC) think of my reaction to the suicide death of a patient, I realize how complicated it is. Three patients with whom I have had relationships have killed themselves. One was a patient I admitted to hospital who killed himself a week later, another was a therapy patient of mine who had clearly improved during his treatment despite a series of recent losses, and another a psychopharmacology patient whom I saw within a day of her suicide. My reactions to each of these suicides differed quite significantly from one another, although I felt a profound sense of shock and dismay with all of them. In order for me to understand my responses to these suicides, I have spent years trying to understand what happened, both why these patients killed themselves and what it has meant to me that they did.

After long reflection, I have come to think of my internal psychological world as a great interconnected web that, in theory, could evoke an infinite number of reactions to any life event, including to the suicides of these patients. However, the event of these suicides plucked on my own web in particular ways, and I realize that, in large part, this is because of the meanings I attributed to the circumstances that surrounded each death. These circumstances contain universal factors: The circumstances of the actual suicide, my role in their treatment, and the reactions of the patient's family members, of my friends and colleagues, and with what was going on in my life at the time. These factors, which were different in all three deaths, evoked different kinds of emotion and degree of emotional intensity within me. As I reflected on them, I felt a clearer sense of my own vulnerabilities as well.

For example, although all three patients did not appear at acute risk of suicide leading up to their successful attempts, the first one was particularly hard to deal with because it was the first time a patient of mine had successfully completed suicide. Although I had several patients who were almost successful in killing themselves, the difference between a patient who almost dies and one that actually does is enormous. The experience of going through an event that was previously held as a theoretical possibility, but then becomes a visceral, emotional reality to live through, evoked responses I could never have imagined and fundamentally changed my relationship to suicide and to all my patients from then on.

The first patient I knew who committed suicide was the one I had admitted to hospital who then killed himself a week later. Although I had no further clinical interface with this patient after the initial admission intake, I nonetheless could not help but feel, in being the one to admit him, some degree of responsibility for his suicide and the subsequent suffering that my colleagues and the hospital went through. The particular circumstances of that suicide happened to touch on certain vulnerabilities in me, affecting me deeply and initiating a long process of reflection and confrontation with aspects of myself I had mostly managed to avoid. I came to see, for example, that being the one to have admitted him, and my sense of guilt for the pain and suffering others felt in response to this suicide, was linked to my experiences as a young child. At the age of three, my father was ill for almost a year in a hospital, and I was witness to the intense worry and fear that my mother went through having to take over as the sole financial support, while seeing myself as adding to her burden and powerless to help out in any concrete way as well as potentially responsible for my father's illness in the first place. The intense shock of this first suicide stirred up dormant memories of this childhood experience, and evoked episodes of a darker mix of self-blame, shame, and doubt. I also had anticipatory fear of going through a repetition of this experience, which cast a shadow over all subsequent admission interviews.

To me, it is remarkable how even small aspects of the circumstances surrounding a suicide can make profound differences in how one reacts, even things that are not really directly connected to the suicide itself. For example, I met with one of my patients just 12 hours prior to her suicide. This was a psychopharmacology patient of mine with a history of serious suicide attempts. I felt we had a good working relationship, and that she and I were watchful in looking together for signs of a potential spiral into a suicidal state. During that last meeting, I felt we covered the important issues that she was dealing with, including her current feelings and thoughts about suicide, and yet I did not feel at that time that she seemed at any acute risk of killing herself.

This meeting took place in the early evening, and I was going to be moonlighting at another job afterwards. I remember debating briefly about whether to write my note about that session then and there, or wait until the next morning, given that I was at that point nearing the time I would have to leave. I chose to spend the 10 minutes I had before I had to leave writing the note, then go off to work. The next morning, a colleague came to my office to tell me the patient had killed herself sometime earlier that morning. Although writing the note had nothing to do with the fact that she killed herself, if I had not written the note before hearing of her death, I know, because of my vulnerability to a punishing superego, that I would have been castigating myself for years to come for not having written that note. Instead, I had documented evidence of her state of mind just hours before she killed herself, which was helpful not just in a medico-legal sense, but also because it was written at a time when I was not thinking that she seemed on the verge of killing herself, and so it is a note that is documenting an encounter in the present looking forward rather than one looking at the past in the context of knowing what happened after. Thus, I was less vulnerable to second-guessing myself after the fact, wondering if I was perhaps missing something or distorting my recollection of what had happened. But, if I had been more rushed, or busy, or if someone had happened to call me at that moment, it would have been very easy to rationalize writing that note the next day.

Because I happen to be someone for whom writing notes has always been a rather tortuous task and one I tend to procrastinate and be very self-critical about, if I had not written that note when I did, I know it would have set me up for much self-recrimination later on. Her suicide would have been forever linked with my self-criticism around note writing, and that would have left me much more emotionally vulnerable to the event of her suicide, even though writing the note in and of itself had nothing to do with her death. But it would also have further intensified my complicated relationship to note writing, something that obviously reflects older internal conflicts. Thus, the consequences of suicide can be compared to a kind of psychological shrapnel, hitting and wounding areas of the mind and heart often quite tangential to the event of the suicide itself.

As with much in life, it is often from very small, seemingly trivial things that more profound, long-lasting effects are created, when at the time they just seemed to be business as usual. I think it is just this kind of circumstance that can make suicide so difficult for those that are left after a person kills himself. The amount of second-guessing after the fact is often because small things are suddenly looked at with new attention and study, as if we can redo the past by closer attention to, and by giving new meaning to, something that at the time seemed not so different than at other times, or at least not so different that we could have predicted someone was going to kill themselves. Yet, afterwards, those very things get analyzed and raked over as if they contain the very information that, if we had only just recognized it at the time, could have led to a different outcome. For example, I know of a colleague who has spent hours reviewing her last meeting with a patient, including whether something in the patient's facial expression was trying to convey she was about to kill herself six days later!

Suicide, by its nature, often seems to carry an intrinsic aura of blame that can becomes amplified in a clinical setting because of the belief, whether justified or not, that a clinician could have done something to prevent it. This belief can rest within the clinician, his colleagues, as well as family members of the patient who killed himself, and thus the therapist may have to deal not only with the anger of family members, but also internal reproaches, and sometimes ineffective responses by colleagues, in a way that can lead a therapist to feel attacked from without and unprotected from within. In my experience, the fact that I had a good relationship with a family member of two of the patients who committed suicide helped enormously in coping with the intensity of my feelings and coming to terms with the limits of my ability to foresee their suicidal behavior.

In the third case, I did not have such a relationship with a family member, and this was one of the factors that led to a breach of my defenses and a sustained period of working through issues that were dredged up as a result. In other words, my reaction to the suicide was partly about the actual suicide and partly about the unconscious/repressed issues the suicide brought to the surface. These issues in me were less about the suicide of the patient and more about my own process, yet the two inevitably became linked, one evoking the other. This confluence of personal and professional issues can be compounded by the shadow of a potential or real lawsuit, another factor that leaves therapists having to deal with the aftermath of a suicide for years after.

When a colleague faced with a lawsuit stated wryly, "That which doesn't kill you will make you stronger," I realized that this was not entirely accurate. Sometimes what doesn't kill you will nonetheless leave you weakened. In my case, I feel I have come away from the experience of a patient committing suicide both stronger and weaker for it. I am stronger in that I have an increased sensitivity to the reality of suicide in a way that only someone who has had a patient commit suicide can have. I think I am a better clinician as a result, both more attuned and attentive to the possibility of suicide and more able to engage a patient about it. I have also come to better terms with the limits of my ability to intervene and prevent suicide. By the same token, I am still in the process of working through some of the issues these suicides have dredged up from deep within me.

Following the suicides of my patients, I have been forced to confront things I might otherwise have kept in the dark. While I am thus better for it, this cleaning-out process has been at a cost. Although I don't begrudge this cost, it has left me at this point with certain questions about how I want to proceed in my work as a therapist that I have not yet satisfactorily answered. In stirring up deeper psychological vulnerabilities, the suicides have also evoked compensatory protective responses. While I feel more expert in the area of suicide, I am less willing to spend the long periods of time it often takes to work in intensive individual psychotherapy with a chronically suicidal patient. Instead, I find myself gravitating to a more short-term role with patients, albeit often quite suicidal ones.

Since the suicides of my patients, I have changed jobs and my clinical practice. I now work in an inpatient psychiatric hospital primarily admitting patients, many of them because of significant suicidal ideation or a recent suicide attempt. I often find myself having a brief conversation with the admitting nurses about their sense of the patient's current suicide risk, and review with them how these conclusions were reached and what their thoughts are about the next immediate step in terms of maintaining that patient's safety, while also discussing my own. I especially like to discuss underlying uncertainties the nurse and I might have in regard to how safe we feel the patient really is, and to make sure that we come to a decision together about the immediate treatment plan that maximizes our sense that we have thought through that patient's potential risk for self-harm and/or suicide. I feel that in this way I am both acknowledging that suicide, although rare, is nonetheless real, and that it can be looked at, discussed, and addressed in a thoughtful, collaborative way, while at the same time recognizing the limits of anyone's ability to completely prevent a suicide.

I also find myself wanting to play a supportive and educative role to other clinicians in the field, who may one day have to go through the suicide of a patient or who already have experienced this. I find that, especially in newer clinicians who have not yet experienced a completed or attempted suicide by a patient in their direct care, a kind of denial exists regarding the reality of suicide and therefore its potential impact on oneself. I recognize that I too once had this denial and find myself wanting to prepare others, knowing of course this is something you can never be completely prepared for. However, knowing others have gone through it too, and survived, is very helpful, and can be a source of support even many years later.

Offering myself as a resource to newer clinicians in regard to the potential experience of patient suicide is a careful balancing act; I do not want to impose my own anxieties onto others, but would rather be there as someone they could turn to with any questions or concerns in regard to their work and the safety of a patient. This reaching out and modeling can be done in the everyday conversations that naturally occur when a less experienced colleague and I are going about the routine business of discussing a patient and preparing his/her treatment plan.

In my career as a psychiatrist and psychotherapist, I have been blessed with wonderful supervisors, bosses, and colleagues. I have found that regular, penetrating attention and discussion of clinical work, examining what is going well, along with things that are not going so well in the work, are values I now bring to my work with other clinicians. Working to create a climate of safety and support is imperative when trying to help clinicians maintain a sense of self-coherence and meaning in the face of a tragic outcome such as suicide. I have come to see myself as a resource to other clinicians based on my experience of what was helpful and not helpful to me and to other colleagues I have spoken with, following the tragedy of patient suicide.

## Suicide as a Challenge to Professional Identity

The formation of an analytic identity is often taken to be very important in the field of psychoanalysis, yet there are few studies of exactly how this happens beyond supposing that the tripartite model inculcates such an identity in practitioners. There is little to explain this process other than identification with one's training analyst and/or supervisors and the ideals and principles of theory and technique. Yet identity is much more complex and deep than a set of habits or technical practices. Kaslow et al. (1992) studied identity formation in family clinicians, finding that various standard training practices culminate in an established professional identity about five years *after* training is completed. From this, we might infer that the suicide of a patient of an early career professional has a potentially significant effect on the evolving identity of that professional. Survey research also supports the finding that early career psychiatrists are more profoundly negatively affected by the suicide of a patient than are psychiatrists with more experience (Ruskin et al., 2004).

In an effort to deepen my understanding of the effects of patient suicide on professional identity, I returned to one of the pioneers of identity development, Erik Erikson, using his paper "Identity and the Life Cycle" (1959) as a hermeneutic lens for revisiting interview data. The developmental psychosocial crises identified by Erikson were a very good fit with what the participants in my study spoke about. While Erikson was mainly concerned with child and adolescent development leading to mature adult identity, his model also lends itself to more circumscribed crises or events occurring in professional life of a clinician. Of course, in his original proposal, Erikson postulated an epigenetic sequence to his stages, or a linear progression. Life is not quite so linear or neat, and the stages are periodically revisited and reworked according to the current life context of each person.

I propose that for some clinicians (indeed, most of the clinicians in my study), the suicide of a patient may provoke a revisiting of Erikson's psychosocial crises in a telescoped and accelerated fashion. For instance, Erikson's first stage, "Trust vs. Mistrust," appears in many of the narratives. Clinicians often spoke about a conflict between trust and mistrust of themselves, their skills, their patients, their organizational structures, and their commitment to long-term work with desperate individuals. The second stage, "Autonomy vs. Shame and Doubt," also presents as a major theme in the data, with some clinicians feeling ashamed of themselves as the psychotherapist who has lost a patient to suicide leading at times to doubts about the value of intensive psychotherapy. "Initiative vs. Guilt," the third of Erikson's stages, is also in the narratives, particularly guilt about "not knowing." Some clinicians in my study questioned their competence ("Industry vs. Inferiority"), while also making presentations and reading as much as they could on the subject of suicide. Some wrestled with their tendency to withdraw and the isolation they sought and also felt from their colleagues ("Solidarity vs. Isolation"). For a time, many clinicians also confronted the crisis of "Generativity vs. Self-absorption," and most wrestled with the grief and the despair they felt for their patients, as well as the integrity they brought to their work and how deeply valued this aspect of their character was challenged by the suicide ("Integrity vs. Despair").

Professional identity is sensitive to events in early training, but the cumulative strain of working with very ill patients and managing crises may become manifest as burnout or exhaustion over the long course of a career as an analyst or psychotherapist. The death of a patient by suicide may lead the clinician to decide to alter the types of patient with whom they will work, the risks they are willing to bear in treating more seriously disturbed patients, and may leave the clinician in a state of traumatic anxiety that disrupts the previous pleasure or satisfaction taken in this intimate work. Whereas Ehrenberg (1992) has talked about the value of working deeply with patients at the "intimate edge," a therapist on the other side of a patient suicide may pull back from these sorts of engagements, feeling that any edge at all is too risky and painful to approach. Other therapists, having endured the pain of patient suicide, report a newfound freedom to work in a more liberated way, knowing what the stakes are, and willing to bear the vulnerability that intimate psychotherapeutic work exposes. Some choose to use their experience to move into research and teaching about working with suicidal patients, perhaps a type of generativity linked to Erikson's epigenetic model.

## Conclusion

If therapists losing a patient to suicide are able to manage the shame and stigma associated with the event, then there is much to teach colleagues who have not had a patient commit suicide about the experience, and also mutual support to give to colleagues who find themselves suddenly in this new territory. The narratives of early career clinicians losing a patient to suicide tell us something about the latent ideals and hopes we bring to our work, and how the suicide of a patient may challenge or restructure those primary ideals. We also have something to notice in our organizations and professions around this topic and our deep ambivalence about preparing ourselves and our institutions for the likelihood of patient suicide. The epidemiological statistics I presented earlier confirm that suicide is an enormous problem in our culture and in our world. This is not a rare event, although our organizational structures often fail to take adequate measures to manage this crisis. Often, when I present on this topic, I ask for an informal show of hands about how professionals have been prepared for the risk of patient suicide. I ask those present if their organization has a protocol or plan in place for managing a patient suicide, or, if talking to students and/or residents, I may ask if a teacher, class, or supervisor has talked to them about this topic, and to both questions there are few who answer in the affirmative. At a presentation to training directors, I asked if they addressed the topic of patient suicide in their training programs; many tentatively agreed that prevention is certainly important, but not many had thought systematically about how to respond over time to a trainee who has lost a patient to suicide. Dynamically, as a profession, we at times seem to be struggling with our anxiety leading to repression and avoidance of a subject that may profoundly affect half of our colleagues.

With a growing awareness in the past decade of the prevalence and far-reaching effect of suicide on survivors, the professional community is now beginning to appreciate just how complex the event of patient suicide may be and the ripple effect it can have on our colleagues and our organizations. Self-care and spaces in which to think and feel about the death of a patient by suicide are especially important. As clinicians, we tend to focus our efforts on providing excellent care for our patients, and often give our own needs short shrift. An unexpected occurrence in response to my writing and speaking on this topic over the past years is that periodically I get telephone calls from psychotherapists who have had a patient commit suicide. Suddenly, with a complete stranger, I find myself listening to intimate details of their experience and reaction to the suicide of a patient. The ones who call describe a number of stressors and strains in relationships with colleagues and, at times, in marriages, relationships, or in mental equilibrium and stability. The shame around the symptoms that may attend a professional trauma often lead clinicians to ignore their own basic needs for rest, vacation, or a return to analysis or psychotherapy.

For those clinicians who are deeply affected by a patient suicide, the repercussions are an opportunity for both self-examination and growth, which may occur over many years in the aftermath. But the process is not tidy, and many therapists are surprised that years later they may have a visceral response or recollection of their experience at unexpected moments. Speaking about the process and trajectory of bereavement, the psychoanalyst Margaret Little (1990) observed:

> [Y]es, you work through anger, self-pity, and remorse, and so on, until you arrive eventually at a relatively peaceful state of pure grief. But, I said, mourning is *for life*, and every now and then the original thing just jumps ups and hits you again and knocks you flat, and for the time being everything else is knocked out.
>
> (p. 301)

The personal meanings, feelings, and conflicts stirred by the suicide of a patient; the projective dynamics of our culture that stigmatizes the survivors of suicide; and the ongoing grief and mourning—all present opportunities and challenges for professional and personal identity growth provided the proper supports are sought out and available.

## References

Begley, M., & Quayle, E. (2007). The lived experience of adults bereaved by suicide: A phenomenological study. *Crisis: The Journal of Crisis Intervention and Suicide Prevention, 28*(1), 26–34.

Bell, J., Stanley, N., Mallon, S., & Manthorpe, J. (2012). Life will never be the same again: Examining grief in survivors bereaved by young suicide. *Illness, Crisis, & Loss, 20*(1), 49–68.

Chemtob, C.M., Hamada, R.S., Bauer, G., et al. (1988). Patients' suicides: Frequency and impact on psychiatrists. *American Journal of Psychiatry, 145,* 224–227.

Ehrenberg, D. (1992). *The intimate edge: Extending the reach of psychoanalytic interaction.* New York: W. W. Norton & Co.

Erikson, E. H. (1959). *Identity and the life cycle: Selected papers.* Psychological Issues, monograph 1, 11–171.

Gutin, N., McGann, V. L., & Jordan, J. R. (2011). The impact of suicide on professional caregivers. In J. R. Jordan & J. L. McIntosh (Eds.), *Grief after suicide: Understanding the consequences and caring for the survivors* (pp. 93–111). New York: Routledge.

Hendin, H., Haas, A. P., Maltsberger, J. T., Szanto, K., & Rabinowicz, H. (2004). Factors contributing to therapists' distress after the suicide of a patient. *American Journal of Psychiatry, 161,* 1442–1446.

Jordan, J. R. (2001). Is suicide bereavement different? A reassessment of the literature. *Suicide and Life-Threatening Behavior, 31*(1), 91–102.

Kaslow, N. J., McCarthy, S. M., Rogers, J. H., & Summerville, M. B. (1992). Psychology postdoctoral training: A developmental perspective. *Professional Psychology: Research and Practice, 23*(5), 369–375.

Little, M. I. (1990). *Psychotic anxieties and containment: A personal record of an analysis with Winnicott.* Northvale, NJ: Jason Aronson, Inc.

Pilkinton, P., & Etkin, M. (2003). Encountering suicide: The experience of psychiatric residents. *Academic Psychiatry, 27*(2), 93–99.

Ruskin, R. R., Sakinofsky, I. I., Bagby, R. M., Dickens, S. S., & Sousa, G. G. (2004). Impact of patient suicide on psychiatrists and psychiatric trainees. *Academic Psychiatry, 28*(2),104–110.

Sveen, C. A., & Walby, F. A. (2008). Suicide survivors' mental health and grief reactions: A systematic review of controlled studies. *Suicide and Life Threatening Behavior, 38,* 13–29.

Tillman, J. G. (2006). When a patient commits suicide: An empirical study of psychoanalytic clinicians. *International Journal of Psychoanalysis, 87,* 159–177.

Wurst, F., Kunz, I., Skipper, G., Wolfersdorf, M., Beine, K. H., & Thon, N. (2011). The therapist's reaction to a patient's suicide: Results of a survey and implications for health care professionals' well-being. *Crisis: The Journal of Crisis Intervention and Suicide Prevention, 32*(2), 99–105.

# 6

# ON BEING THE SECOND ANALYST

## Two Patients Who Suffered Unexpected Loss of Their First Analyst and the Issue of Countertransference

*Madeleine Bachner*

Our patients become very dependent on us as analysts when entering into a deep and transforming psychoanalytic process. For many patients, it takes years to come to the point where they can let themselves depend on us and accept evolving feelings of helplessness and dependency. It is a vulnerable and painful situation, even when everything goes well and the analyst stays healthy and alive.

It is important to keep in the back of our minds how strongly the patient is affected by these feelings when we discuss the loss of the previous analyst. We should stay alive and healthy and be able to bring the analytic process to an end. However, we are vulnerable too, and life can bring us illness that prevents us from continuing our work and bearing the responsibility for our patients. My impression, as I read articles on this subject, is that this issue is rarely, if ever, discussed in our psychoanalytic communities. This silence corresponds to my experience in my own psychoanalytical community. As individuals and as a professional group, we are very unprepared for death.

My purpose in writing this chapter is to illustrate the unfolding of a treatment when the patient has been faced with their analyst's unexpected death. I have had the experience of being the subsequent analyst for two patients whose analysts died suddenly. While my experience does not make it possible to generalize, it can be a contribution to this too often avoided topic. I will focus on what the process can be like for both the analyst and the patient.

In my experience, being the second analyst to a patient who has lost their analyst is complicated. Keeping a balance of letting the first analyst have a central space, along with finding my own space to occupy as a different analyst, is not an easy task. It is also interesting to think about taking over an analytic patient under these circumstances: What kind of analyst are you? It is obvious that there is no specific category for this analyst. This analyst could be called the *second analyst* or the *replacement analyst*, the *new analyst* or the *reserve analyst*. I think it is important to differentiate this analysis from reanalysis. When a patient starts reanalysis he or she has an experience of a full psychoanalytic process with them, the patient I am describing comes with an experience of a broken down psychoanalytic relationship and process that has to be acknowledged and mourned and links have to be made from the first analytic process to the second analytic process. I chose the term *second analyst*, as I was also the patient's second choice. This fact has importance in psychoanalytic work with these patients, as one has to take into account the relationship to the deceased analyst and simultaneously work with the patient to establish a new relationship.

Several authors who have written on the death of the patient's analyst have concentrated on the patient's loss of their analyst, the loss of familiar and reassuring routines when an analyst falls ill or dies, and the relative lack of recognition of the patient's situation (Rendely, 1999; Robutti, 2010; Traesdal, 2005; Ziman-Tobin, 1989). Reading these articles deepened my understanding of my own experience of "taking care" of patients who had lost their analysts. I recognized many of my thoughts in these articles.

After reading Traesdal's (2005) essay about her experience beginning with the second analyst, I realized that I have never discussed with my colleagues the complicated issue of being the second analyst, not even those whom I know have had the same experience. In her paper, Tauber (1989) discusses the dilemmas the second analyst faces when analyzing patients who have lost their analysts to illness and death. She describes the strain she felt as her patient persistently compared to their dead analyst everything she said or failed to say.

I felt inspired by reading these articles. They gave me ideas to emphasize and focus on when writing this chapter about my own experience working with patients who have lost their analysts. In what follows, I will describe my experience with two female patients who were both referred to me after having experienced the unexpected death and loss of their analysts. Although there were differences between these two patients, the circumstances under which they came to me were similar. I will describe the common themes.

## Ms. K.

The first patient, Ms. K., was referred under complicated conditions: her analyst was diagnosed with terminal cancer during the Christmas break. The analyst sent a letter to the patient telling her that she was ill and had to stop treatment immediately. Further, she would not see her for a last session. The patient was unaware of her first analyst's illness and impending death. The colleague who referred the patient to me told me that the first analyst did not want the patient to know that she was terminally ill and dying. I felt uncomfortable with this request, but I wanted to be loyal to my ill colleague. Looking back, I think my relative inexperience led me to agree to this request, and I did not say anything to my patient about her former analyst's situation.

Ms. K. was very unhappy and shocked when she received the letter from her analyst telling her that the treatment had to stop. She understood it was something serious but not how serious. She associated the loss of her analyst in this manner to her childhood experience with her nannies—how suddenly one could be exchanged for another. She had felt completely helpless in this situation without having any means of control over what was happening to her.

I felt I was entangled in some form of denial that her analyst was in fact dying or already dead. I continued to feel more and more uncomfortable with this restriction and felt my first task was to try and build a reasonably stable and secure relationship with Ms. K. Although the circumstances were complex, I came to the conclusion that I had to tell the patient about her analyst, otherwise it would be impossible to work with her. Withholding the information about her former analyst from her would destroy her ability to feel she could trust me. When she again started talking about her former analyst, wondering what had happened, I told her that I wanted to inform her of the facts. The patient was calm and thanked me for telling her about her former analyst; she felt sorry for her and cried silently.

This was the beginning of our psychoanalytical relationship, but there were more difficulties that came along in the form of negative transference. Why had she been referred to me? What made me capable of treating her? She did not choose me, someone else did.

I felt she was right in posing those questions. I also wondered if perhaps I was not the right analyst for her. I felt the need to make up for her loss and abandonment. More precisely, I felt that I wanted to compensate for her loss by protecting her. At the same time, I was aware that those tendencies in me would contradict what I felt she really needed: my neutral psychoanalytical stance and my ability to say what I thought, no matter how painful that might be.

I noticed I also felt guilty for being alive and healthy when my colleague was terminally ill or dead. While I did not know this colleague very well—she was a bit older than I and in the middle of her psychoanalytical career—her death was untimely and felt unfair. Even though it was not strong, I felt preoccupied with the guilt of surviving in the beginning of the analysis.

But, being the second analyst—the analyst not chosen by the patient, referred because of traumatic circumstances—bothered me more. I struggled with the feelings of not being good enough and the fear of being compared to the first analyst; I would always be the one lacking in some respect or another. I could not compensate for the traumatic loss of the first analyst.

A couple of months into the analysis, Ms. K. said that she felt that I was more "soft" than her first analyst, who had been quite hard at times and more strict than I was. What I think the patient meant by my "softer style" was that I was more tentative and her former analyst more confrontational. But this is my fantasy of what the patient meant when she talked about the difference between us. She liked my softer style, but worried that she needed someone who could tell her when she was right or wrong. She felt unsure if I was capable of that. She said that my eagerness to prove that I cared about her, but made her feel insecure at times. She very much needed me to be more firm and clear in my interventions and effectively signaled this to me. But, despite the fact that I was already aware of my tendency not to be, I found it difficult to keep my analytic position and think and speak clearly in her presence.

Ms. K. was married but was unable to bear children of her own. She and her husband adopted a boy at age two, who was about five years old when she started her analysis with me. Her child had severe emotional difficulties resulting from his traumatic upbringing in a childcare center, and was in psychoanalysis four times a week. Much of the material in Ms. K.'s analysis was about trying to be not a good enough mother, but an exceptionally good mother to this very demanding and difficult child who needed a lot of attention from his parents.

I believed that my feeling of wanting to compensate for her traumatic loss of her analyst was a countertransference in two aspects. My patient stirred in me a strong desire to be a good "mother" to her traumatized child, while at the same time I was trying my best just to be a good enough analyst to her, a patient already traumatized by the death of her first analyst. I wanted to make up for that traumatization, compounded by what I believed to have been a poorly managed termination. The tasks I set for myself were made all the more difficult for me, as I was simultaneously struggling with strong negative feelings towards some specific colleagues and the psychoanalytic community in general. I wanted Ms. K. to be able to rely on me and feel that I would not fail her by becoming ill or not being able to be there for her. I wanted to restore her faith in treatment and in psychoanalysis.

Three years into her analysis, Ms. K.'s mother died quite unexpectedly from a stroke. When Ms. K. started analysis with me, she was deeply disappointed with her mother. She was critical of her mother for not caring more about her grandchild or taking enough interest in her life. During the last year of her mother's life, her feelings gradually changed towards her mother, as she saw that her mother cared about her and her family as much as she was able. During the final year, Ms. K. and her mother became closer, and this closeness helped her cope better with mourning the loss of her mother.

After six years—four with me and two with her previous analyst—Ms. K. wanted to terminate treatment. She felt that she had been in treatment for such a long time and needed to see if she could manage on her own. While I agreed, I had mixed feelings about ending at this point. When the last week came, Ms. K. started a conflict with me, feeling I had said something unempathic and wrong. I worried that our parting would be overshadowed by her upset and anger. When the last session came, she was still hurt and disappointed but also sad. She was able to express her gratitude to me.

A year later, Ms. K. called, wanting to see me again. She told me that she had been promoted to a leading position of a home for old and sick people. She felt insecure and had doubts about whether she would be successful in this job. I found myself reluctant to take her back into treatment, but agreed to meet with her to see what she actually wanted. During her appointment, she talked about her strong feelings of insecurity and inferiority. She felt unable to sustain her feelings of being good enough to cope with her situation. She expressed vague feelings of dissatisfaction with me for not helping her enough with her deeply rooted feelings of inferiority that repeatedly surfaced, making life difficult for her.

I agreed to start treatment with her again, initially with mixed feelings. I wondered if it would have been better to show her that I had faith in her ability to cope with her feelings by herself. In fact, I was really not sure about her ability to cope alone, and I worried that I had actually failed her in the previous treatment. My reluctance was very likely a countertransference reaction. That said, I think we achieved a lot during her analysis. She became a more confident mother to her son; she accepted that she was a good enough mother to him and accepted the fact that her son had severe problems that she could not compensate or solve by herself; she became less masochistic when confronted with a problem or a conflict. I wondered if Ms. K. needed to come back and see me just to see if I was still alive. I understood that my feeling of being too "soft" was a countertransference response to her never feeling good enough and her fear of failing her adopted child. One could say that we shared the same fears.

We continued for another two years, and during this time I felt much freer to think and was able to maintain my analytic position more easily and consistently. As I think about it now, it seems to me the first part of the analysis was working through the consequences of her loss of her first analyst, and her wish to terminate was the working through of that loss. The second time she came to see me, it was more of a reanalysis or a new analysis, where she was much clearer about what she needed. *Choosing* to come back to me created a more open and free atmosphere where the process was more dynamic and creative for both of us. In retrospect, her coming back wanting to do further work with me now seems like the start of a new analysis not dominated by the first analyst who had died and "abandoned" her.

## Ms. H.

I was contacted by a colleague who wanted to refer a patient to me; the patient had been in psychotherapy in a public institution. She told me that the both patient and her psychotherapist believed that the patient needed psychoanalysis.

Similar to Ms. K., I was contacted by a colleague who wanted to refer a patient to me; unlike Ms. K., Ms. H. started psychoanalysis, paid by national health care, with an analyst in private practice. National health care rules limit analysis to four years, and the patient was unable to handle a predetermined ending, breaking off treatment at three years in order not to feel abandoned. She later returned to her analyst, and they decided to resume the analysis. However, the beginning was delayed because the analyst had a full schedule. During this time, the analyst very unexpectedly died.

When Ms. H. was informed, she became deeply depressed and was treated at an outpatient clinic where she received psychotherapy and medication. When I spoke with the referring colleague, I sensed that this patient was difficult and demanding and that they wanted to get rid of her.

For complex reasons, I felt very reluctant and cautious about seeing this patient. It was not only what I heard about her from my colleagues, but also because her former analyst was a very important person to me. As my first supervisor during my psychoanalytic training, he meant a lot to me as an older and very highly respected colleague. I felt awkward and strange taking over his patient.

During the consultation, Ms. H. was different from what I had expected. She expressed how important her first analyst had been to her and how abandoned she had felt when she got the news that he had died.

Ms. H., a woman in her mid-forties, lived alone with her son from a previous marriage. During her previous analysis, she met a man and moved in with him. However, after a year of living together, the relationship ended in a very conflictual way. Ms. H. worked for various companies in Human Relations. A very dedicated and ambitious worker, she often ran into conflicts with a leading person in the company, and as a result her employment frequently came to a sudden stop due to her being fired.

The superficial reason she gave for the pause in her first analysis was her new relationship and a new job far away from her analyst's office. She wanted to resume analysis with him because she felt she lacked the capacity to hold on to relationships and work. She wanted to solve conflicts rather than cause catastrophic endings. The strong urge made her resume her analysis, only to discover that it was too late with her chosen analyst. At the same time, Ms. H.'s mother was diagnosed with a very malignant form of cancer, and she had to provide care for her much of the time.

Contrary to what I had expected, I felt moved by this patient. She had an honest and straightforward way of communicating, and I became aware of how much her former analyst meant to her. I wondered if they had come as far in their work as they could, formulating her problems but not as far as looking at alternative ways of dealing with conflicts in love and in work. Also, contrary to my expectation before meeting Ms. H., I did not find it so difficult or complicated that she had been in analysis with my colleague.

In articles on taking over patients from analysts who have died, several authors mention a bridging function, a function that the new analyst has as being in between the patient and the dead analyst. This enables the patient to share memories and to mourn the analyst together with someone who knew and valued that person. Although the needs of the patients vary, in general, Ziman-Tobin (1989) states:

> The most immediate need of such a patient is to share the loss with a "community," albeit a dyad, and preferably with an analyst who knew the deceased. Through such a transitional relationship, the mourning of the patient may be given the time and space in which to begin the dissolution of the transference in appropriate realistic stages.
>
> (p. 437)

My impression was that this was a woman struggling to make her life work, but she had failed in many respects. She very desperately wanted and felt she needed more psychoanalytic work. Perhaps as an act of loyalty and affection for my senior colleague, I felt that I wanted to go on and continue the work Ms. H. and he had started. Meeting this patient was beneficial for me and for her. I also mourned her deceased analyst, but we shared the loss of him from different perspectives. I can add that the patient knew that I knew her former analyst from colleagues of mine. The former analyst and I came from the same psychoanalytical society in Sweden (at the time there were two psychoanalytical societies in Sweden).

At the time of the consultation, Ms. H. was unemployed and disabled because of depression and bodily pain. She had very little money to live on and provide for herself and her son. If I would accept her into psychoanalysis, the government would pay for two sessions and she would pay for two herself. She wanted to start analysis with me, but she would only do so if national health care would guarantee payment for two sessions per week until she was ready to terminate treatment. Once her conditions were approved by national health care, we agreed to start treatment.

Two months later, we began analysis. By that time, her mother had died, and Ms. H. was grieving. Her relationship to her mother had been distant. Ms. H. described her mother as weak, submissive, and very afraid of conflicts. It was almost as if Ms. H. had become not only the opposite of her mother, but also more like a caricature of her. Where her mother was submissive and weak, Ms. H. was offensive but also weak, because she was very vulnerable beneath the surface. Her relationship to her father had become emotionally stronger when she had a son who developed a strong tie to his grandfather. Her father had died some years before her mother fell ill, but she had three younger brothers from whom she had cut off contact. She now felt very lonely.

I expected a challenging analysis with this patient. Would we come to the point when there would be a conflict that made Ms. H. furious? If so, what would happen then? Would she leave the analysis, just cut me off, and never come back? Or would it be possible to work through the conflicts and the negative transference without the relationship ending in catastrophe?

The analysis began in a rather calm way. I think Ms. H. appreciated me very much and felt me to be a good enough analyst, mostly listening to her, getting to know her, and letting her get to know me.

As I described the above with Ms. K., I felt it was a special responsibility to take on these patients who had lost their analysts. I was simultaneously aware that I had not been their first choice as analyst and that someone else had chosen for them.

When I had to present a progress report to the health ministry in order to get additional money allocated for her twice-weekly sessions, I shared the report with Ms. H. After reading it, she agreed with it, but wanted to add something. I do not remember what it was, but at the time it seemed insignificant. After sending the report, I got a phone message from Ms. H. She said she was ill and could not come to the following session but would call when she was feeling better.

She did not call, and she did not come to her next session. The next week she did not call or come to any of her four sessions. I was puzzled at first. Was she seriously ill? In hospital? Despite giving her the opportunity to comment about it, I wondered if her absence was related to the report.

Christmas break was coming up very soon. I decided to call her, but she did not answer. I wrote an email to her asking her to contact me. The last week before the Christmas break, she called and resumed her sessions. When I asked her what made her stop coming to her sessions, she told me that she had noticed that I misspelled her first name when reading the report. She felt furious and hurt. She decided not to come to the next session, but then it grew into something else. She was still very angry and had a fantasy that if she expressed her anger toward me I would become submissive and back down like her mother. If I did that, she would feel contempt toward me and would never be able to trust me again. As a result, she protected herself and me from her fantasized catastrophic ending.

Ms. H. interrupted her first analysis because of external reasons, but I began to wonder if her analysis was at a point where her fantasized scenario could have happened. She protected herself from this fantasy by interrupting her analysis. I speculated that her analysis with me picked up where her first analysis left off. With me, she got the opportunity to work through this traumatic experience with her primal objects and the traumatic experience of losing her analyst when she was approaching him again.

## Conclusion and Discussion

All psychoanalytic work is challenging in many different ways, but being the second analyst requires, as Traesdal (2005) so poignantly puts it, "providing a foster home for somebody else's analysand" (p. 1249). In my experience, it is complicated in a number of ways. One has to bear being not chosen in the first place, and accept and keep in mind that the patient has lost not only a psychoanalytic place and process, but also a person that had deep knowledge of them and of whom they had a deep knowledge. As Traesdal writes:

> The best way to meet the challenge of providing an analytic foster home for somebody else's analysand after bereavement is to regard the situation as a special case, with its own particular dynamics, and not try to make it fit into the category of reanalysis or regard the task as the mere completion of an interrupted analysis with someone else. The patient's needs may be somewhere in between. The particular form of triangulation to be handled by therapist and patient when starting anew is the transferential threesome of present analyst, deceased analyst, and patient. To bring analysis to a fruitful conclusion, the task of the new therapist and the patient in their work together will be to pick up the associative threads from the first analysis and weave them in to a fabric of the new analytic encounter, ultimately to form a complete tapestry, amalgamating shades and colors from the first analysis with those brought forth during the second.
> 
> (p. 1249)

I recognized the special strain involved in taking over work with these patients. However, they have also given me a unique experience, one that is different from other psychoanalytical patients. Working in the shadow of the first analyst made it difficult to keep my own presence, thoughts, and style. I realized that occupying a space of my own and maintaining that space during the work with the patient, as well as allowing the patient to create a space of her own, is of ultimate importance for a successful outcome of the treatment. Room must be made for the relationship with both the old analyst and the new analyst.

The struggle I described with my tendency to be caring and respectful as compensation for my patient's loss is one that I do not feel with other patients. I came to understand that this struggle is linked to endeavoring to keep a space of my own, to allow my own existence, and to think and interact in my own style. At the same time, I needed to remain aware of the patient's need to be with their dead analyst and to persistently measure and compare me to them.

Another significant theme that I think is important in the treatment of patients whose analysts have died is the responsibility to stay alive and be healthy. This feeling of responsibility for the patient is common when dealing with traumatized patients or patients that have lost parents unexpectedly and suddenly. I felt this responsibility even more strongly with these patients since they already had experienced the loss of their analyst. The catastrophic idea that they could be abandoned again surfaced very quickly if they experienced or sensed that something was not as usual. Both patients accentuated this, each fearing the loss of me and worrying that I was ill or would disappear. They were very sensitive to my well-being, anxiously commenting if they thought I looked tired or ill. If I did not open the door immediately when they rang the bell, they both reported catastrophic fears that something had happened to me. I think it is important to address the reality of these fears of abandonment. In my experience, it is not a good idea to merely interpret the fear as separation anxiety or a death wish against the analyst without taking into account the fact that the actual trauma of being abandoned unexpectedly has occurred.

With Ms. K., the theme of fostering was present both in her relation to her child and in my relation to her. Her child had lost his mother; Ms. K. had lost her analyst. We both tried very hard to be good foster parents. I got entangled in this striving to be an "exceptionally good mother." It was not until it was possible to understand the transference-countertransference situation of wishing to make up for her loss that was I able to help Ms. K with her high demands on herself to be a perfect mother to her very difficult child.

The process with these two patients was influenced by my relationship to the deceased colleagues. Ms. K.'s analyst was a person I knew by name, but with whom I had no personal relationship. In her denial of her illness, I thought she did not take responsibility for herself and her patients. By the time she had to give up practicing, it was too late for her to tell her patients about her situation. This made it especially difficult for Ms. K. Ms. H.'s analyst, as described earlier, had made a deep impact on me as my first supervisor and a mentor. His death was a loss for me, and I think this was helpful to me in working with this patient, especially in the beginning of the analysis.

Another issue I have found is the difficulty for these patients in terminating their analyses. Ms. H. said during our last session that she needed to know that she could come back if she needed. While this is quite common among patients terminating their treatment, Ms. H. said this with a pressure that I saw as uncommon. She said that she could not live with the fact that she could never see me again. It remains to be seen if the patient will be able to live with the fact that she does not know if I am alive or dead, or if she will feel she has to return and to try to keep me alive. I hope she can bear the uncertainty of not knowing. With Ms. K., I did not fully understand why she came back to me for more analysis even though she still had some problems in her life. As I think of it now, I speculate that she had a deep need to stay close to me to be sure that I was there for her and that I had not disappeared.

It is not clear, of course, from this material whether the difficulty my patients had in leaving me is a unique picture belonging to patients with this heightened experience of unexpected loss. Nevertheless, my view is that when confronted with having to let go of their second analyst, terminating analysis could be a specific problem for this group of patients. They may bring to analysis an unconscious thought that by staying on they will keep their analyst alive and well and they will never be abruptly abandoned.

More often than not, it is a difficult and emotionally demanding phase for both parties when any analysis enters the termination phase. What I experienced with both Ms. K. and Ms. H., however, differed from what is normally lived through during this phase. They showed that they had to keep coming to see me to assure themselves that I was still healthy, and the thought that they would say goodbye and never see me again was truly intolerable.

But all analyses must come to an end, and with these patients it is crucial that the analyst understands that their fear of catastrophic loss is not only something they are afraid of and in a way are expecting, but also something that really happened to them. Nevertheless, ultimately, they must let go of their object. Then, they can open themselves to the outcome that through letting go of the external object they might be able to create an inner object to turn to in moments of distress and loneliness. In the end, this is how we can stay in contact with our primary objects—letting go, only to find that what was outside now is inside.

## References

Rendely, J. (1999). The death of an analyst. *Contemporary Psychoanalysis*, *35*, 131–152.

Robutti, A. (2010). When the patient loses his/her analyst. *Italian Psychoanalytic Annual*, *4*, 129–145.

Tauber, G. (1989). Re-analysis after the death of the analyst: The problem of countertransference in re-analysis. *Modern Psychoanalysis*, *14*, 171–182.

Traesdal, T. (2005). When the analyst dies: Dealing with the aftermath. *Journal of the American Psychoanalytic Association*, *53*, 1235–1255.

Ziman-Tobin, P. (1989). Consultation as a bridging function. *Contemporary Psychoanalysis*, *25*, 432–437.

# Part III

# THE LONG SHADOW OF RUPTURE

# 7

# LOSING A TRAINING ANALYST FOR ETHICAL VIOLATIONS
## Short-Term and Long-Term Effects[1]

*Elizabeth Wallace*

> Upon the conduct of each depends the fate of all.
> 
> Alexander the Great

My experience as the analysand of a training analyst who was investigated and expelled for ethical violations with another patient, including sexual boundary violations has had profound effects. The impact of these events, which occurred during my psychoanalytic training, has reverberated through my training analyses, my psychoanalytic education, my work, and my relationship with the psychoanalytic community at all levels. Unfortunately, my experience is not rare, although it is seldom discussed. Few psychoanalytic institutes have been untouched by the loss of analysts who commit boundary violations. The study of sexual boundary violations by training analysts has confirmed that these "are not rare phenomena" and that, in the cases studied, "disturbing aftershocks were felt for many years, even after effective action had been taken" (Gabbard & Peltz, 2001, p. 660). Boundary violations have been described as "collective traumas," reverberating dangerously in concentric interpersonal circles that include innocent bystanders such as relatives and colleagues (Ross, 1995, p. 961). This chapter addresses the particular type of trauma that may be experienced by candidates who are affected by the loss of a training analyst for ethical violations, and the longer-term effects post-training.

    The impact that training analysts have as teachers and analysts on generations of analysts makes the investigation of their ethical violations not only of the utmost importance, but also the utmost challenge, within the setting of the institute. With the growth of knowledge and concern about ethical issues in psychoanalysis, national bodies in the United States and Canada have developed codes of ethics and support the development of ethics committees in local institutes. Such committees have the mandate to receive and investigate ethical complaints, tasks that might have previously been referred to external licensing bodies. The multiple roles of the training analyst as an influential senior colleague, faculty member, supervisor, and analyst for trainees amplify the effects of the investigation and expulsion of a training analyst from the community, and underline the necessity for well-formulated institutional responses that take into account these multiple roles. Gabbard and Lester (1996) have outlined four areas of institutional responses to boundary violations: management of complaints, response to victims, assessment and rehabilitation of offenders, and prevention. An additional, but largely unexplored area of institutional response involves the management of educational problems that are generated by the loss of a training analyst who commits ethical violations, and the response of institutes to candidates who are analysands or supervisees of the training analyst in question.

There are several reasons why I have chosen to write about what was for me a painful, albeit eye-opening, experience. While I avidly read the existing literature on boundary violations in the wake of my analyst's investigation and expulsion for boundary violations, I did not find reports by other candidates in my position, which might have been helpful to me and to my institute. I have identified three areas of concern. First, the lack of reports in the literature from a candidate's perspective is a drawback, I believe, for candidates and institutes who must attempt to formulate helpful responses in the midst of a group crisis. Second, because of the dual nature of the candidate-analyst relationship, the issues faced by candidate-analysands are distinct enough from those of other "bystanders" as to merit a separate discussion. The training analysis has been described from the beginning as having dual aims, namely educational and therapeutic. The tension between these aims, which varies among analytic dyads, poses difficulties for both training analysts and educators (Cabaniss & Bosworth, 2006). The training analyst essentially performs dual roles for the candidate-analysand, first and primarily as an analyst, but also as an educator who represents the training program, although attempts are usually made to keep these last roles as muted as possible. It is the existence of these dual relationships and the mounting tension between them that fuels, I believe, some of the particular complications for candidates whose analyst faces investigation and censure, as I illustrate in the chapter.

A third area of concern is the possibility of a domino effect—that is, the loss of a training analyst may be followed by the loss of his/her analysands from the analytic community. It is not clear what typically happens to candidates who lose a training analyst for ethical violations. Do they, in fact, drop out of training, as was suggested by the anecdotal reports of my colleagues, who feared that I, too, might leave training? Even these anecdotal reports suggest that the effect on candidate-analysands is potentially devastating, and sometimes even fatal to training and ongoing participation in the analytic community. My own experience of isolation, in the context of severe strain in the relationships within my institute, certainly led me to consider leaving at a number of points. That I did not leave training was mitigated by several important factors, which I will discuss later.

I propose to offer my particular experience as a springboard for discussion of issues relevant to psychoanalytic institutes that must respond to these events, while taking into account the significant impact on candidates. I am aware that some aspects of my experience reflect my individual circumstances and characteristics, while other aspects may cover common ground. I have divided my discussion into four parts, based on what I felt were somewhat distinct phases in the process with respect to the issues that I faced: namely, the period encompassing the ethics investigation; the announcement of the findings to me and to the institute as a group; the ensuing individual and group dynamics generated by my analyst's expulsion from the institute and subsequent revocation of his medical license; and the period of restabilization that followed over the next year.

## "In the Dark": The Ethics Investigation

Three years into my training analysis, and after the first year of my analytic training, my analyst informed me that he was taking a leave of absence from the institute "for personal reasons." Although my analysis could continue as usual, I would not receive credit from the institute for this portion of my training analysis. My initial alarm and curiosity were reinforced by a follow-up call and meeting with two members of the institute executive committee, who provided the same information and reassured me, as did my analyst, that the situation would likely be resolved within several months. One of these analysts made a simple comment that served me remarkably well over time, namely, "This has nothing to do with you." I was grateful that he anticipated that my fantasies, in the face of virtually no information, could take me almost anywhere. That I knew about the events of the next months at all was a product of my dual position as analysand and trainee, with its inherent costs and benefits. The cost for me was a lengthy disruption to my analysis and training, approximately 10 months from beginning to end, during a period of considerable emotional turbulence and uncertainty. The benefit, as articulated later by the executive members, was the opportunity to alert me to any irregularities in my own analysis, if they had existed.

The following five months "in the dark" were in some ways more difficult than what ensued after the investigation, as all of my worst fears were projected onto this uncertain scenario as if it were a Rorschach. To make matters worse, I experienced the eruption of a symptom that had almost entirely remitted during my previous period of analysis. I include this as a reminder that the disruption of a training analysis has both clinical and educational implications.

Several months after the initial announcement of the mysterious leave of absence, the two executive members informed me that a professional review of my analyst was being conducted, that a committee had been formed to conduct the review, and that the timeframe for completion was unknown. The same two officers of the institute served as my liaisons throughout my ordeal and met with me at intervals, which provided helpful continuity albeit few answers to my many questions. They also conveyed their understanding that I might feel more loyalty toward my analyst, whom I knew better than anyone else, and less confidence in the institute, which proved to be both empathic and accurate as to my state of mind.

The importance of maintaining strict confidentiality was emphasized to me, and I was asked not to share my knowledge of the proceedings with anyone. I was told that no one in the institute would be able to talk with me about the situation. I felt responsible for not putting either the institute or my analyst at risk. The analogy to a child carrying an unspoken family secret was not lost on me, neither were the incestuous connotations of the internal investigation. Not surprisingly, I found it increasingly difficult to go to classes, where I felt anguished but unable to say anything about my predicament to my classmates, a group of seven of us who had grown quite close. I worried that I might "leak" my situation to my class, and put either my analyst or the institute in legal peril—I felt unusually guarded. Despite my subjective experience of distress, I did a good enough job of compartmentalizing that my class remained unaware of the problems brewing.

The issue of confidentiality placed me in the bizarre situation of being able to confide only in my analyst, the very person who was at the center of my anxious speculations. There were no other candidates in analysis with my analyst at the time, with whom I would have sought out discussion. I experienced the double bind of disloyalty to the institute when I talked to my analyst about the investigation, and disloyalty to my analyst when I talked to the institute representatives. My experience of isolation served to create a kind of "cocoon" consisting of my analyst and me "against the world," one that I would characterize now as a kind of "paranoid-schizoid world," in Kleinian terms, in which our work and relationship felt under attack. While I had a faculty advisor who had previously been very helpful, a brief conversation suggested to me that she was likely involved in the investigation of my analyst, which turned out to be the case, thus adding to the conflicts of interest that I was already experiencing. We stopped talking until the aftermath of the investigation, at which time we both realized that I needed a new faculty advisor. My inability to reach such an obvious conclusion much earlier underlines to me how difficult it had become for me to think clearly during this period, which was at least in part a consequence of the isolation I was experiencing.

I was asked by colleagues why I did not leave analysis during this period, as it seemed clear to them that I could not have been doing useful analytic work under the circumstances, whatever the eventual outcome of the investigation. The answer is complex. However, the context was that I was in the middle of what had been a very helpful analysis that I was loath to discontinue. I trusted my analyst, and felt affection and gratitude towards him for his considerable help through a number of life crises. The issue of losing credit from the institute for a portion of my analysis was of secondary importance to me, although it also felt like a punishment for not abandoning my analysis, and perhaps even a "punishment by proxy" of my analyst. I was primarily concerned with not abandoning treatment prematurely, not knowing the legitimacy of the case against my analyst. That I was in the midst of an idealizing transference is much clearer to me now, although we discussed it in my analysis at the time without a thorough analysis of it, which may have been impossible. This particular dynamic configuration predisposed to various splits that I describe below, and was exacerbated by the circumstances of isolation and secrecy, which also served as fertile ground for splits in my thinking and, I suspect, in the thinking of others in the institute.

The "cocoon" of relative isolation from the institute that my analyst and I shared during this time amplified, I think, my identification with my analyst and my sense of a special bond in which our roles were reversed, with me as his loyal protector and advocate, and he as the wounded, perhaps falsely accused victim. I imagined that a complaint had been made against him by a vengeful female patient, as I knew that he had previously worked in a program for severely disordered patients who have been known to complain and litigate. On an unconscious level, I was no doubt projecting a "bad patient" out there, while I remained the "good patient," who would stick with my analyst no matter what. The result was that I felt angry with the imagined patient, angry with the institute, and angry with the investigating committee—in short, I felt angry with everyone but my analyst. Again, I am reminded of the child who cannot afford to be angry with a vulnerable but needed parent. On a conscious level, I was determined to view my analyst as innocent until proved guilty, and I found it hard to imagine that he was guilty. In this respect, I was literally "of two minds," caught in a kind of vertical split: I both knew that it was possible that he was guilty of misconduct of some sort, and did not believe it possible at the same time. Whether this vertical split paralleled a similar split in my analyst is, of course, speculation, but not impossible. Such a split has also been described as part of the dynamics in institutional avoidance, where evidence against a training analyst is scotomized, simultaneously seen and not seen at the same time (Gabbard & Peltz, 2001).

Given the negative consequences of knowing about the ethics investigation while it was in progress, I question whether there is any advantage to informing candidate-analysands, before due process has been served and the investigation concluded. In my case, the long waiting period with minimal information and required confidentiality was highly stressful and disruptive analytically and educationally, and did not offer any material advantage to me, as I was unwilling to make a decision about leaving or continuing my training analysis without the findings of the investigation.

## "Knowing and Not Knowing": The Announcement of the Ethical Violations and Expulsion

My analyst announced his resignation from the institute to me just before the investigating committee was to have its decisive meeting, approximately five months after his leave of absence had begun. This put a rapid end to any hope that I had maintained of being able to complete the training analysis with him in the longer term, and my grief process began in earnest. I soon met with my executive liaisons, who read the findings of the committee to me, which consisted of a list of ethical violations, including sexual boundary violations, as defined by the ethical code of the national psychoanalytic body, and the recommendation for expulsion. I was asked to continue to keep my knowledge of the investigation and the findings confidential, as a meeting of the entire institute could not be convened for approximately a month, until after the winter break. My reaction to the announcement was a complex mixture of grief, concern for my analyst, relief at finally knowing something (however shattering it was), and disappointment about how little I still actually knew. I became aware that I had maintained a fantasy that I would eventually be provided with details that would allow me to judge my analyst's guilt or innocence for myself. I must have imagined that these details would be forthcoming from either the institute or from my analyst if I waited long enough. In fact, even years later, I occasionally have this fantasy of "finally knowing for sure," which remains unrequited.

Still bound by confidentiality in the wake of the findings, I thus continued to confide only in my analyst, who I knew must be suffering much more than he ever revealed. In fact, my resolute idealization and relative absence of anger were fostered by his continuing steady analytic stance with me, focus on my experience, and genuine concern for the impact of these events on me, even in the midst of his crumbling professional status. I was amazed that he could continue to work and function, and I was certainly not going to "kick him when he was down," no doubt fearing that he might really crumble if I became angry due to disappointment in him, or jealous of his having "chosen" another special patient. I verbalized my wish that we could sit down and have a frank discussion about what had happened, feeling that it would help me just to know. He stated that, while he shared this wish, he could not talk about the case. Wanting to know went beyond curiosity on my part: I hoped that in hearing the details of the case I could understand, if not condone, his actions if he were guilty, and forgive him for the betrayal. In addition, my analyst's continued apparent high level of functioning nurtured the small hope in me that a terrible mistake had been made, and that, perhaps, he would be vindicated when his case was reviewed by the medical board, which I assumed would take a year or more to work its way through the complaints system. I had in mind that I would have ample time to terminate over the next year or so, and find another training analyst. That there was a considerable degree of denial at work in my thinking seems obvious now, and perhaps reflected a certain amount of denial on my analyst's part, as my views were not challenged.

I now understand my motivations for continuing rather differently than I did at the time. At the forefront was, I believe, the idea that I would fathom for myself whether the findings of the committee were true, and that I could do this only while still seeing my analyst. After the announcement, I frequently sat up in sessions, as I wanted to carefully observe him to see if I could discern "the truth" from his actions or expressions. I noted over time that no disclosure was forthcoming, and that my powers of discernment were apparently as limited as they had been over the past three years, when I had failed to register that anything was wrong. This experience is in keeping with the finding that it is common for a transgressor's other analysands to report acceptable work even while misconduct is occurring with a single patient, and that such misconduct can occur in an "otherwise ethically sound and competent practitioner" (Celenza & Gabbard, 2003, p. 623).

It finally occurred to me at this point that it would be helpful for me to seek a consultation with another analyst to discuss my view of the situation and my wish to continue the analysis. It seemed that I could only think of this idea once I had been almost released from the "veil of secrecy." My analyst agreed with this plan and suggested a senior colleague in the institute who had no involvement in the case, and with whom I had had minimal contact previously. I considered whether to seek a consultant in another institute or part of the country, but the urgency I felt for another opinion, and my respect for the consultant suggested, led me to choose the local option. My initial meetings with the consultant were painful but extremely helpful, in that I was finally assisted in confronting certain blind spots and areas of denial, such as my assumption about the time required for the case to be adjudicated by the medical board and my fantasies of a leisurely termination process. The consultant also pointed out some of the difficulties I would likely face within the institute while I continued with the analysis. This consultation turned out to be very helpful to me when events unfolded far differently than I had expected.

## "In the Eye of the Storm": Individual and Group Dynamics During the Aftermath

I did not attend the institute meeting in which the announcement about the investigation and expulsion of my analyst was made, as I felt unready to withstand the immediate reactions of the group, which I was certain would be intense. I did elect to go to classes, which directly followed the meeting, with some trepidation. What I experienced was an outpouring of support and concern from all of my classmates, who invited me to share my experience and deferred much of their personal reaction until later. They made it clear that they did not want to lose me. The relief of no longer being alone with "the secret" was immense, as was the validation from my classmates of the difficulty of the experience, all being at similar stages in their training analyses. My analytic class became, for me, a "holding environment" that made it possible for me to weather the stormy dynamics that unfolded in the institute, and was the single most important factor in my ability to continue with training. I had the opportunity to fully process the events with my class because of the willingness of two co-teachers to devote as much seminar time as needed to discuss our reactions over the next month or so. One of these teachers shared his own experience of losing a training analyst under traumatic, although different circumstances, and both teachers were open and responsive. Their input represented, for me, a reassuring positive link to the faculty that also influenced my decision to stay.

I have considered several reasons why my class was able to perform this "holding" function for me. First, I was fortunate to be in a group that "gelled" quickly in the first year, and remained cohesive and close throughout our training. Second, this group had the advantage of "newness" to the institute, with a shorter history of relationships to the larger group, and to my analyst. While one member of my class had been in supervision with my analyst for some months before his leave of absence, she elected to change immediately to another supervisor in order to avoid losing credit, and thus had no further knowledge of the proceedings. Third, all class members were currently in analysis and, thus, had an established venue for working through their own reactions, as well as the ensuing institute dynamics, which would not have been the case at the time for most of the faculty.

To shift from Winnicott to Bion, my class was for the most part a "good container," whereas the larger institute became for some time a "leaky container," under the sway of powerful group dynamics in the wake of my analyst's expulsion. I felt somewhat out of step with the reactions of the rest of the institute in that my grief process was well underway, although I could return to shock and disbelief rather easily at times. I also found myself highly disturbed by the outpourings of hostility and vilification towards my analyst, no doubt in part because I had warded off some of the worst feelings in myself, but also because it seemed that concern and compassion for my analyst, as well as recognition of his contributions to the institute, had at least temporarily been lost. What I was witness to was, as I understand it now, a significant regression in group functioning, with a shift from the "work group," in Bion's terms, to a "basic assumption" group, in this case a "fight-flight group," which is characterized by anger and hate (Lopez-Corvo, 2003, p. 352). My analyst had, in the face of the group's severe disappointment, become the ultimate "bad object," and mixed feelings were not always entertained. These reflections are helpful to me in understanding the pressure I felt to keep my analyst as the "good object." Added to my own reasons was now the implicit pressure from the group to occupy the other side of the split.

A related phenomenon during the aftermath was the emergence of what I have termed a "microbial model" of thinking, in which terms such as *contaminated* and *tainted* were frequently used in conversations. For example, I heard former supervisees or consultees of my analyst state, "I'm afraid the supervision/consultation was tainted." I was asked a number of times, "Aren't you afraid that your analysis was/is contaminated?" It seemed to me that the exposure to the breakdown of boundaries via the ethics case had mobilized some rather primitive and concretized fears akin to microbial invasion, another kind of "boundary violation." In the context of a traumatized group, this translated to group contagion fears. From a Kleinian perspective, this phenomenon may represent the splitting of the bad object into small fragments, such as microbes.

Gabbard (personal communication, 2006) uses a similar contagion model to understand such phenomena, and makes the point that this process, characteristic of the paranoid-schizoid mode, is a result of a projective disavowal of personal vulnerability, either as a patient to boundary violations by an analyst, or as an analyst to boundary violations with a patient. Additionally, Gabbard notes that, since the persecuting objects are perceived as originating from external sources, efforts are made to avoid contact with the contaminated source and other contaminated persons, so one's skin is not violated by the "infected material." The question that arose of whether papers written by my analyst should continue to be included in the seminar curriculum reflects, perhaps, an element of this contamination fear. It is also part of what I experienced as a "purge mentality" that characterized initial reactions of the institute, a seeming wish to expel all traces of my analyst's influence from the group. Again, such a stance is characteristic of the paranoid-schizoid mode of functioning, where ambivalence is not tolerated. In this mode, the group is unable to retain and learn from the experience of the offending member, because the disavowal must be maintained.

While I found these observations fascinating intellectually, the impact on me was quite disturbing, as I was, from this viewpoint, the "most contaminated" of all. Added to my own vulnerable state of mind, serving as a container for the projections of others was difficult, to say the least. Understanding of this contagion model has helped me to make sense of some of the rather agitated reactions of the group to my continuing in analysis with my analyst during the aftermath. While the institute was "circling the wagons" and trying to regroup minus a training analyst, not only was I not closing the circle, but I was also an ongoing potential source of "contagion." Some of the strongest opinions expressed to me came from those who had no direct knowledge of my analysis, but assumed that my analysis must have been substandard and that I should now move on to "a real analysis," which I was not doing quickly enough. It is important to note that such reactions do not represent the totality or even the majority of the input I received, as many of the group expressed interest and concern, without judgment of my analysis or decision to continue.

As well as contamination and tainting, the topic of "intergenerational transmission" came up in early discussions following the expulsion of my analyst, as well as intermittently over the ensuing months. The concept of intergenerational transmission is frequently mentioned in the literature on boundary violations (Gabbard & Peltz, 2001), and is based on anecdotal reports that identify a possible higher occurrence of boundary violations in the analysands of training analysts who violate boundaries than in those without such a history. My sensitivity to these discussions had several sources, one being my own concern that I may have "picked up" something from my analyst of which I was not aware, such as blind spots that mirrored those of my analyst, that could predispose me to problems with my own patients. I worried about the books that I had borrowed from my analyst, and the analytic papers he had given me from time to time. Were these part of a potential "slippery slope," or within the realm of less ominous boundary crossings? Another source of my sensitivity, however, was my feeling that the idea of intergenerational transmission was also being recruited into the microbial model described earlier, and used to validate the contagion fears that came out of a rather regressed state of group functioning, perhaps fuelled by the term *transmission*, which has deeply etched connotations of infectious disease. I also suspected on some occasions that the concept was used defensively, to keep the danger "out there" with someone like me, rather than a vulnerability that lies in each of us.

The concerns within the institute about contamination and intergenerational transmission were factors that led me to seriously question whether I would be accepted by my analytic community in the longer term, or whether doubt would be cast on me professionally, leading to subtle or overt exclusion. My fears were amplified by a conversation with a colleague from another institute, who I ran into at a national meeting shortly after the expulsion of my analyst. He volunteered, without knowing about my situation, that his institute was still reeling from the expulsion of a very senior training analyst for sexual boundary violations some years previously, and that some analysts in the community still refused to refer patients to this man's former analysands, despite there being no evidence of problems in their own practices. This information obviously did nothing to quell my fears, and I decided to meet with several training analysts in my institute to ask for their opinions about my future viability in the institute, and to assist me in understanding the group dynamics that I was experiencing. Both of my consultants expressed confidence that I would be accepted on my own merit by the community once the group had restabilized. That I would be undertaking another training analysis would also be seen as a positive factor in terms of my "safety."

Finally, I want to consider the issue of forced termination, which entered the picture for me soon after the expulsion of my analyst from the institute. My assumptions about an extended termination phase while my analyst's case was processed by the medical board were entirely wrong. Due to the history of lengthy waits within the complaints system, political pressure was being applied to speed up the process. After the institute's findings were referred to the board, my analyst's case was adjudicated within a few months, his license was revoked, and he was directed to close his practice approximately five weeks after the board's decision. The last action, as well as smashing any hopes of vindication of my analyst from the medical board, brought to awareness another line of wishful thinking of which I had hardly been aware. I had assumed that the medical board, as a benevolent authority, would take into account the long-term nature of psychoanalytic practice, and not subject patients to such a rapid termination process. In many ways, it felt like another punishment for the innocent bystanders. Fortunately, my first consultant agreed to become my next training analyst, and I had immediate follow-up when I most needed it. I wondered if my analyst's other patients, who were unprepared, had been as fortunate. Dealing analytically with a forced, rapid termination is significant in itself and, combined with the added meanings when the termination involves an analyst expelled for boundary violations, may require a considerable period of further analysis to deal with the unfinished and iatrogenically generated business, as I will discuss later.

## Restabilization

Fortunately, a period of restabilization occurred over the next year, in which I was able to engage in a new training analysis and to reinvest my energies in analytic training. Not surprisingly, my initial response to my next analyst was negative, hostile, and distrustful, as I brought to him the full force of the previously unexpressed negative transference. I spent several months sitting up and felt anxious about any cancelled sessions, expressing fears that this analyst might also be "up for review." At the same time, I was concerned that my new analyst not demonize or denigrate the earlier one, as I also felt concern and affection towards my previous analyst, and a deep sense of loss of that analysis. My new analyst, who proved to be resilient and focused on the challenging analytic task at hand, helped me work with the anger, grief, and betrayal that I was finally able to feel after termination, and after the pressure of projection and splitting in the larger group had diminished. I undertook to write several letters to my former analyst, expressing some of the intense mix of feelings I was experiencing during this period, and even requested a refund of the fees that I had paid for treatment after his expulsion. While my request was denied, I felt relief in asserting my own reasonable boundaries and needs, once the idealization of my former analyst had receded.

The fuller unfolding of a grief process occurred during these next months. My next analyst was crucial in helping me to work through the traumatic, rapid termination that I had endured, a termination that was unique in several respects. While the analytic literature has questioned whether training analyses ever fully terminate, due to ongoing contact with one's training analyst as a colleague, I knew in my case that the termination was final. My expectation that I would run into my former analyst at meetings and conferences for years to come, and that I would have the option of returning for "tune-ups" if needed, also had to be mourned. A once prolific writer of papers and books, the absence of my former analyst's name in print is something that I still mourn.

My analytic class remained a steady and nurturing support that helped me to weather the institute dynamics until a degree of equilibrium was reestablished. I came to feel welcome and accepted by my analytic community, and left with sadness when I later had to move for unrelated reasons. I was able to hold onto the good analytic work that was accomplished before the investigation, and felt grateful for my analyst's help, along with the anger, disappointment, and betrayal that I felt about his unethical behavior. I felt that, with assistance, I had been able to emerge from the circumstances as a healthy (although bruised), well-trained, and contributing member of the analytic community.

## Reflections a Decade Later: Longer-Term Impact and Process of Recovery

With the publication of my paper on my experience of losing a training analyst for ethical violations (Wallace, 2007), I learned that there was great interest in the analytic community about the impact of ethical violations; I received many communications and I was asked to present at several international meetings. I was afforded the opportunity to discuss my experience with colleagues from around the world, some who served on ethics committees, many who had experienced the loss of analysts from their institutes due to ethical violations, as well as some who confided their own experiences of losing training analysts for ethical violations, during or after training. I learned that I was definitely not alone in my experience, and that, while some aspects of my experience were unique, many themes were shared. These conversations resulted in a panel presentation at the International Psychoanalytical Association Congress in Chicago in 2009 by three of us, from three countries, on the collateral damage caused by losing a training analyst for ethical violations (Wallace, 2010), chaired by Glen Gabbard and the first of its kind. Thus, our knowledge about the impact of boundary violations on the larger community is steadily expanding as more conversations and papers appear by those who have been affected.

I will consider here four areas concerned with longer-term effects of losing a training analyst for ethical violations: subsequent recognition of boundary problems, impact on subsequent analyses, effects on formation of analytic identity, and changes in clinical practice. These areas were highlighted in my discussions with other candidates and analysts who suffered similar losses, as well as in the questions posed to me by others who heard or read about my experience. My reflections are informed by a decade of subsequent experiences, including those as an analysand, analyst, psychiatrist, and teacher, which have demonstrated to me that important consequences of collateral damage due to boundary violations may manifest, and come into awareness, only slowly over time.

I have been asked many times whether, in hindsight, I recognize any boundary problems in my work with my former analyst. At the time of my analyst's expulsion, I would have said no. Now, the answer is yes, and my awareness comes out of subsequent analyses in which the boundaries were clearly maintained. I am now aware that my analyst disclosed far more personal and family information than any of my subsequent analysts. I was shocked after these events to hear Glen Gabbard state, in a talk I attended, that many of the boundary-violating analysts he assessed made reference to Ferenczi's concept of "mutual analysis." My analyst had also spoken with me about Ferenczi, in reference to him (the analyst), feeling understood by me!

At the time of my analyst's expulsion and after, I was loath to look at several events in my analysis as boundary crossings. I suspect I was reluctant because I was still under the sway of idealization, and wanted to hold onto feeling special to him, perhaps particularly in the face of not having been "chosen." My analyst asked me on one occasion to review and critique a paper he had written, before presenting it at a meeting. He initiated what seemed like avuncular hugs on several occasions, and made several inappropriate comments. After his expulsion from the institute, but before revocation of his licence, he allowed me to page him after my traumatic Friday analytic classes and encounters at the institute, and I would debrief at length with him on the telephone, sessions that were never referred to during the week. He also agreed to my request for "double sessions" just before he closed his practice, which were my useless—and expensive—attempts to give myself more time. I now think that these extra sessions fostered my ongoing idealization of him, and foreclosed on my anger, which he was also actively avoiding. Of course, I have subsequently questioned if the extra sessions were given out of compassion for me, out of his guilt about having done damage, or out of concern for his dwindling bank account. In the opposite direction, my analyst phobically avoided discussion throughout the analysis of my at times erotic transference, which was heightened by the above boundary crossings and my resulting sense of specialness. Thus, there were not only acts of commission, but some important omissions that seemed related to my analyst's history of boundary violations with another patient.

My rationalization of these behaviors unravelled only slowly over the next years, in the context of my experience of subsequent analysts who did not do any of these things. My resulting feelings of shame and guilt for participating in the aforementioned boundary crossings necessitated a subsequent analyst reminding me that it was my analyst's job, not mine, to preserve the boundaries. While I doubt that the boundary crossings with my analyst would have progressed to serious violations, I remain humbled by the power of transference, and the vulnerability of the analysand under the sway of these powerful forces. Sitting on the other side of the couch now, I remind myself of the serious responsibility I hold to preserve a safe working space for my patients and myself.

A second important area concerns the effect of losing a training analyst for ethical violations on subsequent analyses. I learned from other candidates in similar situations that all of us worried whether other analysts would want to treat us. We felt like damaged goods in the eyes of the analytic community. I was uncertain whether such fears were realistic, or a manifestation of "contagion fears," or perhaps both. My experience would support the latter; others and I indeed left the ruptured analysis feeling "tainted" to some degree, and the task for our next analysts was also realistically quite daunting. Some candidates are so disillusioned that they do not return to analysis, or do so only briefly, or perhaps look for an analyst of the opposite gender to the offender.

I wonder if I was able to continue with other helpful analyses because, despite the aforementioned boundary crossings, I also experienced genuine help and change in the previous analysis, and was thus keen to try again—that is, I lost faith in my analyst, but not in analysis. Notwithstanding, I also believe that these events complicated and lengthened my subsequent analytic treatments. It is important that we continue to be aware that boundary violations do significant collateral damage, and that those affected continue to pay the price, sometimes in costly treatment, for years to come.

I have also considered the impact of these events on the formation of analytic identity. I realized only a decade later that my change in theoretical orientation soon after these events, a change that has endured, was a direct result of unconscious dis-identification with my former analyst. One of the reasons I sought out my analyst originally was that we shared similar theoretical interests. After the end of that analysis, I turned firmly away from that shared theory, and embraced a different perspective. I was impressed by one of the few comments my analyst made to me about his difficulties, subsequent to his expulsion. He said, "I made some serious mistakes. I never appreciated the powerful role of aggression," and indeed my aggression was not analyzed by him. I understood from his comment that he had failed to analyze the aggression of the patient with whom the transgression occurred; others have suggested to me that he may have been also referring to his own aggression. More importantly, however, I think my move away from my analyst's theoretical orientation was not because of a belief that any particular theoretical orientation predisposes to boundary violations, but that it was an attempt to put some concrete distance between us, especially our minds.

Subsequent to this experience, I made conscious efforts to connect with admired analytic figures whom I could use as mentors, supervisors, and role models. Of note, none shares my former analyst's theoretical orientation. I have come to think of one's relationship with theory as a kind of "object relation," as any theory is animated by knowledge and fantasy about historical figures, personal analysts, supervisors, or teachers associated with it. The theory that I had linked with my analyst could no longer serve a holding or containing function for me after the rupture in our work, and I parted ways with it, as I had with my analyst.

My experience has also had important effects on my clinical practice. At the beginning of my analysis, my analyst told me, "I will stick with you no matter what," which I experienced as an expression of his commitment to and belief in me. After my analysis terminated, I read in one of his books that he said this to all his patients. This served not only as a painful disconfirmation of the specialness that had infused the analysis, but as a stimulus for de-idealization and differentiation. It also spoke to me, in retrospect, of a potential for masochistic surrender, a dynamic to which I suspected my analyst had succumbed. I make the same statement to none of my patients. In fact, I say something like this to myself, when starting with a new patient: "I will stick with safe and ethical practice. I will not stick with you if either of us is endangered by the treatment. I will not attempt to rescue you with extraordinary measures, as the risk to me and my other patients is too great." No doubt this is, in part, another kind of dis-identification with my analyst, but, for the most part, I believe that it has served me well clinically. I highly value ongoing supervision and consultation with peers. In an effort to reduce the illusion of treatment occurring in a bubble of secrecy and isolation, I have an item in my treatment agreement that states that I routinely discuss all my cases with peers, who are also bound by confidentiality.

In recent years, I chose to become more involved in education and treatment involving boundary violations. I have assessed professionals who have committed boundary violations for several professional bodies, as well as treating some offenders as part of my practice. Potential countertransference pitfalls notwithstanding, which have included voyeuristic and vengeful wishes on my part at times, I hope and believe that I am using my experience to do some good. I give lectures on boundaries to trainees in various disciplines, and make a point of teaching about erotic and hostile transferences to those I supervise in psychotherapy. In my clinical work, I have moved to a somewhat more formal and less self-disclosing style than before these events, which reflects both a stepping away from what I now consider problematic aspects of my former analyst's style, and a move toward a consolidation of my own analytic identity, which, as in life, has been woven from a full range of "good-enough" analytic experiences to those encompassing suffering and disappointment.

## Conclusion

The effects of boundary violations by training analysts reverberate not only collaterally, but forward in time, via their analysands who go on to psychoanalytic careers. I have outlined the immediate, short-term, and longer-term effects that my training analyst's boundary violations with another patient had on me as a candidate-analysand, and on me as an analyst. My hope is that my experience will contribute to the expansion of our knowledge about the consequences of such events for candidates, for training programs, and for the larger psychoanalytic community. My experience suggests that complex consequences, including effects on subsequent analytic work, practice, and identity formation, manifest only slowly over time.

## Note

1 Portions of this chapter have been previously published in Wallace, E. M. (2007). Losing a training analyst for ethical violations: A candidate's perspective. *International Journal of Psychoanalysis, 88*, 1275–1288; and Wallace, E. M. (2010). Long-term effects of losing a training analyst for ethical violations. *Canadian Journal of Psychoanalysis, 18*, 248–254.

## References

Cabaniss, D. L., & Bosworth, H. (2006). The aim of the training analysis. *Journal of the American Psychoanalytic Association, 54*, 203–230.

Celenza, A., & Gabbard, G. O. (2003). Analysts who commit sexual-boundary violations: A lost cause? *Journal of the American Psychoanalytic Association, 51*, 617–636.

Gabbard, G. O., & Lester, E. P. (1996). *Boundaries and boundary violations in psychoanalysis*. New York: Basic Books.

Gabbard, G. O., & Peltz, M. (2001). Speaking the unspeakable: Institutional reactions to boundary violations by training analysts. *Journal of the American Psychoanalytic Association, 49*, 659–673.

Lopez-Corvo, R. E. (2003). *The dictionary of the work of W. R. Bion*. London: Karnac.

Ross, J. M. (1995). The fate of relatives and colleagues in the aftermath of boundary violations. *Journal of the American Psychoanalytic Association, 43*, 959–961.

Wallace, E. M. (2007). Losing a training analyst for ethical violations: A candidate's perspective. *International Journal of Psychoanalysis, 88*, 1275–1288.

Wallace, E. M. (2010). Collateral damage: Grief and recovery after losing a training analyst due to an ethical violation. *International Journal of Psychoanalysis, 91*, 963–965.

# 8

# COLLATERAL DAMAGE

The Fallout from Analyst Loss Due to Ethical Violations

*Candace Young*

Collateral damage, ground zero, nuclear fallout, psychic shrapnel: these wartime metaphors of attack and damage permeate the personal accounts of candidates who have lost their training analysts due to boundary violations. The metaphors of lingering nuclear winter—contamination, fallout, and radiation—find themselves in the voices of these victims of the collateral damage created when training analysts are lost due to ethical violations, particularly those of a sexual nature. This unique type of analyst loss shares the structure and affects of other types of analyst loss, yet has elements that differentiate it powerfully due to the collapse of idealization of the analyst and the attack on the professional identity of the analysand (Burka, 2008; Wallace, 2007, 2010; Gabbard & Wallace; 2010; Young, 2009).

Psychoanalysts who have written about boundary violations have focused primarily on the individual analysts involved, the direct victims, and the institutional response (Celenza, 2007; Celenza & Gabbard, 2003; Gabbard & Lester, 1995; Margolis, 1997). Relatively little focus has been placed on the indirect victims of these events: the analyst's remaining patients whose trust has also been betrayed, the profession that has been blackened, and the candidates who have been traumatized by the abrupt loss of an analyst as certainly as to a sudden death, yet robbed of the consolation of a benignly idealized analyst to remember and internalize.

Celenza (2007) has drawn attention to the scope of the collateral damage to a transgressing analyst's colleagues and institute, and more particularly to the analyst's other analysands. Wallace (2007) has written of her personal experience of losing a training analyst due to ethical violations, focusing on both the personal loss as well as the particular role of institutional dynamics in compounding the loss. She describes her experience of grief, anger, disappointment, betrayal, professional dis-identification, and disillusionment.

Burka (2008) has described her own experience with the same dilemma, compounded by breaches of her confidentiality by her analyst. She reports that through the process of learning of her analyst's boundary violation, as well as his violation of her confidentiality, she suffered not only grief, but also traumatic de-idealization and dis-identification, as well as feelings of mistrust and shame. She worried how others in her institute would view her if they knew she had been in analysis with a boundary-violating analyst and subsequently undertaken a lawsuit against him.

Wallace and Burka found that, in the wake of these events, they developed deep questions about psychoanalysis as a profession and suffered doubts about continuing to practice as analysts. Anticipating the possibility of another analytic betrayal, both experienced initial mistrust of the analysts from whom they sought treatment after the loss of the boundary-violating analyst. Considering institutional fallout, Wallace (2007) describes what she calls a "microbial model" to capture the sense of contamination involved in such a violation, with a potential for an epidemic spread from person to person.

In this chapter I offer an alternative working model that proposes a more pervasive mode of transmission of the pain and disruption created by these professional dilemmas. This model is one of nuclear fallout, where no one is safe from the contamination that is spread: not patients, not colleagues, not institutes.

We as analysts are particularly vulnerable to the stain of sexual transgressions by other analysts in our institutes. Sexual violations by analysts loom large in the imagination of the public, tending to confirm their deepest unconscious fears about what could happen if an analyst plumbed the depths of *their* souls. The cultural ambivalence about psychoanalysis as a profession that deals with sexuality, secrets, and hidden knowledge, makes us vulnerable to the fears and projections of the public. These events tend to publicly underscore our power over our patients and their great vulnerability when in our care. Fallout and contamination are very real concepts for all of us (transgressors, victims, colleagues, and institutes) when professional ethics are involved.

My discussion will focus on issues of personal and institutional grief and recovery from this singular trauma. A personal narrative will be followed by a consideration of the intrapsychic dilemma faced by analysands who have lost analysts in this fashion. I will propose that following any sudden loss of the analyst, whether to ethical violations or to death, a fractured transference may emerge, laying bare the underlying beating heart of a psychoanalytic relationship. I will explore the unique configuration and dynamics of the fractured transference, as well as the fractured countertransference, which follows a mid-phase rupture of a psychoanalytic relationship. A discussion of termination and trauma follows. Finally, the institutional effects of the collateral damage of boundary violations will be addressed.

## Personal Narrative

In the second year of my psychoanalytic training, and what was the third year of my analysis with a senior training analyst, I was contacted by my institute's director. He told me that my training analyst had been accused of, and had admitted to, an ethical violation. I was told that I would need to find another training analyst, although I would have a grace period in which to terminate my analysis.

The faculty and students of my institute were informed of the situation the following day, so that I had only a brief period in which to process this painful revelation before having to deal with it with my colleagues or my analyst himself. Without being told that such was the case, I immediately was certain that the violation was sexual in nature. My analyst had a warmth that had an underlying flirtatious energy to it that I had previously found enlivening. These qualities in him made this assumption a natural one, and the assumption later proved correct.

Prior to this call, I had felt that my analyst was quite helpful and that the analytic process was vital and productive. I felt that we had had a deep, mutually respectful connection that had sustained me well in my training and allowed me to deal with central personal issues. Our productive work had given me no hint of what was to come. After the news from my director, I was plunged into profound despair.

I returned to my analyst the following day, personally distraught and deeply worried about his state of mind and his ability to continue the analysis with me. I appreciated that he greeted me in the waiting room a few minutes before our scheduled time, and invited me to start the hour then. He thus signaled to me that he was stepping into this issue rather than backing away from it. I appreciated his not shying away from the crisis between us. It was the first of a number of modifications of the analytic frame that occurred as we terminated our work together, many of which I welcomed. The walls of the analytic frame had been blasted wide open by the revelation of his boundary violation, which so centrally announced to me his vulnerability and his frailty, and provided indisputable evidence of his personal/erotic life outside of our work.

My analyst appeared totally present and engaged in this initial hour in which he faced the first blast of my anger and disillusionment. When I directly asked, he acknowledged to me the truth of the accusations, although he said he was not free to talk with me about the details. He implied that if I knew the whole story I might understand or accept his role in it, due to extenuating circumstances that he said he was not free to clarify. I was relieved to not be burdened by his explanation, yet I knew that there was nothing he could tell me which would adequately rationalize a sexual boundary violation.

What was particularly telling to me was his response to my question about whether or not he was surprised that a report had been made to the institute. He responded that he had been very much surprised. His admission of surprise clarified for me the depth of his denial about his own behavior and its potential repercussions. I felt that if an analyst had suffered a lapse in judgment sufficient to allow him to have a sexual relationship with a patient, his own guilt and common sense should foresee the consequences of that behavior moving towards him as surely and unstoppably as a locomotive hurtling down a railroad track. I later learned that such denial of the self-destructive impact of sexual violations is common among analysts who engage in these behaviors (Gabbard & Lester, 1995).

I was given an open-ended timeline from my institute, which proved both helpful and problematic. My analyst had not yet had his license suspended; this would not happen for months, leaving my status with him and my institute in limbo. He told me he believed that he would be exonerated of the charges once the extenuating circumstances were known, and that we might be able to continue together.

I appreciated that we had the time to work together on this profound rupture prior to this untimely termination, to allow me to express my anger and disappointment with my analyst, who, if anything, welcomed it. I learned that the institute had asked him if were willing to voluntarily self-report to the licensing board, and he did so. I later learned that the female patient who had been the direct victim of this ethical violation had never made a report herself. According to our state statutes, an analyst could neither lose his license nor have it suspended without a report from either the patient directly involved or the analyst himself. By self-reporting, he brought on a punishment he would have not otherwise received.

Midway through this process, I sought consultation with an analyst in another community, who was helpful in allowing me to sort through my own distressed emotional states and reactions. I was relieved that this consultant did not vilify my analyst, but instead expressed concern about his scrupulosity and failure to protect himself legally.

Throughout this process, I experienced a kind of emotional whiplash. I vacillated between anger and a desire to see my analyst punished, and a strong loyalty and protectiveness toward him. I felt gratitude for the considerable help he had provided for me prior to these events and still felt a strong bond to him. His state of mind seemed similarly disrupted, with swings between his previous warmth, insight, and sturdiness, and periods of diminished, anxious, and self-protective states of mind.

I was struck by remembering a prescient dream I had had earlier in my analysis. In the dream, my analyst had died. But I was able to meet for five more sessions with him after his death, during which I was able to deal with my grief together with him. Having earlier in my life sustained the sudden death of a loved one, I found this dream unbearably poignant. While my analyst's age may have stirred in me worries of his death, the dream also seemed to be a healing one.

The spectral visit of my analyst in the dream addressed the unbearable longing to see that lost loved one "just one last time." A loved one's death impacts us in ways we cannot anticipate before that death. We cannot know what questions and feelings it will leave us with. There remains an incredible longing for the healing balm of sharing our grief with the one for whom we grieve. And, in many ways, that is just what happened in my analysis. His death to me was a foregone conclusion, and we grieved it together.

Compounding this loss was the fact that friends and family who were unfamiliar with psychoanalysis were unable to comprehend the nature or the profundity of the grief involved. This loss remained largely invisible to my significant others, leaving me feeling further isolated. This element of isolation, I discovered, is present in the accounts of almost every published case involving the premature loss of an analyst, either to death or to ethical violations (Galatzer-Levy, 2004; Rendely, 1999; Traesdal, 2005).

We began a prolonged period of work permeated by a shared grief, as well as my outrage and feelings of betrayal, and his feelings of regret. His receptiveness to my hostility allowed me to be rageful with him in a way that I had never been before, enabling me to deal with new depths of aggression in myself. The depth of my anger was equal to the depth of the trust that had been betrayed. While previously there had been strong idealizing elements in my transference with him, which suppressed my anger, his ethical failure made this idealization impossible to maintain, ushering in a strong negative transference. The unleashing of my previously over-contained aggression was paradoxically an aspect of this ruptured process that I came to see, in part, as therapeutic and growth-promoting.

Despite my analyst's concern about the impact of this event on me, I began to sense his deep, growing preoccupation with his own future and grief for himself at what he had lost, which at times made it difficult for him to listen to my own sense of loss. At one point, I struggled to draw his attention to the depth of my own feeling. I told him: "To you, I'm just collateral damage. But for me, I'm Ground Zero." The power of the psychoanalytic process, of which I felt oblivious when safely embedded in the analytic relationship, was a revelation to me as it came undone. This was not conventional power, but nuclear fission.

There was a deep poignancy to the sense of impending doom to our relationship that was reinforced by my analyst's openness and immediate responsiveness to receiving after-hours phone calls from me. My sense was that he welcomed these calls, which seemed to help ease his own sense of loss, isolation, and guilt. His increasing frailty contributed considerably to my sense of protective loyalty and my reluctance to leave him.

I swung between loyalty and anger, love and hate, protectiveness and outrage. These multiple contradictory feeling states and self-states played havoc with my sense of sanity. There was no as-if space surrounding these feelings to allow the consideration of where fantasy and transference played into these events. The collapse of the emotional play space of analysis was absolute. The deadly seriousness of the analysis at this point was palpable.

Ogden (1997) suggests that in a fruitful psychoanalysis, the analysand, and to some extent the analyst, "loses his mind," his capacity to think and experience himself as a fully separate individual. He contends that the blending of subjectivities that leaves the analysand (and the analyst to a lesser degree) temporarily "out of his mind" creates a deep vulnerability in the patient to loss of the analyst. The patient who suffers a premature termination then suffers a unique type of insanity because he has not yet "retrieved his mind."

Ogden's comments specifically address the experience of those in productive analytic relationships who lose analysts to death. But my experience of losing my analyst to a boundary violation was similarly unmooring and unbalancing of my sanity, which had so recently been anchored in the safety and shared space of an intact analytic relationship.

Although the unraveling of my analyst as he faced professional and financial failure might suggest that the considerable period of my analysis prior to this crisis was troubled as well, my own subsequent analysis of this period suggests otherwise. As both Gabbard (1999) and Celenza (2007) note, analysts who engage in boundary violations with one patient often concurrently have conducted competent and ethically boundaried analyses with their other patients. Celenza (2007) suggests, moreover, that for these analysts accused of boundary violations, the sequelae of having their reputations impugned and their livelihoods threatened may include a posttraumatic stress reaction, potentially leading to a devolution of any continuing work with patients. It was my observation that this happened with my analyst as well. So I not only ultimately lost the real relationship with my analyst through premature termination, but also, before that end, lost the competent and helpful analyst I once had. I indeed had "lost my mind" to this analyst, not once but twice.

This event reawakened and magnified in me previous losses in my life, in a way that I was quite unshielded from, as the very person who might have helped me process the loss was the very one responsible for it. I had the particular sense of losing time in my life dealing with this blow to my heart, my psyche, and my developing identification as a psychoanalyst. Elise (2010) has suggested that an essential element of psychoanalysis is its timelessness and the freedom it gives us to play in a fluid temporality which allows us in a single hour to revisit our very beginnings and to anticipate our future and our ultimate death. She notes that the loss of an analyst can bring psychic time to a careening halt and leave the analysand frozen in time, until such time as the process of mourning can allow the analysand to once again find his ability to return to the past in order to move into the future. This very stuckness in time was striking to me, so that I felt that I had lost a full year of my life in my deep preoccupation with the loss of my analyst.

Despite my analyst's wishful anticipation that he would be exonerated and that we would be spared a goodbye, the situation devolved predictably as he became more troubled by the looming prospect of loss of his career and livelihood, which powerfully overshadowed any concerns he had about me. His previous vigor and good humor were replaced by a vulnerability and anxiety that I could recognize yet not act on by leaving, out of a continuing sense of protectiveness and loyalty toward him. While I had initially felt that I had been given a reprieve from the looming loss, it merely delayed, and in some ways compounded, the inevitable.

His fragility and his own unmoored countertransference became more evident when I talked with him one day about my remaining feelings of love and loyalty towards him. He shared with me, uncharacteristically, his association to the scene in the film *Saving Private Ryan* in which the Allied troops swarm ashore amid chaos, death, and bloodshed. While neither he nor I understood what this association meant, it made something clear to me about his internal turbulence and disarray. It also seemed clear that my love for him was in some ways experienced as disorganizing and potentially damaging.

His association communicated to me that his distress was overpowering his ability to tolerate the intensity of even my positive affect. I ventured my own interpretation that love had derailed his life and that perhaps he was afraid of the power of love at this point, and he agreed. I recognized then that my own shift into an interpretive/therapeutic stance with him was one more signal that it was time to end my analysis. At that point, I set my final termination date with him.

I began the difficult job of looking for a new training analyst in a professional community in which I knew everyone far too well. I ultimately consulted with an analyst who was new to our community. She had the unwelcome experience of being the court of last, and only, resort. I initially met with her occasionally while still meeting with my old analyst as well, straddling the chasm of loss into which I feared falling.

The bridging between the two analysts, although my choice, created an untenable situation for my new analyst. She had to be extremely artful in not devaluing my former analyst while engaging a very reluctant analysand who was once burned, twice shy. Struggling to mourn the loss of an analyst who was still alive, yet lost to me, while trying to establish a relationship with what still felt like his unsatisfactory replacement, was a wearisome task for both me and my new analyst.

My subsequent analysis was characterized by hypersensitivity to cancellations, latenesses, distractibility, and any indications that something might be amiss with my new analyst. The high anxiety and negative expectations on my part had the power and specificity of posttraumatic experience. My heart could start racing when my analyst was two minutes late for a session, or when she started to inform me of a future cancellation. I had a hypervigilance about minor shifts in her behavior and moods, and a narrowness in what I could tolerate from her, which tended, I think, to restrict her freedom of thought and action initially. Any misstep on her part seemed to signal another impending therapeutic rupture.

The literalness and collapse of symbolic meaning that had occurred in my termination with my first analyst thus carried forward into this work. At times, I felt my new analyst was speaking a different language in which I could understand the words she was saying, yet not be able to understand their meaning. I frequently asked her what she meant by something she had said. I was not asking for the deeper meaning but the *apparent* meaning of her words, which eluded me. It was as if my mother tongue were that of my first analyst, and my new analyst was speaking a cognate language, in which I could understand the words but not always discern their meaning.

My new analyst, for example, frequently used metaphors to capture underlying meaning. Ultimately, I came to appreciate this aspect of her communication as both evocative and affect-deepening, but initially it just perplexed me. I just did not "get" what she was saying to me, because this aspect of her style was so different from that of my first analyst. I was struck by how distinctly each analytic couple develops its own language with its own particular verbal rhythms, tonalities, idioms, and idiosyncrasies.

Deutsch (2011) writes of the death of her analyst and describes a similar unsettling experience with a new analyst: "Choking on words that used to be familiar ... the tone, cadence and rhythm of my thought and dialogue felt foreign" (p. 528). Ralph Greenson (1950) also wrote of the mother tongue of childhood and its power as a carrier of affect and early experience. He proposed that ideally one should be analyzed by an analyst who spoke one's childhood language (if different from English), as one's first language is literally the language of the mother. As with mothers and infants, analysands and analysts in their intimate dyads develop their own language that carries the embodied affect of the analysis (Harris, 2011). This linguistic intimacy of my original analysis left the language of my new analyst initially feeling hollow, dry, and emptied out.

My second analysis, nevertheless, ultimately proved very helpful to me. In time, I became well-engaged with this analyst so that I could continue my psychoanalysis. We gradually developed a common language, and eventually we were able to revive the sense of psychological and symbolic space in the room in order to reengage in meaningful analysis. I felt restored to life. But to return to productive analytic work required a huge amount of patience, empathy, and tolerance on my new analyst's part. I came to understand that taking on the role of the replacement analyst is a thankless but lifesaving role, to be undertaken only by someone with considerable emotional resilience and tolerance for anger.

## The Fractured Transference

Psychoanalysis is designed to create deep regressive experiences, to allow conscious suspension of disbelief, and to allow transferences to have full play. One is never clearer about the power of the analytic relationship than when reading the accounts of those who have lost it. The vulnerability of analysands becomes painfully evident, and the responsibility of analysts becomes abundantly clear. This is nuclear energy, with the power to create and drive enormous change, and the power to damage or destroy as well.

Psychoanalysts who have written about loss of the analyst due to death further shed light on the vulnerability of patients to mid-phase analyst loss due to analyst ethical failures. Traesdal (2005) observes that these patients are particularly traumatized because their defenses have become weakened by the analytic work, which has allowed access to deeper analytic material. Rendely (1999) writes that due to the deep and regressive transferences of mid-phase analysis, the loss of the analyst may be experienced much as the loss of the mother for an infant, leading to existential terror in the analysand. Deutsch (2011) reports that she suffered the temporary loss of her own interpersonally constituted analytic voice after the death of her analyst.

The deep distress and the sense of catastrophic loss experienced by those who lose their analysts give us a glimpse into a private world that in many ways disappears from view after planned terminations of analyses, during which patients emerge more gradually from the therapeutic regression. These stories of loss of an analyst, whether by death or ethical violation, reflect a fractured relationship structure, a delicate eggshell cracked or broken open. Metaphors of damaged shells, wombs, and cocoons are evoked in many of these narratives (Rendely, 1999). The deeply dyadic and interdependent nature of the analytic relationship is also revealed clearly in these accounts, which emphasize such elements of the lost analysis as voice, breath, and physical presence.

If we take a close look at these cracked-open relationships, we see the deeply interpenetrating and biologically resonant dyad evoked by Harris (2011), who writes:

> Over the course of a long and highly orchestrated, repeating relationship in analysis, the analytic pair comes into highly synchronized and deeply enmeshed biorhythms and somatic resonances . . . a process in which individuals in some deep ongoing relationships become entangled at levels that range from the metaphoric and soaringly symbolic right down to breath, voice, metabolic process and the body.
>
> (p. 537)

The analyst and analysand have created a world together, a culture of two, to which the rest of the world has little access. The enduring transference-countertransference patterns that have developed over many hours, many months, many years, have their own structure, voice, and deep familiarity. It is this predictable, deeply familiar structure, this protective shell, that is broken open and shattered in the fractured transference.

Sudden terminations of analyses leave patients without the benefit of the gradual process of separation and individuation from this intense bodily and interconnected structure. When the analyst is lost, the shattered shell spills its contents: the dissolved defenses, the primitive love and hate, the deep and infantile dependency, the infantile objects, the unmodulated affect, and the regressed cognitive functioning—all those elements that carry the power of a deep analysis.

## Termination and Trauma

To understand the impact of traumatic ruptures in analysis, whether due to analyst ethical violations or analyst death, one must consider why these endings are so traumatic, while planned terminations are not. What transpires between the prolonged mid-phase of analysis and the ultimate planned ending that makes the loss of this profound relationship become tolerable? Grand (2009), in discussing termination, notes the paradox that we enter into an analytic relationship *knowing* that we are developing closeness only to lose it at termination. She notes, "In constructing psychoanalysis, we have conceived an intimate pursuit with ruptured bonding at its core" (p. 728).

If one accepts that ruptured bonding is a part of every analysis, one must consider what makes a sudden termination so much more devastating. What makes a mid-phase loss of an analyst uniquely painful among the many losses that one suffers in life? Davies (2009) offers us a framework for considering this question. She suggests that in analysis, through our ordinary analytic love, we as analysts create the illusion of timelessness in a potentially healing space that exists somewhere between fantasy and reality. She suggests that through our reliable presence and care, as well as our sustained attempt to listen empathically, we have waged war on the "anti-libidinal forces" of the internalized bad objects of our patients, which otherwise might lure them into detachment and despair. She states:

> I would like to suggest that the delicacy of termination, the sense that so much could go so right or so wrong depending upon the tact and sensitivity of this mutual separation process, proceeds from the very difficult task of transcending this illusion, transforming it into something healthy, fertile, vital and alive, a slow and partial undoing that hopefully proceeds without incurring a catastrophic descent into

a hellish world once again ruled and defined by our spurned and vengeful bad objects.

(p. 737)

She suggests that the mutual decision to terminate an analysis tends to occur when patient and analyst feel confident that the patient can carry on the task of fending off the return of those bad objects and their "always ready passion for subverting engagement, attachment, love and eros" (p. 738).

Davies thus provides us with a scaffolding for understanding the fractured transferences of those who lose their analysts without the benefit of a termination process. Without the sustaining illusion of bounty and goodness provided by the analyst's ordinary care and attentiveness in the mid-phase of analysis, the analysand easily becomes prey to those internalized bad objects that attack hope and create despair.

The acute pain suffered by the analysands who have lost an analyst has two aspects. First, they experience the pain of loss of a treasured and singular intimate relationship. Second, they experience the painful return of those unleashed bad objects that are no longer bound by the analytic relationship and that attack the self, other potential therapeutic relationships, and psychoanalysis itself. It is no wonder, then, that potential second analysts are wary of taking on these patients whose capacity for idealization and desire for attachment have temporarily abandoned them.

This collapse of the internalized good objects is all the more powerful in the case of analyst loss due to boundary violations. The element of the analyst's betrayal of professional standards and the emotional betrayal with another patient further incites the analysand's troubling inner objects that have not yet been integrated sufficiently. While a dying analyst has not chosen his lot, a boundary-violating analyst most certainly has done so.

An effective analysis generally allows a gradual de-idealization of the analyst as negative transferences are more deeply explored and worked through. However, a mid-phase termination due to a boundary violation aborts this process by abruptly and painfully deflating the idealization. If a patient's idealization has served the function of suppressing negative transferences, as in my case, an ethical violation may uncloak these unexplored feelings, leaving the patient feeling swamped with negative affect. While the death of an analyst may leave a patient with his positive vision of his analyst intact, the loss of an analyst due to an ethics complaint shatters any illusions a patient might have.

For candidate analysands, this internal dilemma is further compounded by their professional identification with their analyst, and the potential collapse of this identification. Burka (2008) and Wallace (2007) both have described how this professional dis-identification constitutes another loss to the analysand.

## The Fractured Countertransference

A final consideration concerns the fractured countertransference, which one may speculate mirrors the transferential configuration. I have described my once sturdy analyst who began fraying at the emotional seams, overstepping the analytic frame, revealing personal concerns, and reacting out of guilt and grief. The literature on dying analysts as well as boundary-violating analysts is rife with similar stories (Barbanel, 1989; Galatzer-Levy, 2004; Simon, 1989; Tauber, 1989). They describe individuals who were once competent and admirable analysts, but who, in the face of illness, acted in a manner that was quite dramatically at odds with their previous practice. In the face of the dissolution of the intense dyadic intimacy of analysis, many of these analysts are reported to have behaved inappropriately, stepped over boundaries, violated the analytic frame, and confided their concerns to patients. Many dying analysts patently denied the reality of their illnesses, thus failing to prepare their analysands for the looming loss.

These accounts suggest that derailed analyses contribute not only to fractured transferences, but also to fractured countertransferences that are internally disorganizing to the analyst as well as the patient. It is as if the sense of impending loss sets loose in the analyst what Davies has described as the "anti-libidinal bad objects." When my analyst evoked the image of storming the beachheads at Normandy, I heard in his association the power of his internalized bad objects that were threatening to overwhelm him and me, as well as the internal force of the army of Allies trying to reclaim and save the territory that had been lost. His image powerfully conveyed to me that we were in deeper water than was safe for me to be with an analyst from whom I would soon be parting.

In the end, we all, analysts and analysands alike, hope that if we must say goodbye, we will have the compensations of the fictional termination portrayed by Amy Bloom in her short story "Psychoanalysis Changed My Life" (1993). In this story, an elderly analyst abruptly asks her patient to sit up and acknowledges to her that she will undoubtedly not live to the end of her analysis. The analyst hastens to share with her young patient what she knows about her, over a few weeks confronting her about her inhibitions in love and reminding her that life is short. When the analyst later collapses in the office, she coaxes her patient to drive her home, where the young woman meets the analyst's husband and her son. It becomes clear that the son will be the new love of her life, facilitated by the analyst's interpretations, so that the analyst can die, knowing that her son and her analysand will be happy together.

The story seems to embody the fantasy of both analyst and analysand facing a sudden termination. This is what we who lose our analysts long for: to make our analysts real and substantive so that we can hold onto them, to condense our work so that we might complete our analytic transformation, to be compensated for our loss with a new love, and to find in ourselves the capacity to love again. Bloom's wishful story is so entrancing because it embodies our impossible longings when we lose an analyst or a patient or, for that matter, anyone we love.

## Institutional Fallout

The final focus of this chapter is on the institutional fallout from the loss of a training analyst, the widest circle of the blast of damage.

Prior to this sequence of events, our institute was a young one, and I was in one of the first few training classes. Our group had the buoyancy and enthusiasm of an idealistic new venture among like-minded people. Our candidate class was a strong one, and our classes were characterized by intense, free-thinking, and creative dialogue. The classes and faculty were uniformly excellent, and there was a palpable institutional *esprit de corps*, accompanied by a benign and seemingly healthful sense of inflated group narcissism. The community's good spirits matched my own prior to this disruption. My training was exhilarating.

The structure of our institutional group was a particular one. The training analyst involved was a senior analyst and more experienced than many of the other training analysts, who for the most part were fairly young in their psychoanalytic development. He had served as analyst, supervisor, and mentor to a number of faculty, as well as students. Because of the size of the institute, our young faculty members found themselves pressed into service doing enormous amounts of administrative and committee work when they were still in the process of coming into their own psychoanalytic identities. This situation was often burdensome to the younger faculty members, who nevertheless were sustained by the enthusiasm of the venture, as well as the support and encouragement of their mentors and leaders.

When a report was first made to the institute about a potential boundary violation, a number of young faculty members found themselves in the very painful position of having to investigate the situation and potentially discipline a beloved colleague. They struggled with their grief and worry about this man. The experience of role reversal, in which their mentor became the unboundaried child and they became the limit-setting authorities, strained this younger generation of faculty enormously. Beyond the emotional impact on them, they also found that they needed to take on more work to compensate for the loss of their colleague from the faculty.

A community-wide sense of deflation and loss ensued, with a sense of guilt that no one had recognized what trouble their mentor had been in. In most cases, grief predominated over anger. Although the faculty was able to reconsolidate and continue the training of our class to its conclusion at a very high level, their exhaustion was evident as our class graduated. Despite a strong potential candidate pool and a well-developed program and curriculum with a successful track record, there was little energy or enthusiasm for taking on another training class. The faculty tended to explain their lack of initiative as fatigue from the hard work of training the previous classes and a desire to rest and pursue other interests.

While indeed they were tired, the discussion surrounding these issues was characterized increasingly by a sense of disheartenment and cynicism. Yet the dialogue remained focused on the burdens of the work. There was rarely any mention of the defrocked analyst who was previously their beloved mentor. Little overt connection was made between their disillusionment, fatigue, and emotional deflation, and the failure of the analyst involved.

The situation mirrored the dilemma faced by the character Biff in Arthur Miller's play *Death of a Salesman* (1949). Biff suffers a traumatic disillusionment with his father when, as a young man, he is exposed to his father's sexual transgressions. He subsequently finds his own ambition, previously sustained by his idealization of his father, inexplicably collapsed. The lack of psychic linkage of these events leaves Biff unable to take hold or recover his earlier ambition.

The inability in our institute to more clearly connect these threads of disillusionment and failed ambition was striking because the collapse of morale was so absolute. A colleague later commented on the confusion about what had transpired with my analyst and the multiple conflicting stories surrounding these events. She suggested that even at the institutional level, there was a "fractured mind" that could not cognitively hold onto the shifting stories and fragments of information about the beloved colleague who had created so much havoc (Steif, personal communication, June 10, 2012).

A subsequent more minor boundary violation by a younger faculty member reawakened the initial group trauma, highlighting how unmetabolized and unformulated the trauma remained, leading to this return of the repressed. The initial ethical violation by their older mentor was painfully reawakened. This second individual drew some of the anger and disparagement that had never fully been directed at the original offending party. This last turn of events seems to have administered the *coup de grâce* to our institute, which subsequently closed its doors. My analyst's sexual boundary violation, I believe, had set in motion a cascade of events ultimately leading to the collapse of our institute.

## Conclusion

The radioactivity of such events in psychoanalytic institutes has a very long half-life that extends well beyond the original ethical failure of one analyst. The transgressing analyst harms not only the patient with whom he commits a boundary violation. His ethical failure generates expanding circles of damage, as surely as a nuclear blast. While the initial patient is Ground Zero in the destruction, the shock wave rolls over the analyst's other patients powerfully as well, particularly candidate analysands. The fallout descends further on the analyst's family, colleagues, friends, and institute, ultimately irradiating the larger psychoanalytic community.

Traumatic de-idealization is one of the distinctive features of the collateral damage to candidates whose analysts commit boundary violations. The collapse of the image of the analyst is absolute, and is accompanied by the analyst's public fall from grace and into censure and deep stigmatization. This is a crushing load for a candidate to bear, as candidates are so often identified with their training analysts in institutes. The shame and humiliation of the analyst may radiate to his candidate analysands, who may feel contaminated by association and by the very love they hold for their analysts.

For colleagues, the fallout is potent as well. Nicholsen (2010) has described how the toxic effects of learning of an admired colleague's boundary violation may lead to disillusionment, cynicism, and a hatred of psychoanalysis even in those not directly affected by these events. Celenza (2007) also has noted the deep feeling of betrayal that colleagues and friends experience on learning of the transgression, as if the transgressor violated the boundaries of the friendship itself. Gabbard concludes: "A boundary transgression by a training analyst poisons the well for all of us. In its wake, analysts and candidates alike become steeped in doubt about their chosen profession" (Gabbard & Peltz, 2001, p. 660).

Psychoanalytic institutes are fragile institutions. They survive in a cultural environment that is increasingly hostile to the deep exploration and recovery of the human spirit. As Reeder (2004) describes in *Hate and Love in Psychoanalytical Institutions*, group ties and mutual identifications help sustain us in our difficult and lonely work and become increasingly important to the pursuit of that work. The traumatic loss and de-idealization of a valued training analyst can damage the very fabric of psychoanalytic communities and set off unanticipated posttraumatic sequelae, leading to damage or destruction of these sustaining ties. Patients, colleagues, and the larger psychoanalytic community suffer from a sense of contagion of the unethical analyst's "badness" so that we all are blackened with the same brush, in what Ross (1995) has called a "collective trauma" (p. 961).

In recounting my personal experience of losing a training analyst due to a boundary violation, I have attempted to clarify the cost of such events, as well as a path towards recovery. The possibility of loss that is embedded in all intimate relationships is particularly poignant in analysis. This vulnerability is at the core of every deep analysis and needs to be safeguarded by us as psychoanalysts with the utmost care. Just as nuclear power has the potential for both creation and destruction, so does the considerable power of the psychoanalytic relationship. Respect for that power calls on us to be vigilant with ourselves and with our colleagues about the circumstances, both personal and institutional, which allow each of us to practice in the most ethical and humane manner with our patients.

## References

Barbanel, L. (1989). The death of the psychoanalyst (panel presentation): Introduction. *Contemporary Psychoanalysis, 25*, 412–418.
Bloom, A. (1993). Psychoanalysis changed my life. In A. Bloom, *Come to me: Stories* (pp. 163–190). New York: HarperCollins.
Burka, J. (2008). Psychic fallout from breach of confidentiality. *Contemporary Psychoanalysis, 44*, 177–198.
Celenza, A. (2007). *Sexual boundary violations: Therapeutic, supervisory, and academic contexts.* Lanham, MD: Jason Aronson, Inc.
Celenza, A., & Gabbard, G. O. (2003). Analysts who commit sexual boundary violations: A lost cause? *Journal of the American Psychoanalytic Association, 51*, 617–636.
Davies, J. M. (2009). Love never ends well: Termination as the fate of an illusion. Commentary on papers by Jill Salberg and Sue Grand. *Psychoanalytic Dialogues, 19*, 734–743.
Deutsch, R. (2011). A voice lost, a voice found: After the death of the analyst. *Psychoanalytic Inquiry, 31*, 526–535.
Elise, D. (2011). Time to say goodbye: On time, trauma and termination. *Psychoanalytic Inquiry, 31*, 591–600.
Gabbard, G. O. (1999). Boundary violations and the psychoanalytic training system. *Journal of Applied Psychoanalytic Studies, 1*(3), 207–221.
Gabbard, G. O., & Lester, E. (1995). *Boundaries and boundary violations in psychoanalysis.* New York: Basic Books.
Gabbard, G. O., & Peltz, M. (2001). Speaking the unspeakable: Institutional reactions to boundary violations by training analysts. *Journal of the American Psychoanalytic Association, 49*, 659–673.
Gabbard, G.O. & Wallace, E. (2010). Collateral damage: Grief and recovery after losing a training analyst due to an ethical violation. *International Journal of Psychoanalysis, 91*, 963–965.
Galatzer-Levy, R. M. (2004). The death of the analyst: Patients whose previous analyst died while they were in treatment. *Journal of the American Psychoanalytic Association, 52*, 999–1024.
Grand, S. (2009). Termination as necessary madness. *Psychoanalytic Dialogues, 19*, 723–733.
Greenson, R. R. (1950). The mother tongue and the mother. *International Journal of Psychoanalysis, 31*, 18–23.
Harris, A. (2011). Discussion of Robin Deutsch's "A voice lost, a voice found": After the death of the analyst. *Psychoanalytic Inquiry, 31*, 536–542.
Margolis, M. (1997). Analyst-patient sexual involvement: Clinical experiences and institutional responses. *Psychoanalytic Inquiry, 17*, 349–370.
Miller, A. (1949). *Death of a salesman.* New York: Basic Books.

Nicholsen, S. W. (2010). Too close to home: Countertransference dynamics in the wake of a colleague's sexual boundary violation. *Canadian Journal of Psychoanalysis, 18*, 225–247.

Ogden, T. (1997). *Reverie and interpretation: Sensing something human.* Lanham, MD: Jason Aronson, Inc.

Reeder, J. (2004). *Hate and love in psychoanalytical institutions.* New York: Other Press.

Rendely, J. (1999). The death of an analyst: The loss of a real relationship. *Contemporary Psychoanalysis, 35*, 131–152.

Ross, J. (1995). The fate of relatives and colleagues in the aftermath of boundary violations. *Journal of the American Psychoanalytic Association, 43*, 959–961.

Simon, N. P. (1989). The second analysis after the first analyst's death. *Contemporary Psychoanalysis, 25*, 438–447.

Tauber, G. (1989). Re-analysis after the death of the analyst: The problem of countertransference in re-analysis. *Modern Psychoanalysis, 14*, 171–182.

Traesdal, T. (2005). When the analyst dies: Dealing with the aftermath. *Journal of the American Psychoanalytic Association, 53*, 1235–1255.

Wallace, E. (2007). Losing a training analyst for ethical violations: A candidate's perspective. *International Journal of Psychoanalysis, 88*, 1275–1288.

Wallace, E. (2010). Collateral damage: Long-term effects of losing a training analyst for ethical violations. *Canadian Journal of Psychoanalysis, 18*, 248–254.

Young, C. (2009). Collateral damage: Personal and institutional fallout when a training analyst commits a boundary violation. Paper presented at panel at the 46th Congress of the International Psychoanalytical Association, Chicago.

# 9

# A CHORUS OF DIFFERENCE

Evolving from Moral Outrage to
Complexity and Pluralism

*Jane Burka*

## Introduction

I am going to tell a disturbing story about ethical violations committed by my analyst, "Dr. M.": sexual misconduct with another patient, "Ann," and breach of my confidentiality by talking to Ann about me. Learning of his betrayal led me to end my very helpful long-term analysis abruptly. I filed a lawsuit that ultimately led to a civil trial before a jury that found him liable. I not only wanted him held accountable for being unprofessional and unethical, I was filled with a righteous moral outrage that propelled me through the ordeal.

I have been changed by this experience: both scarred by the trauma and healed by my actions. The emotional scars, such as loss of faith that someone I trust is trustworthy and loss of confidence in my treasured intuition, have faded but not disappeared. However, I also discovered a gritty determination to take personal and professional risks that challenged my Southern ladylike upbringing and strengthened my confidence. The benefits of my perseverance in spite of certain exposure and uncertain outcome have remained a pillar of my foundation.

Of the many aftereffects of the betrayal, lawsuit, and trial, this chapter will focus on the evolution of my moral attitudes. As a victim who challenged my betrayer, I needed the armor of a blunt morality: he is wrong, I am right. Yet that armor, stiff and unyielding, interfered with my thinking flexibly and with more empathy for other perspectives.

In this chapter, I will trace chronologically the evolution of my moral attitudes from a powerful but restrictive subjectivity to broader, more nuanced and complex perspectives on ethical violations.

These moral transformations occurred unexpectedly through several evocative experiences: I wrote a paper about the betrayal by my analyst using my dreams to trace the psychological impact of traumatic de-idealization and dis-identification (Burka, 2008); I confronted my own temptation to cross a professional boundary; as a member of the board of my analytic institute, I had to contend with two formal complaints against two analyst members; and, later, I was part of a committee that interviewed members of the institute about their experiences during the two ethics investigations. Through these engagements, I developed new perspectives on my convictions about how perpetrators should be viewed and treated, and I developed a greater appreciation for moral attitudes that differed from my own. I will introduce the concepts of moral complexity and moral pluralism as ways of thinking that might help individuals and organizations grapple with the traumas of ethical violations.

## Breach of Confidentiality

In 2001, two years after I graduated from my analytic institute, my analyst, Dr. M., told me that he had to take a "forced sabbatical" from his duties at his institute, one different from my own. I asked why, and he said softly, "You'll never know." But I *needed* to know. I asked some of my colleagues if they had heard anything about his "sabbatical," and within days someone told me that my analyst had had an ongoing sexual relationship with a patient. Disbelieving, I confronted him with what I had heard, and he confirmed it by replying, "I guess it's a small town." I was shocked and horrified that he had been sexually involved with a patient, an outrageous offense, and I was dismayed that he held the illusion it could remain a secret.

My idealization of Dr. M. was demolished abruptly. I lost confidence in him, in myself as an analyst, and in the field of psychoanalysis. Since he took the stance that he was being unfairly treated by his institute and his professional organization, and that his "mistake" had nothing to do with his work with me, I recognized that he was no longer functioning as an analyst with me, and I quickly ended my analysis. I grieved the loss of my respect for him and the loss of my reliable, intimate, long-term relationship with him. I felt compelled to learn more about what had happened, to learn who he really was.

Researching online, I saw that a complaint had been filed against his license, and I ordered a copy. I had heard speculation about the patient's identity, and when I saw Ann's initials on the complaint, the speculation was confirmed. The 21-page complaint alleged, among other accusations, that Dr. M. had talked to Ann about many of his patients, breaking their confidentiality. I was very upset by the multiple accusations, but I did not know whether to believe them. If true, I needed to know if Dr. M. had talked to Ann about me, and I arranged a meeting with Ann. She brought a list of 13 statements she remembered he had said about me, specifically using my name. Any doubt I had had about the veracity of the complaint vanished, as everything she remembered was either something accurate about me or words I had actually spoken in my analysis.

My disillusionment after learning of Dr. M.'s unethical sexual misconduct and my grieving the analysis gave way to intense moral outrage: this was personal; this was a transgression against me directly. I filed a complaint against his license and considered also filing a lawsuit. I was ambivalent about initiating legal action, not only because of the trauma and exposure I knew it would entail, but also because I was reluctant to expose the dirty laundry of psychoanalysis. I feared being criticized and ostracized by my analytic community. Facing both psychological conflict and a stressful moral dilemma, I consulted with the chairperson of the ethics committee at my institute. He encouraged me to make my decision based on evaluating the consequences for myself and not to feel responsible for the reputation of psychoanalysis. The consultation was reassuring but still left me in a difficult dilemma.

As I struggled with my decision to file a lawsuit, I experienced a conflict of two moral positions. On one hand, I approached the decision with an "ethical attitude," a necessary internal position "that involves depending on oneself to carefully and thoughtfully embrace a stance that may not be approved by others" (Allphin, 2005, p. 458). At the same time, I was filled with a contemptuous moral perspective based on strong conviction: I know right from wrong, and he does not, and I am going to hold him responsible. I had been devastated, and I wanted revenge. I was not willing to excuse him based on whatever complex emotional dynamics or difficult life circumstances had led him to behave unethically. I could not let myself be sympathetic with the suffering his misconduct must have caused his family and close associates. With this narrow focus, I used the fuel of my moral outrage to drive my determination to file the lawsuit in 2002.

My moral indignation helped me persevere through three years of traumatic experiences. I was interviewed for six hours by the psychiatrist who would testify as my expert witness. I attended depositions at which I heard Dr. M. claim that he had indeed talked about me with Ann, but the conversations were for the purpose of "informal consultation with a colleague" (since Ann was also a therapist), and he maintained that he had not used my name. An attempt at mediation failed, because Dr. M. refused to discuss a settlement. Ultimately, the case was heard in 2005 in a two-week trial before a jury. Ann's testimony contradicted Dr. M.'s testimony, and I believed her. I testified for several hours, but I could not remember most of what I said. Although the evidence seemed convincing, it was difficult to predict what the jury would decide. This was not a jury of my peers. Some had been in therapy, but the idea of a four-times-a-week analysis was quite foreign and almost astonishing to them. During the trial, some jurors paid attention and some were barely awake.

The jury determined that Dr. M. was guilty of "professional negligence" and "breach of fiduciary duty." They granted me a financial award that did not cover the cost of my long-term analysis. They declined to pay for future analysis, because, as one juror told the lawyers in a post-trial debriefing, "These people are in therapy all the time anyway."

Although having sex with a patient and breaching my confidentiality clearly went against professional standards, I also thought Dr. M. was morally corrupt. From a current perspective on moral development, I engaged in "initial simplistic, concrete, black/white reflexive intuitive thinking . . . i.e., what is perceived is assumed to be a single, true reality" (Narvaez, 2010, p. 20). I rejected opinions that did not coincide with mine. It was obvious to me that having a sexual relationship with a patient was not only unethical, it was damaging to that patient and to other patients, even though I knew that some analysts married their patients and some of their careers and marriages survived. I was convinced that Dr. M. could not be working effectively with his other patients, and I wished I could protect patients who did not know he had been sexually involved with a patient and was under ethical investigation. Yet Celenza and Gabbard (2003), experts in the field of boundary violations, comment: "It is common for a transgressor's other analysands to report acceptable analytic work being done concurrently with his ongoing sexual relationship with that one patient. In other words, the misconduct, though an extreme ethical violation, can occur in an otherwise ethically sound and competent practitioner" (Celenza & Gabbard, 2003, p. 623). I could not accept this: I believed that breach of confidentiality not only broke professional rules, it reflected a perverse relationship with the patients who were betrayed as well as with the patient who heard the betrayal.

Feeling moral outrage carried the weight of self-righteousness that made me ashamed and uncomfortable, but it served a purpose. It helped me survive the loss of my analyst, the end of my analysis, and the risky and humiliating process of the lawsuit and trial. Dr. M. had acted unethically and did not take responsibility for the harm he caused, and I had to separate myself—both internally and publicly—from his actions and from his view of reality.

Moral outrage has other value. In the literature on women who are trying to extricate from abusive relationships, there is recognition of the contribution of anger and contempt. Contempt of someone else's wrongdoing reveals and illuminates our own moral code, which may then allow us to take action on our own behalf, like my filing a lawsuit. "Contempt gives a person the right to set up a code of conduct and judge whether someone has violated it; this capacitates agency in the subordinated person" (Stein, 2011, p. 83). Sometimes extreme or rigid moral opinions are necessary and function to reveal the moral positions that we hold.

## Writing to Metabolize Trauma

Two years after the trial, I decided to write about my experience. Part of my motivation was to continue to process the trauma, as writing helps move the writer from chaotic emotional experience to symbolic, conceptual consciousness. Writing captures what we do not know we know until we write. Writing about trauma is especially valuable, because a traumatic situation is one in which "'good supplies' are withdrawn, 'bad' things are done, and everyone pretends that nothing unusual is going on" (Akhtar, 2011, p. 185). I lost my analysis and my good object analyst; he sexually exploited a patient and talked to her about my analysis; and my analyst contended he had not used my name and characterized me as overreacting. At my institute, aside from my closest confidants, no one spoke to me about my ordeal, even if they had heard about it. There was no official acknowledgment toward me from his institute or mine. I did not want to carry on as if nothing unusual had happened. I desired publication, "the private fact made public" (Bion, 1992, p. 197), so that a thought can be translated into action. I wanted to act on the psychoanalytic community, which has focused primarily on the violators among our ranks, not on the damage experienced by the victim. I hoped to create something positive out of the destruction.

As I was planning my paper, I talked with my writing group about presenting the chronology of events. One member asked, "What will make it psychoanalytic?" I responded, "He's bad; I'm good. What's psychoanalytic?" When we are dealing with traumatic experience, our capacity for symbolic thinking can be impaired (Brown, 2005; Schore, 2003), and we need help working our way back to symbolic, complex, representational thinking. My colleague's question was the first step in moving me away from my concretized victim stance to consider other perspectives. At this point, while I could not venture beyond my experience, I could engage my observing ego to reflect on my experience, and I decided that nothing was more psychoanalytic than exploring one's dreams. I read the record of my dreams that I had kept during the demise of my analysis and the waking nightmare of the lawsuit. I analyzed the themes and read the literature on the issues that emerged from my dream life: collision of love and hate, traumatic de-idealization, dis-identification, identity confusion, psychic permeability, and death anxiety (Burka, 2008).

Studying and associating to my dreams opened "collaboration with the unconscious other" (Rather, 2001). This dreamwork enabled me to activate the psychoanalytic function of my personality (Bion, 1962a, p. 89), to re-engage curiosity and self-reflection, to think more flexibly and complexly, and to conceptualize the experiences I had been living. Writing about my dreams organized and gave deeper meaning to my experiences, moving me from feeling overtaken by trauma to developing psychic growth.

As the exploration of dreams is a natural challenge to a self-righteous view of oneself, I was able to recognize more of my feelings, not just my righteously held feelings of violation and betrayal, but aggressive feelings of vengeance and retaliation. In addition, I saw in my dreams a concern for the welfare of my analyst that I had consciously tried to suppress, as my empathy presented a challenge to my determination to pursue the lawsuit. The movement from relying on my conscious emotions to engaging my internal analyst made my moral stance much more complicated: I both hated and loved him; he was both wrong and damaged; I felt both contempt and gratitude. Accepting the emotional ambivalence represented in my dreams signaled a shift from moral certainties to a greater tolerance of ambiguities and helped me reclaim a sense of others' humanity and my own. Unconsciously, I was working my way back to my pre-trauma capacity for both/and. I was relieved to feel less heavily armored but sad that I had publicly exposed someone I used to love.

## Temptation

Unexpectedly, I developed visceral empathy for the desire to violate boundaries. A few months after the lawsuit was resolved in 2005, I was approved as a personal and supervising analyst at my institute. Almost immediately, I was asked by a candidate to supervise her training case. I had taught the candidate, and I respected and enjoyed her. I had been eager to supervise an analytic case, so I was ready to agree and begin. However, I was aware of a relational conflict: I had a close relationship with someone to whom the candidate was also close. I knew about this overlap, but the candidate did not.

I recognized that supervising the candidate would compromise the effectiveness and closeness of both relationships, but I felt compelled to join the ranks of my colleagues who were supervising training cases. I rationalized multiple convoluted ways of making it work: I imagined complex scenarios that involved keeping certain secrets from each party, and I minimized the potential interferences these deceptions would create for the candidate's learning. Gradually I realized that this was the exact process that a professional goes through when contemplating crossing an ethical boundary of a more egregious nature.

While my dilemma did not involve breaking a code of professional ethics, it was an ethical dilemma, and my moral high ground was eroded by my desire: "I want this, so I can make it work." Pressured by the wish to have what I wanted, I regressed in this dilemma to a more primitive stage of moral reasoning, typical of young children. The classic theory of moral development by Kohlberg (1969) is a linear stage model, unfolding in a predictable pattern of moral reasoning that becomes more sophisticated as children mature and interact with others. In Kohlberg's developmental scheme, the second stage is the stage of self-interest: "If it's good for me, it must be okay." In this frame of mind, correct behavior is evaluated by consequences that serve the interests of the individual. I recognized in myself the temptation for analysts, including Dr. M., to rationalize bad behavior, disregard misgivings, and suppress guilt in the interest of getting what they want. Gabbard (2002) writes that boundary-breaking analysts "are characterized by a vertical split that keeps their unethical behavior from being integrated with a conscience that is ordinarily functional" and adds a warning: "the capacity for self-deception in all of us is extraordinary" (p. 383). I did not believe I was capable of similar self-deception until I lived it.

While Kohlberg's theory is one of linear stages, from a postmodern perspective, moral development is not linear but fluid and bidirectional, a mixture of moral perspectives that can vary depending on the context. In the context of my strong desire to become a training analyst, I regressed to a primitive self-interested morality that does not see beyond the self. I was also situated in a morally compromised social context: perhaps I was unconsciously influenced by the disorganizing experience of Dr. M.'s violations of the rules of psychoanalysis, sliding backward into a primitive moral orientation as I lost faith in the social order of the analytic community (Bronfenbrenner, 1979). However, I simultaneously held higher principles of morality that respected ethical behavior and had concern for the consequences for others. I struggled to achieve a decision about supervision that was not based on self-interest but on the higher principle of avoiding potentially messy and hurtful relationships. I concluded that I could not supervise this candidate, and I told her there was a relational conflict she was unaware of. I was humbled and chastened by the powerful forces of denial and rationalization that pushed me close to crossing a professional line I would typically hold.

## Learning Through Leadership

A few years after my lawsuit was adjudicated, I was on the board of my institute. During my board tenure, the institute's ethics committee investigated two separate formal ethics complaints against two analyst members. These ethics investigations had profound and disturbing effects on the whole institute community. For me it was retraumatizing: Not here, not again. I was thrown back into a state of moral outrage almost equivalent to what I had felt toward Dr. M. In a traumatized state, concrete thinking prevails, "characterized by a narrowing of perception and rigidity of mental processes" (Boulanger, 2007, p. 115). Simple answers are appealing. The splitting defense of the paranoid/schizoid position bolstered by "an assumed omniscience" creates definitive categories of right and wrong, good and bad, "a false dictatorial affirmation that one thing is morally right and the other wrong" (Bion, 1962b, p. 308). After hearing rumors but before I knew the identities of the alleged violators or any facts about the investigations, I formed strong opinions about guilt and commensurate punishment.

Like many people at my institute, I first heard about the ethical complaints through informal social channels well before the ethics committee finished its investigations and presented its reports to the board. As is typical of analytic institute ethics committees, all aspects of the investigatory process were confidential, including the names of complainants and respondents, the charges, and the details of the process. Institute leaders who were aware of the ethical complaints were also supposed to keep all information private. However, the complainants and the respondents were not held to a standard of confidentiality, so they were free to talk to friends and colleagues. Bits and pieces of information spread through social networks inside and outside the institute. The information that seeped through our community was incomplete, frequently inconsistent, and sometimes biased toward either a complainant or a respondent, with conflicting stories about what had occurred.

Even though I was not certain of their names and did not know the full extent of the charges or what had actually happened, initially I firmly identified with the complainants. I was outraged at the alleged unethical behavior I heard about. I hoped that if the accused analysts were found guilty of serious ethical violations, they would be censured and perhaps excluded from membership in the institute. I formed these opinions while I had no direct knowledge of the ethics committee's work.

The ethics committee conducted formal investigations of each case, found both analysts responsible for ethical breaches, and reached separate agreements with the respondents on remediation. They presented the resolutions of each case for the board's vote of final approval. They also maintained confidentiality about identities, the violations, and the processes, in accordance with their separate agreements with the two analysts. In both cases of ethical violation, the board unanimously agreed to accept the resolutions the ethics committee had reached with both accused analysts.

Casting my vote put me in a dilemma: I had intense judgmental reactions that were emotionally powered by my experience of Dr. M. and his boundary violations, but I was also a member of the board that had responsibility for the organization as a whole. This conflict awakened my appreciation of complexities I had not been considering. I began to recognize important differences between my victim-identified stance on ethical violations and my position as a board member with responsibility for the well-being of the institute. My determination to pursue my lawsuit had been so driven by moral righteousness that I was single-mindedly committed to following it through to the end regardless of the outcome or consequences. Taking the perspective of a board member, I recognized that decisions about penalties for ethical violations would have complicated, long-term consequences for the institute—for individuals, subgroups, groups, and the organization as a whole. As a victim, I had needed to hold onto my emotional certainty, but as a board member, I had to tolerate the uncertainty of ambiguity, incomplete information, and emotional confusion. As a victim, I felt despair at being betrayed by my loved analyst, but as an institute member, I felt despair at the betrayal of the whole community. A victim is typically alone in losing an internal good object, but a community member joins others who feel the loss of an idealized organization: we are not immune from ethical violations.

When protection of confidentiality is the highest priority, people who do not know the privileged information are necessarily left in the dark and may be quite confused or draw unsubstantiated conclusions. Yet I understood the rationale for the ethics committee's promise of confidentiality. During an ethics investigation, psychoanalytic institutional culture tries to protect the participants from rumors and misinformation that become less factual and more distorted as conversations spread. In addition, promising confidentiality to the respondents in a formal ethical investigation is intended to encourage members to cooperate with the ethics committee.

However, well-intended procedures also produce unintended consequences. The adherence to confidentiality over transparency can create a cautious, strained atmosphere in which discussion is constricted, and people are afraid to ask questions or bring up issues. A culture of anxious silence (see Sinsheimer, this volume) keeps people from engaging in productive discussions about the ethical issues, the investigatory process, or the final recommendations.

In moral dilemmas, there is a tension between "moral enormity," i.e., outrage at an extreme offense, and "moral complexity," i.e., understanding the personal, social, and historical conditions that contributed to the offense (Fellman, 2006). The board's task, to decide whether to approve the ethics committee's resolutions that included disciplinary action, emphasized moral enormity—punishment for ethical wrongdoing. I was ready to support restrictions, but, given my history as a victim of boundary violations, I was concerned they might not be strict enough. The lack of institutional group discussion did nothing to move me from my stance that had developed more in response to my experience with Dr. M. than to the current complaints, which remained opaque. Since people outside the ethics committee could not have a discussion about the complicated personal, social, or historical issues, we did not have perspective on the issues of moral complexity, and I did not have the opportunity to learn if these violators were more deserving of my forbearance than Dr. M.

(Being vigilant about confidentiality is an elusive challenge. In the first draft of this chapter, I described the atmosphere in the board meetings when we were voting on the ethics committee's recommendations. Neither I nor several colleagues who read my paper remembered that we had voted in executive session, meaning there were no minutes taken, and therefore the proceedings were confidential! I made revisions as soon as I realized my error.)

While board members were asked to keep the final ethics committee reports confidential, after participating together in the climactic meetings we finally felt freer to talk with one another. As I began to have conversations with friends and colleagues on the board, I learned that some had very different opinions and reactions from my own. I found these conversations very stressful. I had to grapple with the opinions of others I respected who disagreed with me or who endorsed more leniency than I felt the violators merited. These difficult conversations opened up previously collapsed spaces in my mind, shifting my focus from my own subjectivity to one of increased empathy for the experiences of all concerned: the emotional burdens and complex deliberations of the ethics committee, anxieties that might have led the inner circle of leadership to make decisions I did not understand or agree with, and what I assumed were painful experiences of both complainants and respondents during the investigations. While these additional perspectives did not alter my judgment that the two analysts had engaged in unethical behavior, they did create new pathways of thinking.

Through conversations with others, I was confronted with reasonable alternative ideas about how ethics investigations should be handled and about the possibilities for rehabilitation of the offending analysts. I developed more curiosity, empathy, and concern for everyone involved than I had had when I was alone with my thoughts that were colored by the traumatic involvement with Dr. M. These interactions helped me begin to separate the past from the present, to further metabolize my difficult experiences, and to think in more complex and nuanced ways.

## The Gift of Witnessing

The investigations of the ethical violations by two analysts at my institute had devastating effects throughout our organization. Everyone was affected to some degree, whether they had been at the eye of the storm or on the outer bands. The ethics committee felt beleaguered and unappreciated; the leadership was weary and anxious about holding together different factions in the community; a number of candidates were disillusioned with the organization and felt uncontained and unattended to. Some members raised questions about aspects of the institute's ethical guidelines, which the ethics committee followed in reaching their determinations. In the aftermath of the two investigations, the board voted to form a committee that would suggest a process for reviewing the institute's official ethics guidelines. I volunteered to be on that committee, as I was eager to be part of a group that was actively reviewing and discussing ethical principles and procedures. It offered a productive application for my preoccupation, as well as an opportunity—finally—to be with colleagues who shared my interest in defining and dealing with ethical violations.

Our group of eight[1] began by exploring the impact that the ethics investigation had produced on our members. We decided, with approval from the board, to conduct individual, confidential interviews and invited every member of the institute to participate. About half of our members volunteered to be interviewed, choosing interviewers from among our group. I interviewed

14 people. I could not have predicted at the outset that I would be so transformed by the cumulative experience of these intimate interviews.

Each interview consisted of 10 open-ended questions and typically lasted one to two hours. As interviewers, we explained that we were not going to give any information or state our opinions; we were only interested in listening to their experience, hearing their reflections on what went well and their suggestions for a better process in the future. Both the identities of the interviewees and their specific responses were kept confidential from others on the interviewing committee, but as a group we generated categories for scoring the anecdotal data, and each interviewer then scored our own transcripts. Finally, we aggregated the responses and reported the results to the community in summary form.

"Every story deserves telling" (Rozmarin, 2011, p. 343). The interviews were private, intense experiences. I had the profound privilege of entering into the moral universe of many different people, an *in vivo* lesson in moral complexity. Each person had a unique, coherent, understandable perspective on the same events, and they were very different from each other and from my own. Whether people knew quite a lot about what had happened or very little, were closely involved or considered themselves peripheral, they expressed strong reactions to the events that had shaken the institute, and they had many suggestions for how the process could go better in the future.

As I helped these stories unfold, I became completely immersed in each person's perspective, however similar to or different from my own. Usually when we hear our patients' painful experiences, we are not part of the story, but in this circumstance I was part of the story. Sometimes it was jarring to hear an opinion or suggestion I did not agree with or support, but by the end of each interview I understood how the interviewees came to hold their views. After listening and clarifying, I respected their feelings, their conclusions, and their suggestions. When I was interviewed by another member of my committee, I welcomed the opportunity to describe my experience and express my opinions about how ethics investigations should be handled. But while conducting my interviews, I managed to bracket my own feelings and convictions and empathically took on the perspective of each interviewee.

In retrospect, I realized that during each interview I served the psychoanalytic function of a witness, "an other who maintains an actively observing presence, who recognizes and grasps the emotional activity in the mind of the patient at work, and who is seen and recognized by the patient as a distinctly separate person" (Poland, 2000, p. 21). There are two aspects of the witnessing function: being a "beholder," who serves as a catalyst for the other to achieve self-knowledge and discover meaning, and holding "a position of separated otherness," with respect for the other's uniqueness and autonomy (Poland, 2000). In my role as interviewer—with the task of listening, empathizing, and clarifying but not adding information—I was in the position of beholder, inviting the interviewee to explore his or her experiences and feelings without intruding my own. In order to remain separate, I had to suspend my own convictions about the ethical violations and the ethics investigation process. Otherwise, I would have been engaged in an internal dialogue or argument with the interviewees, which would have interfered with my capacity to fully receive their experiences.

"*Witnessing develops from holding but implies letting go*" (Poland, 2000, p. 21; emphasis in original). Because of temporarily letting go of and suspending my opinions in order to fully recognize and respect my interviewees' ideas, I could see the validity of their perspectives toward the respondents, the complainants, the institute, and the investigatory process. Of those who were aware of the behaviors in question, no one expressed doubt that the actions were unethical. But people had very different convictions about many issues, and these reactions reflected different moral perspectives. Interviewees held diverse positions on issues such as whether or not to remain friends with the respondents and complainants (I had chosen not to), whether someone found guilty of an ethical violation should remain active in the institute or even be a member of the institute (I had been in favor of expulsion), whether transgressions should be made public after a finding (I supported transparency), or whether an inhouse ethics investigation was fair to all involved (I had doubts about an inhouse investigatory committee). While being with the interviewees, each of their viewpoints made perfect sense to me, even when they did not coincide with my view.

I was also exposed to this moral diversity within the committee that created, conducted, and summarized the interviews. Many of our meetings were emotionally charged and challenging, as we shared our different personal experiences during the ethical investigations. Our group represented a variety of roles played during the investigations, including leadership, candidates, people highly involved in formal capacities, and people who were close to respondents or complainants. We continually confronted our different perspectives about what was most salient and what was most traumatic. We learned that each member's personal experiences during the ethics investigations shaped their philosophy about what must be emphasized in our data summaries and what must not be overlooked, and ultimately we developed compassion and respect for each other's attitudes.

The cumulative experience of the interviews and the variety of viewpoints expressed by our committee members contributed to my receptivity to diverse moral perspectives and to my readiness to give full credence to opinions that were different from mine. This transition illustrated Kohlberg's (1969) fifth stage of moral development, the "social contract" stage, in which it is expected and respected that people hold different and unique opinions and values. My open-mindedness caught me by surprise. Released from the grip of rigid, trauma-based patterns of moral judgment, I was more able to think freely, symbolically, and metaphorically.

## Reverie and Metaphor

An image occurred to me that organized my experience of this chorus of difference. I began to see each of us as points within a three-dimensional cube that represented our reactions to the ethical violations in our institute. One dimension represented our roles at the institute during the ethics investigations. A second dimension represented our personal histories with boundary violations, betrayal, and trust. The third dimension represented our private, often implicit, dearly held values about good and bad, right and wrong. Everyone occupied a different point of intersection within this imagined cube, and my point suddenly seemed to be no more or less valid than anyone else's. The imagined cube, with its dotted array of equally valued points, seemed to suggest that I had been working internally to develop receptivity to and tolerance for difference, uncertainty, and complexity.

As I thought about the first factor—one's place in the institute during the ethics investigations—I reflected on how my roles as teacher, supervisor, and analyst had led me to feel protective of the candidates and want to safeguard them from unethical analysts. The second factor—personal history with boundary violations, secrecy, and betrayal—resonated with me as a victim of an ethical betrayal by my analyst and contributed to my harsh judgments.

But the third factor that emerged during the interviews—our implicit moral stance—was more elusive to my understanding, so I began reading about psychological approaches to morality. I discovered that my imaginary cube was an example of both moral complexity (Latimore, 1987) and moral pluralism (Mason, 2011; Samuels, 1989). Moral complexity takes into account the social, cultural, and historical context for individual moral convictions. In thinking about the three vertices—each person's role in the institute, the history of their experiences with boundary violations, and their family histories of moral attitudes and behavior—I was intuitively exploring moral complexity. When I sensed that each point in the cube could have equal value, I was unknowingly subscribing to the theory of moral pluralism. The theory of moral pluralism holds that there is a value of what is good, but there are many reasonable interpretations of good and bad, and they may be in disagreement or conflict with each other.

Pluralism, by definition, means diversity, and multiple interpretations of what is right moral behavior do not necessarily share one ideal or pattern in common. Pluralism accepts multiplicity and the inherent conflict multiplicity entails: "If values are plural, then choices between them will be complex" (Mason, 2011, p. 2). This view also implies that each moral approach is respected: "Pluralism enables us to see that irresolvable disagreements are not due to wickedness on the part of our interlocutor but may be due to the plural nature of values" (Mason, 2011, p. 4). I noted that moral pluralism in philosophy seemed parallel to theoretical pluralism in psychoanalysis—a dominant value in our institute and one that is thoroughly integrated into our curriculum.

Despite our comfort with theoretical pluralism, many of our members had difficulty accepting moral pluralism. Typically, when moral issues dominate a group, different moral biases are activated. Members had strong convictions and disagreed about what was or was not moral, whose moral attitudes were or were not correct, and what was the best course of action based on these views. We tended to get locked into our own positions on "truth," without acknowledging our personal biases and without supporting the validity of others' moral priorities. People with different moral positions began to mistrust each other and distance themselves: Relationships suffered. It is difficult to have calm and curious interchanges that respect differences when there has been a breakdown in the social fabric that threatens the integrity of the community.

For example, during meetings and informal social conversations, some of us expressed primary concern for the welfare of our candidates when a senior analyst was undergoing an investigation for an ethical violation. We questioned whether a respondent in an ethics investigation should continue to teach, analyze, or supervise candidates while being investigated for a formal complaint of wrongdoing. This concern reflects the value that the moral good should be to protect the most vulnerable and least powerful members of the community, the candidates. Other members held different moral priorities. Some did not support any actions (such as preventing a member involved in an ethics investigation from teaching, analyzing, and supervising) that might risk legal repercussions or threaten the solidity of the organization, reflecting the value that the good of the community lies in maintaining the cohesion of the institute. An array of alternative moral essentials is referred to as "value pluralism" (Mason, 2011).

Social and cultural psychologists have identified six "psychological systems as the foundations of intuitive ethics" (Haidt, 2001, 2012). I found the categorization of different value systems very helpful in understanding the conflicts that disrupted relationships among institute members. We were all striving to do the right thing, but we had different ideas about how to go about it, because we privileged different ethical values. My primary concern for the protection of the candidates fell into the moral foundation of "care vs. harm." When people in leadership made decisions that protected the organization but did not privilege the candidates, they were acting from a different moral foundation, "loyalty vs. betrayal," expressing loyalty to the organization as a whole. Some members automatically respected the decisions of the leadership, reflecting the moral foundation of "authority vs. subversion," whereas others automatically distrusted the leadership and felt their freedom was being constricted, reflecting the moral foundation of "liberty vs. oppression." Those who wanted stringent punishment for transgressors were seeking their version of justice, coming from the moral foundation of "fairness vs. cheating." And people who wanted the violators excluded from institute membership were following the moral foundation of "sanctity vs. degradation," hoping to purify the community of toxic elements. All of these different principles have moral value.

Although someone might hold several of these values on a particular issue, we do not usually hold multiple moral foundations equally. We have a tendency to weigh some factors more heavily and to act, react, or make recommendations consistent with our primary moral point of view. However, we do not usually recognize that we are operating from one value system while others are operating from a different but also ethical system. These value differences make it very difficult to reach consensus within a community about ethical violations, because each of these moral foundations leads to a different solution to the problem of how to handle an ethics investigation and what to do about transgressors. Organizations facing ethical complaints might avoid judgment and fragmentation if they could recognize that different moral foundations are likely to be distributed among the group and that there is more than one ethical road to morality.

I wondered how we could have such different views of what is right and yet be so convinced of our rightness. A comic version of this attitude is what political satirist Stephen Colbert (2005) dubbed "truthiness," an unthinking attachment to one's opinions because they "feel right." A current theory of how we come to our foundational values is the Social Intuitionist Model. Like psychoanalysis, it takes into account emotions, social interaction, and the unconscious. The model proposes that "moral judgment is generally the result of quick automatic evaluations (intuitions)" (Haidt, 2001, p. 814). The process of arriving at our intuitions is unconscious; the conscious process of reasoning comes later (Haidt, 2001, p. 818). While we may believe we have solid, rational reasons for our moral values, Haidt's research suggests that "the reasoning process constructs post-hoc justifications, yet we experience the illusion of objective reasoning" (Haidt, 2001, p. 815). We invent reasons after the fact that support the correctness of our automatic intuitive moral conclusions.

Altering our automatic moral judgments, or intuitions, usually requires an interpersonal exchange (Bronfenbrenner, 1979; Haidt, 2001; Kohlberg, 1969). Haidt (2001) recommends that we rely on others to help us improve our moral reasoning:

> By seeking out discourse partners who are respected for their wisdom and openmindedness, and by talking about the evidence, justifications, and mitigating factors involved in a potential moral violation, people can help trigger a variety of conflicting intuitions in each other. If

more conflicting intuitions are triggered, the final judgment is likely to be more nuanced and ultimately more reasonable (p. 829).

My interviewees became my "discourse partners," even though I did not have an overt dialogue with them. Listening to them with an open mind stimulated an internal dialogue in which I questioned my moral foundations. As I helped others explore the nature and origins of their moral attitudes about the institute's ethical investigations, I recognized how my earlier judgments had been greatly influenced by dealing with the boundary violations of Dr. M. My view had been darkened by the shadow of the bad object. I had to question the definiteness of my opinions that had seemed so clear, so right. "We need to approach our own experience with the same uncertainty with which we approach that of the patient [or interviewee]" (Frank, 2012).

It was through the cumulative experience of taking on the perspectives of my interviewees that I developed full understanding and respect for attachment to moral foundations that were different from my own. Over time, I gradually developed an attitude of curiosity about the violators at my institute, so that I could keep them separate from my attitudes toward Dr. M. I also became more curious about the attitudes of those who disagreed with me. Instead of wondering, "How can you think that?" I became interested in "How do you think that?" Interviewing was a little like being an anthropologist, immersed in different countries with different cultures, confronting different moral systems and accepting the validity of unfamiliar moral conventions, then being moved to reexamine my own. Although my interviewees and I were members of the same institute, deeply witnessing their emotional and moral perspectives was akin to entering different psychological cultures. These empathic confrontations generated in me an internal dialogue that challenged my convictions and unexpectedly led me to give up my illusion of certainty and accept the moral complexities of my institute's ethical dilemmas.

## Conclusion

I will never know exactly what violations occurred between Dr. M. and Ann. Neither will I know if he talked to anyone else about my personal and professional life. I have to live with many uncertainties. I have given up wishing I could know what "really" happened, and this relinquishment brings relief. "Establishing the truth once and for all is not possible and is in fact a dangerous goal to maintain" (Stern, 2011, p. 349).

I do not have to accept moral pluralism when it comes to Dr. M.'s unethical behavior. Clearly, he broke the ethical standards of our profession by committing sexual boundary violation and breach of confidentiality. My judgment of his wrongdoing remains unchanged, and I have no regrets about filing my lawsuit, testifying in court, and publishing my paper.

But can I accept the moral complexity of Dr. M.'s violations? I have been through a gradual process of internally reworking my relationship to Dr. M. In Faimberg's (2007) explanation of *après coup*, she identifies two phases: first, an event occurs and leaves a trace that is outside of awareness; second, at a later time, something happens that gives meaning retroactively to the trace that was left. At the time of the lawsuit, I knew Dr. M. well enough to have speculated on what led him to his professional misconduct, and I was attached enough to worry about him, but these thoughts and feelings remained unknown in the background until I worked through fresh confrontations with ethical violations. Gradually, I could afford to have ideas about Dr. M. that had remained unthought, because they posed too great a threat to my purpose and my psyche. Now I can construct coherent theories about how his life situation, character, psychological issues and history might have led to his unethical actions. Given all that I knew about him, I think his vulnerability to boundary violations and his obliviousness to the consequences were almost inevitable. I view his downfall less as a triumph for me than a tragedy for him and all who were affected.

I lost my analyst, but I gained perspective. I went from seeing myself as a victim to appreciating the complexities of my ethical attitudes and the insoluble dilemmas in our ethically complex profession.

## Note

1 The other members of the Ad Hoc Ethics Review Task Force were Barbara Baer, Chuck Brandes, Josie Gallup, Sharon Karp-Lewis, Julie Leavitt, Patricia Rosbrow, and Angela Sowa.

## References

Akhtar, S. (2011). Editor's introduction: Besides perpetrators. *International Journal of Applied Psychoanalytic Studies, 8*, 185–186.

Allphin, C. (2005). An ethical attitude in the analytic relationship. *Journal of Analytic Psychology, 50*, 451–468.

Bion, W. R. (1962a). *Learning from experience*. London: Tavistock.

Bion, W. R. (1962b). The psycho-analytic study of thinking. *International Journal of Psycho-Analysis, 43*, 306–310.

Bion, W. R. (1992). *Cogitations*. London: Karnac.

Boulanger, G. (2007). *Wounded by reality: Understanding and treating adult onset trauma*. Mahwah, NJ, & London: Analytic Press.

Bronfenbrenner, U. (1979). *The ecology of human development: Experiments by nature and design*. Cambridge, MA: Harvard University Press.

Brown, L. (2005). The cognitive effects of trauma: Reversal of alpha function and the formation of a beta screen. *Psychoanalytic Quarterly, 74*, 379–420.

Burka, J. (2008). Psychic fallout from breach of confidentiality: A patient/analyst's perspective. *Contemporary Psychoanalysis, 44*, 177–198.

Celenza, A., & Gabbard, G. O. (2003). Analysts who commit sexual boundary violations: A lost cause? *Journal of the American Psychoanalytic Association, 51*, 617–636.

Colbert, S. (2005). Tonight's word: Truthiness. Available online: http://www.colbertnation.com/the-colbert-reportvideos/24039/October-17-2005/the-word-truthiness. Also available at: http://www.en.wikipedia.org/wiki/truthiness (accessed August 2, 2012).

Faimberg, H. (2007). A plea for a broader concept of Nachträglichkeit. *Psychoanalytic Quarterly, 76*, 1221–1240.

Fellman, M. (2006). The case for moral complexity. in P. A. Tabensky (Ed.), *Judging and understanding: Essays on free will, narrative, meaning and the ethical limits of condemnation*. Aldershot: Ashgate.

Frank, K. L. (2012). Strangers to ourselves: Exploring the limits and potentials of the analyst's self-awareness in self-and mutual analysis. *Psychoanalytic Dialogues, 22*, 311–327.

Gabbard, G. O. (2002). Boundary violations and the abuse of power. *Studies in Gender and Sexuality, 3*, 379–388.

Haidt, J. (2001). The emotional dog and its rational tail: A social intuitionist approach to moral judgment. *Psychological Review, 108*, 814–834.

Haidt, J. (2012). Moral foundations theory. Available online: http://www.moralfoundations.org (accessed August 10, 2012).

Kohlberg, L. (1969). Stage and sequence: The cognitive-developmental approach to socialization. In D. A. Goslin (Ed.), *Handbook of Socialization Theory and Research*. Chicago, IL: Rand McNally.

Latimore, C. (1987). *Patterns of moral complexity*. Cambridge: Cambridge University Press.

Mason, E. (2011). Value pluralism. Online in E. N. Zalta (Ed.), *The Stanford encyclopedia of philosophy* (fall 2011 edition). Available online: http://plato.stanford.ude.archives/fall 2011/entries/flue-pluralism/ (accessed August 10, 2011).

Narvaez, D. (2010). Moral complexity: The fatal attraction of truthiness and the importance of mature moral functioning. *Perspectives on Psychological Science, 5*, 163–181.

Poland, W. S. (2000). The analyst's witnessing and otherness. *Journal of the American Psychoanalytic Association, 48*, 17–34.

Rather, L. (2001). Collaborating with the unconscious other: The analysand's capacity for creative thinking. *International Journal of Psychoanalysis, 82*, 515–531.

Rozmarin, E. (2011). To be is to betray: On the place of collective history and freedom in psychoanalysis. *Psychoanalytic Dialogues, 21*, 320–345.

Samuels, A. (1989). *The plural psyche: Personality, morality and the father*. London: Routledge.

Schore, A. N. (2003). *Affect dysregulation and disorders of the self*. New York: W. W. Norton & Co.

Stein, A. (2011). The utility of contempt. *Contemporary Psychoanalysis, 47*, 80–100.

Stern, D. B. (2011). Ethics and liberation: Commentary on paper by Eyal Rozmarin. *Psychoanalytic Dialogues, 21*, 346–353.

# Part IV

# RUPTURES' IMPACT ON ORGANIZATIONS

# 10

# SILENCING

## When a Community Loses an Analyst to Ethical Violations

*Kathy Sinsheimer*

> The most damaging response to violations of sexual taboo is silence.
> Ruskin (2011, p. 105)

A tsunami, churning deep and wide, can engulf an institute when it is revealed that an analyst is leaving because of committing ethical violations. Without an explanation from the analyst—often a significant, powerful figure in the community—members are left without adequate information to successfully navigate the raging waters. There are pressures to both speak and not speak of what one knows. This phenomenon, which I call *silencing*, emerges from many locations. Although silencing can arise from external pressures due to individuals' roles within the institute, such as those requiring confidentiality, there are other, more subtle forces at work, with members sometimes finding that they cannot speak out but also cannot locate the source of the prohibition. Silencing also arises out of members' own interpersonal and intrapsychic dynamics coming out of their backgrounds. These prohibitions—coupled with individual and group dynamics and then combined with the departing analyst's secrets—create a powerful silence that insidiously works to destabilize and, ultimately, rupture the institute.

In this chapter, I will discuss the history of silencing in institutes following reported ethical and sexual boundary violations; the power structures within such an institute and how they affect members' freedom to speak; and the ensuing dynamics within the institute. I will include examples of these dynamics, including a personal experience with silencing.

## A History of Ethical Violations

The recorded history of ethical violations in psychoanalysis begins with letters between Jung and Freud regarding Jung's liaison with his patient, Sabina Spielrein (Freud, 1909). The term *countertransference* was coined by Freud during this exchange. For many years, ethical violations were dealt with privately and, at times, without professional consequence. In early psychoanalytic relationships, analysts were caught off guard by the powerful feelings they experienced in transference-countertransference dynamics. What we now think of as ethical or boundary violations occurred between Jung and Spielrein as well as Ferenczi and Elma Palos, among others.

Freud was involved in attempts to sort out the complexities that arose in these early treatment relationships (Gabbard, 1995). Louise de Urtubey (cited in Llopis-Salvan, 2008) is critical of Freud's negligence concerning his followers, "such as Jung and Ferenczi, the first transgressors in the history of psychoanalysis" (p. 464). She feels his indulgence to be a "heavy legacy to bear that contributes, if not to such acts, at least to a silent complicity by colleagues concerning those who commit them" (p. 464). It is possible that this silent complicity is one of the precursors of the silencing we experience today. Years later, there is Masud Khan, whose ethical violations were notorious. But he was not fully investigated until after his death, when the British Psycho-Analytical Society held a posthumous ethics investigation after the publication of an essay by his former analysand, Wynne Godley (2001), who both witnessed and experienced multiple violations by Khan.

Silencing can also occur in extra-institute situations involving publication. Grosskurth (1998) described her experience working on her seminal biography of Melanie Klein as one of seduction followed by exclusion. The exclusion began to occur when she discovered secrets about Klein's history and made it clear that she would be including these in her biography. The Kleinians had initially embraced her and her project, coming to call her an "honorary Kleinian"; she states, "It is embarrassing to confess, but I began to believe I was a member of this privileged group" (p. 90). After reviewing materials given her by Klein's son, Grosskurth said she was "shocked out of my private fantasy. The Kleinians began to become alarmed, fearful that I had stumbled on family secrets" (p. 90). Meetings were held and plots hatched to discredit Grosskurth's biography. "This was a very painful episode in my life ... My youthful naïve assumption that analysts were grown-up mature people capable of tolerating ambivalence was destroyed forever" (p. 90). In addition to being excluded from her group, Grosskurth lost her idealized view of psychoanalysts. She concludes by emphasizing the need for analysts to be "mature enough to accept that there have been sorry incidents in [psychoanalytic] history from which perhaps some wisdom can be garnered" (p. 95).

While there are further recorded instances of ethical violations in the literature, analysts do not appear to have written about the institutional difficulties related to ethical violations until the writings of Gabbard, Peltz, Margolis, Ross, and Rutter in the 1990s. Noting the severity of the impact on an analytic community, Ross (1995) declares, "boundary violations constitute collective traumas that live on in the psychic and political lives of generations to come" (p. 961).

## Power Structures and Silencing

Many efforts have been made to modernize the power structures at psychoanalytic institutes, but, as in all groups, inevitably there are members who hold greater power and status than others. Junior members, who have graduated and wish to become faculty members or training analysts (TAs), feel intimidated by senior members of these groups because their ability to secure positions is contingent on the support of senior members. Kernberg (1986) speaks to the difficulties between the generations at institutes with the elders being an "in group" who are "in the know," in contrast to the "out group" of junior faculty who are not TAs and the candidates. While specific members of the "in group" may know more than members of the "out group," even knowledge within the "in group" will likely be uneven.

Candidates are in an especially vulnerable position, since they are dependent on the ethical behavior of senior members to help them progress through their training. Having to proceed through established trajectories of growth and development to advance, their progress is subject to the evaluation of senior members of the community. This structure and approach, no matter how reasonable, produces a power differential that all members of the institute experience and internalize.

Sandler and Godley (2004) cite the dual relationships within any analytic community. In the previous example of Masud Khan, members of the British Society were patients of Masud Khan, while a prominent member, Winnicott, was Khan's analyst. During that same period, Khan acted as Winnicott's editor, and the two became entangled in a *folie à deux*. Many members were so grateful for Khan's actions as a benefactor in the Society that, caught up in his enactments and omnipotence, they overlooked his infringements and did not address his transgressions. All analytic communities have similar overlapping roles, with analyst, analysand, supervisor, supervisee, advisor and advisee relationships intertwining with collegial and social connections.

These power differentials affect the community in at least two ways. First, the group may be reluctant to acknowledge the possibility of a senior member violating boundaries, as this disrupts the power dynamics in the institute. Rutter (1989) reports having noticed problematic behavior on the part of a senior analyst in his community for years before that analyst's multiple sexual boundary violations were finally discovered. Rutter learned that others had wondered about this behavior as well and had not spoken. Sandler and Godley (2004) suggest that avoiding recognition of problems is common, describing the discovery of misbehaviors as an attack "on the basic frame of the profession" (p. 37) and therefore psychically unwelcome. They also describe self-silencing due to disbelief, echoing Rutter's observations of his own behavior. Second, members at this senior level may wish to keep such allegations quiet after being revealed in order to present a united front to the wider community, unstained by unethical conduct on the part of a member.

### *Case Example: Dr. S. and Ms. T. are Silenced*

Ms. T., a trainee, became concerned about her analysis with a junior analyst, Dr. J. Ms. T. was alarmed at the increasing boundary enactments between her and Dr. J. She consulted with a previous supervisor, Dr. S., who was a senior analyst at their institute. With the support of Dr. S., Ms. T. took her concerns to the appropriate committee at their institute. As Ms. T.'s allegations, as well as Dr. S.'s support of Ms. T., became more widely known at their institute, silencing began to occur. Ms. T. felt silenced and excluded following the public knowledge of her complaints regarding the violations. Dr. S., as a senior analyst, experienced difficulties that have not been detailed in the literature. Dr. S.'s silencing involved being excluded from previously offered positions of leadership; being denied the possibility of hiring a consultant to help the institute with their difficulties; and being excluded from entering into dialogue with powerful members who seemed unwilling or unable to consider multiple points of view regarding the allegations. Supporting the trainee proved costly to Dr. S. This example illustrates some of the ramifications for senior members who attempt to address ethical violations at an institute that is unable or unwilling to face the challenges and controversies of allegations of unethical behavior in their midst.

## Institute Dynamics that Generate Silencing

### *Family Secrets*

In Gabbard and Peltz's (2001) paper "Speaking the unspeakable," they write of two cases of alleged ethical violations and the institutional reaction, "Although the candidates were quite distressed, they were reluctant to say anything. They feared that revealing the 'family secret' might jeopardize their training" (p. 664). For good reason: the candidates had learned that a particular training analyst, Dr. B., was having sex with at least one female patient. One complaining candidate was labeled psychotic and two junior members were told that they would not be appointed training analysts if they continued their demands for an investigation.

It seems likely that institute members who experience the ethical violations as family secrets may feel that if the secret is spoken out loud—not in hushed tones—they are betraying their family. Gabbard (1997) also registers this incestuous-like dynamic when he calls sexual boundary violations a "professional form of incest" (p. 379). Family dysfunction, including keeping secrets and curating or grooming history, is a well-known but hushed phenomenon in psychoanalytic history.

Margolis (1997) asks:

> Why has there been such silence about this issue? I would like to suggest that our silence has been due to the same forces within us that for so long kept the issue of actual clinical incest relegated to the realm of fantasy, namely, that the main cause of our reluctance to deal more openly with this phenomenon is our horror of actual violations of the incest taboo which is at the psychological core of these ethical violations. We do not wish to acknowledge this in our colleagues or in ourselves.
>
> (pp. 349–350)

Gabbard and Peltz (2001) describe colleagues confessing to "a feeling that they were revealing well-guarded family secrets. They were speaking the unspeakable" (p. 660). They also found that, within some institutes, behavior that violated ethics codes was "fairly well-known within the analytic community and was gossiped about at length ... Pervasive denial was rampant and threats of litigation often deterred any definitive action. A sense of paralysis and helplessness swept over education committees and ethics committees alike" (p. 660). They conclude, "No one wants to breach the veil of privacy surrounding training analysis" (p. 662).

### *The Threat of Legal Action*

Often, an analyst who has committed or who has been accused of committing ethical violations will seek legal counsel, subsequently threatening to sue the institute. These threats can have the effect of silencing individual members or the group as a whole. Gabbard and Peltz (2001) state:

> Some dynamics of institutional avoidance hide behind the fear of litigation that so often emerges in discussions about the boundary-violating analyst. Attorneys retained by the accused may demand a moratorium on any discussion of the case, which is conveniently appropriated by members of an ethics committee or education committee as a way to avoid talking about their own anxieties concerning the case. Attorneys often advise their

clients to deny the allegations or to be completely silent about them.

(p. 667)

The legal-ethical rule of confidentiality seems to contribute to silencing. As analysts, we perform the function of protecting the confidentiality of our patients. We hear information daily that is protected by our rules of confidentiality. We regularly hold secrets and confidences of many individuals—it is part of what we do! It is possible that we overgeneralize this concept and carry it into our professional lives in ways that are unnecessary and harmful. Members become confused about whether or not their knowledge of an analyst's ethical violations is confidential or can be shared, even if they did not come by this knowledge in a confidential relationship.

This may be all the more confusing due to overlapping roles at institutes. If a member is a training analyst, he may be analyzing a candidate (a confidential relationship), advising another candidate (not confidential), sitting on the ethics committee (confidential), sitting on the board (sometimes confidential, sometimes not), and so on. This overlapping may make members cautious and sometimes think that information is confidential when, in fact, it is not.

## *The Idealized Analyst*

To enter into analytic training, it seems likely that one must have in mind a version of the analyst one wishes to become. When I decided to train to become a psychoanalyst, I had my own vision of the perfect analyst. The analyst was bright, highly trained, analyzed, and extremely insightful—a master of his[1] own mind and the inner workings of his patients' minds. When I was in the thick of my own personal analysis at the beginning of my training, I felt indebted to my analyst for the help she had given me thus far. I superimposed my image of the perfect analyst over her: I idealized her mind, her training, and her position in contrast to my own—the lesser trained but desirous junior clinician. This idealization inhibits the understanding of the analyst's vulnerability.

To learn that a potential teacher has committed significant ethical violations is a blow to that image of the idealized analyst. Nicholsen (2010) states:

Candidates in analytic training, who may not yet have gone through a gradual and tolerable de-idealization of the profession, may be particularly vulnerable to the kind of traumatic de-idealization and de-stabilization that abuse, in any form, including contact with sexual boundary violations, brings with it.

(p. 227)

When the ethics-violating analyst is introduced into a candidate's training experience, it brings forth challenges for the candidates, faculty, and institute. The candidate's image of the idealized analyst is immediately brought into question.

Although many analysts have difficulty acknowledging their own professional vulnerabilities, the analyst is made vulnerable by his active role with his patients, his community, his family, and his internal life. Slochower (2003), Harris and Sinsheimer (2007), and Celenza (2010a) have written about the analyst's vulnerability in daily work and in the profession. Working day in and day out in his office, he is subject to myriad psychological pressures, including the analytic ideal that psychoanalysts are always "present as full and feeling persons in the treatment relationship while always aiming to use our humanity in the service of our patients' needs" (Slochower, 2003, p. 467). Slochower describes learning of how analysts responded to their sense of various types of deprivation in their lives and in their consulting rooms with "misdemeanors." If an analyst works too much, does not have a satisfying personal life, and is faced with difficult internal challenges due to his countertransference reactions in his treatment relationships, he may come to see his patients as having the potential to fill his needs.

I liken this dynamic to the tripolar relationship in the tale of Little Red Riding Hood. Many of us can imagine being Little Red Riding Hood, skipping through the forest with treats for Grandma, or as the loving grandmother who is receiving her granddaughter. However, there is another figure in the story we are far less likely to empathize with: the Big Bad Wolf. Split off in our consciousness, he is a whisper of appetites and envies that may spring forth unbidden in analytic hours. If we keep our own appetites out of consciousness, we may be surprised by their appearance when we are fatigued, isolated, and under personal and professional strain. Is this denial part of our silence—the difficulty we have acknowledging our selfishness, our own appetites?

If the analyst comes to his consulting room too drained from professional activity, or with problems in his personal life, he is vulnerable to being knocked off-center, succumbing to the slippery slope (Gabbard, 1995) that leads to ethical violations. Erotic transference and countertransference contribute further to this instability. Celenza (2010b) compares this to keeping one's balance while dancing. A seasoned analyst knows these pressures. Candidates may not yet realize that they will be facing these balances and imbalances throughout their careers. They may imagine that, as fully trained individuals, they will always be able to maintain or reclaim their balance. They are not yet aware of the strains of many hours, possibly isolated, in the consulting room and the pressure that will put on them. Thus, it comes as a shock when a senior community member has not been able to keep his balance.

Analysts find that the many hours in the consulting room do weigh on them, heavily, at times. One example comes from Celenza (2010a), who describes becoming "waiting impaired" (p. 65). She finds herself wanting to make all family decisions right away once she has finished her clinical day. Celenza also describes a friend who will not wait at intersections for the light to change, instead turning right on red in order not to have to await the green light. Our patience may be strained at the end of a long day of listening, reflecting, interpreting, and restraining ourselves. In the television series *In Treatment*, burnt out psychotherapist Dr. Weston tells his consultant that he has "No patience for my patients." He is soon to commit a sexual boundary violation (García, 2008).

There is also a de-idealizing of the analyst as he is removed from his institute. More than one author (Ruskin, 2011; Wallace, 2007) reports members objecting to citing the body of work previously generated by the ethically violating analyst after the revelation of his behavior. Ruskin reported that members did not want texts used in teaching that had been written by the offending analyst. This appears to be another instance of silencing, which now includes the analyst who has committed the offense.

## *The Idealized Institute*

In the same way that analysts and analytic function can be idealized, so can analytic institutes. Members likely wish, and may believe, that the institute will function as a safe container of analytic life. Candidates will be supported and protected while learning the exquisitely intricate function of becoming psychoanalysts. Graduate members (TAs, faculty, etc.) will be supported, and will support one another, while working rigorously in their private offices. Yet, even with the safeguards of ethics committees, leadership groups, structures, regulations, and rules, individual members can have difficulties with boundaries.

The functioning of the ethics committee is complex, and their work is profoundly challenging. They are working within systems that have been developed in anticipation of ethical concerns within the institute, but these systems are more or less effective depending on the actual challenges the committee faces. The ethics committee, along with the board, while functioning at its best, may still be challenged to offer emotional safety to the institute. Perhaps this is not even its task. In addition, these committees are generally designed to protect the confidentiality of the individuals with whom they are working—those who may have had difficulties with boundaries. When they communicate with the community through official channels, their typically brief statements will reflect their rules of confidentiality. While confidentiality is beneficial to the individuals in question, it may undermine the sense of safety for the remainder of the institute, where, likely, news will begin to flow through social, rather than official, communication. I will describe these two levels of communication later in this chapter.

Once this information begins to enter the realm of social communication, rumors and truths will begin to circulate and create instability in the protective frame of the institute. Personal friendships and psychoanalytic "genetic" relationships—Analyst W. was analyzed by Analyst X., who is supervised by Analyst Y. and is in a consulting group with Analyst Z.—complicate the picture. Blasdel (2010) states, "It was very hard to decipher the incoming data, deal with our mixed loyalties and multiplicity of roles, and work through our confusions about how to proceed with a nuanced balancing of transparency and confidentiality" (p. 14). This "genetic" overlap brings about internal struggles for those in the middle of multiple relationships within the community. This strain affects the group as a whole. The individuals who are caught between conflicting loyalties—such as being a friend of an individual who is bringing a complaint as well as being a friend of an analyst who is alleged to have committed an ethical violation—are in a position not even Solomon could remedy.

Groups such as these experience significant strain attempting to contain their anxieties. In the case example of Dr. S. and Ms. T., members fell into two factions: those who wanted to attend to the concerns regarding the alleged ethical violations, and those who felt the need to silence the discussion. In Bionian terms, the group in power—those who felt the need to silence—became a "fight or flight" basic assumption group (Bion, 1961). In order to preserve itself, the members of this group prevented (fight) and avoided (flight) discussion of the allegations of ethics violations. The group not in power had proposed a process to organize the institute into a "work group," hoping to facilitate members' movement into generative discussions regarding the ethical matters that faced their community. The minority group (the potential initial work group) proposed structured community dialogue facilitated by an outside consultant. This proposal was turned down by the basic assumption group, which used its power to block the minority group's recommendation.

In a basic assumption group, thinking cannot occur. In order to become a work group and begin to think, a number of institutes, such as Toronto Psychoanalytic Institute, Boston Psychoanalytic Institute, and Psychoanalytic Institute of Northern California, held meetings using group process to examine how difficulties with ethical violations affected their functioning. Group process offers a forum to express and work through feelings and reactions to both the ethical violation and the groups' reactions to that violation. It gives the community a chance to speak together and to try to work through differences. Such group process is the opposite of "silencing." And yet, even after significant processing, friendships will be altered due the individual and group pressures inherent in group dynamics arising out of boundary violations in an institute. Celenza (2007) states, "The membership of an institution has needs for recovery. If these are not addressed in some direct manner, there will be an unhealthy level of confusion, anger and alienation from within the institution itself" (p. 126).

### *Case Example: My Experience of Swimming in an Institutional Tsunami*

So far in this chapter, I have primarily been referring to boundary violations that have been published. However, I will be best able to illustrate post-violation dynamics through describing my own encounter with just such an experience.

As an active member in my institute, I heard about ethical violations in two ways—through my official capacities and through social communication. What I was hearing appeared to put candidates at risk by placing them in a situation that was potentially ethically misguided, destabilizing, and detrimental to their psychoanalytic education. I felt that I had to take action, but the different information channels confused and then silenced me.

I have scrutinized whether what I learned was through confidential official communication, which I may not write about, and what was communicated through social communication, which I may write about. These levels of communication are actually key components in the dynamics I am describing. Official communication regarding ethics violations is typically of two types. The first type of official communication occurs within the official bodies that confront allegations, and possibly findings, of ethical misconduct. Almost all of this communication is confidential. The second type of information is issued by the board and is not confidential; it is brief and limited. Outside the official communications, there lies social communication. This is communication that typically occurs between members over coffee, on walks—at times when members get together to socialize. Although I have clarified for myself that the information I am writing about was learned in non-confidential settings, the dynamic of silencing continues, even now, as I feel personally concerned about displeasing those who would prefer that these sensitive matters be kept private.

Several years ago, while functioning in an official but not confidential capacity, I learned of a broadcasting of previously confidential information regarding the unethical conduct of a faculty member, Dr. F., who previously had a formal complaint lodged against him with the institute's ethics committee. It had been determined that his behavior had been unethical. When the ethics committee has determined that a member has committed an ethical violation, the committee, along with the board, has the power to forge an agreement with that member to undertake further, remedial steps. Whether Dr. F. was asked to do so is confidential. By agreement, Dr. F. continued to function in some of his capacities within the institute, including teaching. What I learned was that the previously confidential information about Dr. F.'s ethical violations, as well as information about additional allegations, had been brought into the candidate group by an affected outsider who was not bound by confidentiality. The candidate group was soon to have Dr. F. teach them a course that was both clinical and didactic. I was distressed to learn that the candidate group was in this predicament, and because I was in an official role, I felt it was my duty to inform Dr. P., a senior member of the community. At that time, I was naïve and unaware of the troubled waters in which I was swimming.

At this point, an enactment occurred within the institute. Although I had requested confidentiality for my source, within the hour Dr. P. had shared the information, including the source, with Dr. D., another senior member of the community. Once this information became known, it seemed impossible to protect confidentiality, and it seemed equally impossible for senior members to think clearly once they learned that the information had become known within the candidate group. Gabbard and Peltz (2001) state: "Colleagues who hear this information may find their ego functioning affected. Rational, clear-headed thinking may be compromised" (p. 668). While they are referring to members' initial hearing of the analyst's transgression, the dynamic they describe also applies to the secret once it is let loose, even at a later time, outside of confidential settings.

Drs. D. and P. subsequently asked me not to share this information beyond the contacts I had made with them, and they informed me that Dr. D. would help the class metabolize its new knowledge. This request came to feel like silencing to me. I felt the matter needed to be more out in the open. How was that going to happen if I was quiet and the matter was being "contained" within the class? Was Dr. F. still going to teach the class? Should he?

Dr. D. began to try to help the candidate group metabolize this new, disturbing information. However, when Dr. D. spoke about the matter with this particular group of candidates, at least half of the group felt they had been silenced while the other half did not have that experience. Those who believed they had been silenced felt they had been told to keep the information within the group and not to speak even with other candidate groups about what they had learned. Dr. D. was certain that she had not told them to be silent. Something powerful had affected communication, and it seemed that no one was able to escape this dynamic—not the senior members, not the candidate group, and, then, not other members of the community who came to learn that something was wrong.

Since it appeared Dr. F. would still be teaching the candidates, I worried what the class dynamics were going to be like. Was Dr. F. going to be told that the candidates knew? What discussions were the class members going to be able to have with the teacher about his violations? Was the class going to have to keep a secret from the rest of the community? All of this appeared to be a potentially toxic learning environment.

Candidates wondered if they were putting themselves in professional danger by learning about clinical work from an individual who had committed ethical violations. Would there be missing, incorrect, or even corrupt content in the teaching? Might the instruction contaminate them? Wallace (2007, 2010) coined the term "microbial model" to characterize this fear of contamination from an ethically violating analyst. For the candidates not to be free to speak within the community about these questions was untenable.

I felt, if I kept quiet, I was abandoning my community—my family—to enact its dysfunction. I felt compelled to speak in order to prevent further family dysfunction. Through my work with families dealing with incest, I know the danger of family secrets. I know how these secrets stop people from thinking and speaking. Nicholsen (2010) describes the state I was in as "heroic fantasies of omnipotent responsibility" (p. 233).

We were in the midst of silencing dynamics. How had we gotten here? Akin to being under a spell, the group becomes possessed by these dynamics. What are the ingredients of the spell? Unspeakable acts, the downfall of a powerful individual, confidentiality requirements, the pressure of a secret. Who or what takes possession of individual and group consciousness (and unconsciousness) and infuses silencing? Could an ethical violation indicate the presence of the uncanny—experiences (emotional, physical, and mental) that come from an unidentifiable source? Harris (2011) states, "When Freud deployed the term 'uncanny' he meant to be saying something about unconscious communication" (p. 539). This unconscious communication takes place between members, giving a sense of being overtaken or not being able to identify the source of one's response. Once the transgression becomes public knowledge, the lack of thinking and presence of acting spreads throughout the institute. Individual members react in unique ways: some feel an acute urgency to speak; others maintain silence; many feel shame, guilt, worry, and anxiety.

Our histories come to haunt us. The ghosts of each individual member come forward in an interplay that expresses conscious and unconscious responses: "In clinical impasses, we often see how the analyst similarly arrives in the work to cure old injuries, bury the undead, undertake the final repair of history" (Harris, 2012, p.10). Since it is impossible to completely work through trauma and loss (Gerson, 2009), we each carry unmetabolized responses to traumatic events. These get triggered when we are in the presence of the secret of an ethical violation and we begin to enact our responses to our earlier wounds. Villela (2005), writing of profound ethical difficulties at a Brazilian institute, states: "What is repressed in everyday speech finds other forms of expressing itself in the real—producing symptoms, fantasies, hallucinations" (p. 808). At my institute, we repressed and suppressed ourselves and one another.

After I learned the secret, I became convinced that I needed to help the candidate group metabolize this information. I felt an urgency to "protect" the candidates, even at the risk of offending senior members who wished to have this matter be quieted down, which I thought of as "hushing up." Though there was an argument for silence as a way to contain and protect the candidate group, I did not see it that way. Rather, even though I had been asked not to, I began to speak of what I had learned to other senior members of the community. I chose members who already knew at least some details of the matter and who might have power to intervene on behalf of the candidate group. Cognizant of the power structure, I chose people whom I thought of as allies. While those whom I told seemed very glad to hear from me, others were unhappy that this information was traveling within the community and that the matter was coming to a head.

The spell, and the allure of truth, pushed me onward. I felt that the well-being of the candidates depended on my speaking up and that the entire institute would suffer if I did not. The candidates needed clarity (truth) in order to be free to learn. I also believed that the institute's reputation in the community would be affected once it became known that candidates were going to be taught by someone found guilty of ethical violations. (This certainly appears to be an omnipotent fantasy, and the results of my speaking up were indeed mixed—not at all my fantasy of rescuing the candidates and the institute.)

Even though one aspect of the difficulties of the candidate group was resolved—Dr. F. resigned from teaching the class—other difficulties remained with this group for the four years of their candidacy. My intervention helped bring some resolution to the conflict, but it also created new difficulties for the group. The group members struggled for months with their differing perceptions of whether or not they needed to keep their knowledge of the senior analyst's ethical violations within their group, or if they could let other candidates know. Their sense of group identity, combined with their mixed perceptions of their prohibition against speaking, led them to be silent in the larger candidate group. The larger candidate group found itself unable to function as a work group until the silence was finally broken.

Has there been fallout for me for having brought an aspect of the secret back into the institute? I angered members, but I also brought something into the light that, it seemed to me, was best not kept hidden. I experienced shame and guilt for waiting too long to speak, and yet I still felt fear of repercussions from speaking. Despite those feelings, I can live better with my moral self. I continue to have questions about my actions. While some issues were resolved, difficulties lingered for the candidates for a significant period of time. There are no simple solutions to what is a deeply complex problem, and each one is personal. This was mine. Even writing now, I have the uncomfortable feeling that I am breaking a rule, and/or that members of the community will be upset with me. As I speak out, I feel the weight of silencing.

## Conclusion

In summary, in using the term *silencing*, I am speaking of a phenomenon in which members of a community, for known and unknown reasons, feel they are not free to speak of ethical violations in their midst. Multiple pressures, from within and without, come to bear on each individual community member, who responds in his/her own unique way.

Members learn of these violations through various channels, including official and social communications. In each instance, there can be confusion about what information one might freely share, and the concern about the specific unethical behavior can also add pressure to what is already a volatile mix. Gabbard's (1997) calling professional sexual ethical violations "a professional form of incest" sends a clear message about the severity of the transgression, as well as the impact it may have on the system in which individuals are trying to metabolize knowledge of disturbing information. Because we are all in what I call "psychoanalytic genetic relationships" binding us closely to one another, this intense connection both facilitates and hinders communication. As with family systems, familiarity does not always breed excellent communication. Within our institutes, these relationships reflect the prevailing power structures, with senior analysts holding the greatest power and the candidates being the most vulnerable. Vulnerable candidates who idealize senior analysts are particularly disillusioned when they come to understand that senior analysts are vulnerable as well. Recognizing the analyst's vulnerability is key to establishing more realistic views of ourselves and our work.

There are many dynamics that contribute to silencing and speaking. Wallace's (2007, 2010) "microbial model" describes the fear of any work created by the ethical violating analyst; it is as if by committing an ethical violation, he negates his ability to function and contribute. The silencing then extends to his entire volume of work, as if he should never be heard from. Finally, my own "heroic fantasies of omnipotent responsibility," to use Nicholsen's (2010) term, emerged as a wish to bring clarity to a murky situation. Where I may have added some clarity in one arena, I created more murkiness in another, and many difficult matters lingered far beyond my attempted intervention to bring speech to the silence.

Silencing in the face of ethical violations is a complex phenomenon with multi-determined sources and many areas for acting and enacting. It casts a long shadow over the community it holds in its spell. In addition to institutional dynamics, members bring personal experiences of silencing that affect the group as a whole. Our shock or horror regarding ethical violations is intensely personal and professional. We are disappointed in the analyst. We are afraid of being victim and perpetrator. We are vulnerable and outraged. The pressures from within individuals as well as from the organization create a combustive mix that can bring about a tsunami within the institute.

Those institutes that have made use of group process were able to find improvement in their communication and understanding of their situation. Further work and education can help individuals and groups heal from the effect of an ethical violation and move beyond the dynamic of silencing. We must find our voices if we are to heal.

## Note

1  The ethics-violating analyst will be referred to as "he" throughout this chapter, as the greater number of reported violations occur between male clinicians and female patients (Rutter, 1989).

## References

Bion, W. R. (1961). *Experiences in groups*. New York: Basic Books.

Blasdel, B. (2010, April). Psychic fallout from ethical disturbances within an analytic institute: The creation of one analyst's ethical dilemmas. Paper presented at Division 39 Spring Meeting, Chicago.

Celenza, A. (2007). *Sexual boundary violations: Therapeutic, supervisory, and academic contexts*. Lanham, MD: Jason Aronson, Inc.

Celenza, A. (2010a). The analyst's need and desire. *Psychoanalytic Dialogues*, *20*, 60–69.

Celenza, A. (2010b). The guilty pleasure of erotic countertransference: Searching for radial true. *Studies in Gender and Sexuality*, *11*, 175–183.

Freud, S. (1909). Letter from Sigmund Freud to C. G. Jung, June 18, 1909. In W. McGuire (Ed.), *The Freud/Jung letters: The correspondence between Sigmund Freud and C. G. Jung* (pp. 234–235). Princeton, NJ: Princeton University Press.

Gabbard, G. O. (1995). The early history of boundary violations in psychoanalysis. *Journal of the American Psychoanalytic Association*, *43*, 1115–1136.

Gabbard, G. O. (1997). Discussion. *Psychoanalytic Inquiry*, *17*, 371–386.

Gabbard, G. O., & Peltz, M. L. (2001). Speaking the unspeakable: Institutional reactions to boundary violations by training analysts. *Journal of the American Psychoanalytic Association*, *49*, 659–673.

García, R. (Writer, Director) (2008). *Paul and Gina: Week one* [television series episode]. Los Angeles, CA: Paramount Studios.

Gerson, S. (2009). When the third is dead: Memory, mourning, and witnessing in the aftermath of the Holocaust. *International Journal of Psychoanalysis*, *90*, 1341–1357.

Godley, W. (2001). Saving Masud Khan. *London Review of Books*, February 22, 3–7.

Grosskurth, P. (1998). Psychoanalysis: A dysfunctional family? *Journal of Analytic Psychology*, *43*, 87–95.

Harris, A. (2011). Discussion of Robin Deutsch's "A voice lost, a voice found": After the death of the analyst. *Psychoanalytic Inquiry*, *31*, 536–542.

Harris, A. (2012). Regarding the uncanny. Unpublished manuscript.

Harris, A., & Sinsheimer, K. (2007). The analyst's vulnerability. In F. S. Anderson (Ed.), *Bodies in treatment: The unspoken dimension* (pp. 255–273). New York: Analytic Press.

Kernberg, O. F. (1986). Institutional problems of psychoanalytic education. *Journal of the American Psychoanalytic Association, 34*, 799–834.

Llopis-Salvan, N. (2008). Si l'analyste passe à l'acte [What happens when the analyst acts out?]. *International Journal of Psychoanalysis, 89*, 460–464.

Margolis, M. (1997). Analyst-patient sexual involvement: Clinical experiences and institutional responses. *Psychoanalytic Inquiry, 17*, 349–370.

Nicholsen, S. W. (2010). Too close to home: Countertransference dynamics in the wake of a colleague's sexual boundary violations. *Canadian Journal of Psychoanalysis, 18*, 225–247.

Ross, J. M. (1995). The fate of relatives and colleagues in the aftermath of boundary violations. *Journal of the American Psychoanalytic Association, 43*, 959–961.

Ruskin, R. (2011). Sexual boundary violations in a senior training analyst: Impact on the individual and psychoanalytic society. *Canadian Journal of Psychoanalysis, 19*, 87–106.

Rutter, P. (1989). *Sex in the forbidden zone: When men in power—therapists, doctors, clergy, teachers, and others—betray women's trust*. New York: Fawcett Crest.

Sandler, A., & Godley, W. (2004). Institutional responses to boundary violations: The case of Masud Khan. *International Journal of Psychoanalysis, 85*, 27–42.

Slochower, J. (2003). The analyst's secret delinquencies. *Psychoanalytic Dialogues, 13*, 451–469.

Villela, L. (2005). The chalice of silence and the case that refuses to go away. *Psychoanalytic Review, 92*, 807–828.

Wallace, E. (2007). Losing a training analyst for ethical violations: A candidate's perspective. *International Journal of Psychoanalysis, 88*, 1275–1288.

Wallace, E. (2010. Collateral damage: Long-term effects of losing a training analyst for ethical violations. *Canadian Journal of Psychoanalysis, 18*, 248–254.

# 11

# TROUBLE IN THE FAMILY

## The Impact of Sexual Boundary Violations in Analytic Institute Life

*Donna Fromberg*

In writing this chapter, I am trying to reckon with the impact of a senior analyst having sex with a patient. As a candidate and early career analyst, each time I receive news of an analyst's resignation due to claims of sexual misconduct, I feel dread. My heart stops and time slows down as I reread the stark one- or two-line email stating the person's name and announcing his resignation from institute membership and professional licensure. I feel unable to think. This dramatic response always puzzled me. The more I talk with my peers, my mentors, and my analyst, the more complex this question became. Why am I and everyone I know so upset? At the time, senior people are always empathic with my experience, but I never feel satisfied with what they have to say. Initially, my mind feels clouded and confused. Slowly, over the course of many conversations, my mind has cleared and brought me to writing this.

Since I began psychoanalytic training at the Boston Psychoanalytic Society and Institute (BPSI) in 2004, I have received three resignation emails from my institute; each analyst was a well-known, well-respected, and even revered supervisor and mentor, and all were men. I remember precisely my reaction to each email and exactly what I did. Just as I called my mother on 9/11, when someone resigns I immediately call peers. I want to share my shock. Knowing and deeply respecting the legal and privacy protocol that calls for silence, I nevertheless feel thirsty to find out as much as possible. This reaction puts me at odds with my better judgment, which is to let the leaders do their job and not to give in to the temptation to talk. I tell myself that what I am being told has nothing to do with me, knowing full well it does. Although I personally know none of the individuals involved in these resignations, taking in this news and experiencing the aftershocks affected my analytic development and my relationships with colleagues, teachers, and mentors. My journey processing, reviewing, and assigning meaning to why these events have shaken me so deeply is what this chapter is about. I am hoping that writing it will clarify why my analytic conviction and my sense of belonging in my institute are irreparably disrupted.

Of course, I am not alone in my response to an email with this news; there are after-effects throughout the institute. Never explicitly stated, each email communicates that a serious ethical violation has come to light—an analyst has had sex with a patient. The sudden shock, like an earthquake, sends out aftershocks for a long time to come—rumors in hallways and emails, discussions in classes and among peers—the time spent trying to make sense of what happened. In my cohort of six classmates, enormous amounts of time have been spent trying to process these resignations, grappling with questions of what happened and of how these breaches could have occurred. It seems to me our attempts to understand the impact of these boundary violations took up more time than reading Freud!

I sat down to put into writing what happened to me and my institute. What I discovered, in retrospect, was a long journey beginning with panic and fear, then a search for understanding and sense. A trusted colleague had broken a taboo. I wanted to know what had happened in detail, but realized that I never would. Even if I learned the facts, I would never know what had been in the minds of the perpetrator or victim. Whatever I learned would be unsatisfying, inconclusive. Whatever I came to understand about the institute, or myself, I also would need to find a way to live with the ambiguity of not knowing. I had both witnessed and been part of a catastrophe. People had been harmed, but I could not know what had led to the tragedy.

Sexual misconduct within my analytic community damaged my idealization of psychoanalysis and my conviction about its possibilities. Psychoanalysis is more than a professional or intellectual enterprise. The analytic endeavor involves all aspects of who we are —our past, present and future, our conscious and unconscious life, our emotional and intellectual life. Hearing that a member had sexual contact with a patient causes a crisis involving all dimensions of us as well. It is not simply problematic professionally—being and becoming a psychoanalyst is deeply personal. When there is sexual misconduct, I am deeply shaken.

In this narrative, I will explore the effects of sexual boundary violations on me as an individual, as a group member, and as a member of a profession I value deeply. In the first part of the chapter, I use personal and collegial examples of how these connections develop to highlight the nuances and complexities of the process that create these deep and enduring relationships. This bonding process, I argue, inhibits each member's ability to see clearly when confronted with troubling news about a colleague.

As part of my effort to make sense of these crises, I turned to psychoanalytic theory, and, as I relate in the second part of this chapter, I discovered that Bion's theories not only helped me begin to understand the fierce unconscious forces stirred up in groups, but also helped me frame my response to sexual misconduct. Bion's ideas, taken from his work with psychotherapy groups, illuminate what unconscious dynamics are at work in group members, how individuals identify with the group's mission, and what the consequences of that membership are on the individual's identity and intellectual functioning. Bion's constructs also provide a way to understand how stress within a group affects the subsequent functioning of the group and of each member. A severe rupture such as sexual misconduct, Bion's theories show, changes group functioning, the relationships between individuals, and the relationship of members to the group as a whole. These alterations caused by sexual misconduct affect one's faith in analysis and, as Bion helped me to see, influence the institute's ability to be of use to members during these times when members and trainees need the organization the most.

This chapter illustrates my journey to make sense of my reactions to sexual misconduct within my analytic community. What started out as shock and dread led to the process outlined here—a search for a frame to capture my experience. In the end, I am more certain what had happened to my institute and me. I also conclude the chapter considering how differences between male and female analysts and early career and later career analysts cope with these traumatic events. Then, given the insights I discovered, I outline some ways to smooth the impact of these ruptures on members and trainees.

## Joining and Belonging

In my process to uncover why these crises are so disruptive to me, I started thinking about the depth of my attachment to BPSI and psychoanalysis. Understanding this attachment quickly became a key to understanding parts of this disruption. The attachments to our institutes are deep and multifaceted. These ties illuminate to me why our profession has difficulty addressing sexual boundary violations in an ongoing way within our analytic community. With ties this deep, it is painful to imagine something as toxic as a sexual breach. Understanding how these connections form is critical to appreciating the depth and power of the effect of sexual misconduct on analytic development.

As within our families, our training institute becomes a place to which we pin many of our hopes and dreams. Our personal and professional growth takes place under its wings. We come to analytic training with aspirations, willing to make a tremendous commitment of time and money in order to meet spoken and unspoken wishes and ideals. Regardless of each person's motivations, members share a commitment to deep clinical work and self-knowledge. We explore and expose ourselves, growing within the context of our analytic home. Idealization and longing, both necessary for growth, start before we begin our analytic journey. For many, me included, a romance emerges. We want to be accepted and included. Because of the intense intimacy of the application and educational process, these familial transferences deepen. There are elders to guide us, our parents, those ahead of us in classes to model, and our cohort of analytic siblings for company. The training takes enormous time and deep relationships are built; four or five years of classes alongside the private discovery in our training analysis, and then the numerous personal relationships in supervision and mentoring. Although the same is true for a person wanting to join any group, I think psychoanalytic training evokes a particular passion because of the depth of both the personal and professional meaning.

This intensity begins with the application process, illustrated in the experience of a colleague. She began the process ambivalent about the investment of time and money that analytic training required. She also worried whether she could be a good analyst and if she would be accepted into the institute of her choice. Then, she felt fascinated and impressed to see the offices of the three established analysts who interviewed her. My colleague was full of fantasies about her own analytic office. What analytic couch would she purchase? How would she talk with her patients about becoming an analyst? As she interviewed, a transformation occurred: she became aware of her fear that she would not be accepted, and became more and more invested in starting the next fall. The application process left her enveloped in idealization of and positive transference with the institute. She longed to be part of an organization of people who valued thinking deeply and openly about the self and who were intellectually curious. In the meantime, her ambivalence about the investment of time and money vastly diminished. The intensity and excitement of her interviews made her long for acceptance. She wanted to be part of a group of smart, sensitive, and accomplished people, where she felt understood and listened to. Her analytic journey had begun. Whatever the history she brought from her life, by the end of the interview process she knew she wanted an analytic family. She wanted a seat at that family table; the beginning process had enticed her. Her sense of affiliation and idealization may, as I suggest here, turn out to be the same qualities that keep her from being able to identify problems that are divergent from her wish to see the institute and its members as beyond serious blemish.

During this process of induction, one is accepted to be part of the rich legacy of psychoanalysis; each candidate becomes the younger generation being guided by the elders. Becoming the younger generation of solid thinkers and clinicians is disrupted when a senior analyst is accused of sexual misconduct. The anxiety that emerges is reminiscent of Oedipal fears and wishes. A trusted senior member crosses a sexual boundary with someone under his care, very often a therapist generations behind him; all three victims at my institute were candidates or therapists. It feels as if incest has occurred, especially to the younger generation of trainees, and, as with incest, it feels as if this violation cannot be acknowledged, processed, or talked about.

The perception of lack of transparency and elusive decision making further complicates the feeling these "taboo" subjects cannot be spoken about openly. In our idealizing state, this mysteriousness is either overlooked or accepted as private. I believe this vagueness about how the organization operates can communicate a "keep out" sign when it comes to disturbing events. It starts with how we open ourselves up from the application process without knowing what criteria are required or how selections are made. What personal or professional qualities make a good analyst? There are inherent judgments made on admissions committees about our character and future potential. Further, these individuals are on other committees and will be our teachers and supervisors if we are accepted. Many will remember us from the admissions process. While we can find out who is on the admissions committee, we can be left feeling that we are known in ways we do not know about. For some, this feels protective and warm; for others, it can breed suspicion. Further, our analysts are close friends and colleagues of our teachers and mentors. Whether or not there is acknowledgment or communication about these private relationships, it is very provocative to candidates and adds to the perception of secrecy and lack of transparency. We live with this sense of mystery—some more bothered by it than others—but it adds to the strain and anxiety when a member is accused of sexual misconduct. Sex with a patient always starts with a secret—what other secrets are there?

The training analyst (TA) system, a group within the group, exemplifies the mysteriousness of how psychoanalytic institutes work. The training analyst group members, most often the leaders and the majority of the main decision-making body, are like parents—our analytic future lies in their hands. They guide us in supervision, mentoring, and teaching. They evaluate our suitability to be analysts, decide the rate of progression, and the time for graduation. Initially, I felt shy and deferential. Questioning the authority or judgments of the TA group would be like challenging my parents. After a boundary has been crossed, however, the perceived secrecy of the training analyst group feels alienating. The brevity of the initial communication of a resignation makes me wonder what they are doing and how injured they are. As with my parents, I want to imagine all is well with them and they know what to do in times of crisis.

The mysteries about the TA system and admission criteria evoked a positive, familial transference in me. I felt taken care of left in this nurturing, warm, and receptive environment. I wanted to shine and be known. For other candidates, of course, the experience is different; the mysteries cause suspicion and uncertainty. Either way, the vulnerability in the face of professional advancement is agonizing. Many, including me, feel opened up and exposed. The perception, at least, of a solid and secure base is essential for the vulnerability to be growth-promoting. When a leader commits a heinous abuse of power, I feel that necessary base eroding. The foundation I relied on is disrupted. Trust is breached. It is painful and confusing.

Our investments are tremendous, and our options for advancement are often limited to other analysts for referrals, teaching, and consultation. This furthers our reluctance to see difficulties—one's career and livelihood are at issue. Fear of not being liked or respected can keep us from seeing or speaking up about smaller boundary issues such as lateness or a teacher's not seeming prepared. It is unusual to take steps for specialized training and then remain so reliant on that same group of individuals for professional advancement. In a job, if you are not excelling or getting along with your employer, you can look for employment elsewhere. In contrast, most cities have only one analytic institute. Even if you are lucky enough to live in a city with two or three, there is always cross-fertilization. Analysts teach and supervise at one another's institutes. This is another reason why when there is an ethical breach we are all affected, and some of us traumatized; we represent analysis to each other and to the wider world.

When there is an incident of sexual misconduct, I look around me and imagine who knows what and who is trustworthy. The cohesiveness I felt in the group—the safe, open, and holding feeling—is gone. In its place, there is strain and uncertainty. Faculty look stressed; there are myriad questions but few answers. The mysterious dynamics of the leadership group and TA system that felt peacefully in the background now loom large. The undercurrents and complexities of these dynamics now feel like a foreshadowing of the deep unquiet that fills the halls. Just as there is intimacy among my cohort, there is intimacy among the leadership group as well, inviting further fantasy. Questions swirl in my head as I look to see who my analyst is sitting with at lectures and meetings. My curiosity about these relationships is acutely stirred under times of deep stress. The events that led to this person's resignation provoke in me deep and alarming anxiety. I realize the depth of my connection to the institution and my mentors, supervisors, and colleagues. I seek out steady connection and reassurance. It is just then when I feel dumbstruck, confused, and in need of help that I feel most alienated.

## Bion's Constructs: Basic Assumption and Work Group

Reading Bion was an integral part of my metabolization of these events at my institute. His description of group functioning, which I read in the aftermath of the reports of sexual misconduct, helped me understand why institutional fallout is traumatic to members.

Bion (1961) states, "The individual is, and always has been, a member of a group, even if his membership to it consists of behaving in such a way that reality is given to an idea that he does not belong to a group at all" (p. 168). We are born into some groupings, such as our families, and others we chose, including our analytic training site, our professional home. Membership, Bion believed, requires ongoing work: "The adult must establish contact with the emotional life of the group in which he lives; this task would appear to be as formidable to the adult as the relationship with the breast appears to be to the infant" (p. 141). Like the infant with the breast, the relationship between the group and the individual requires ongoing negotiation and adjustment, a mutual accommodation. During the admissions process, for example, the tone of voices on the telephone, the ease or difficulty of scheduling interview appointments, and interactions with the institute are all subtle reciprocal influences that help shape thoughts and behaviors that are acceptable within the institute's culture.

According to Bion, there are two elements of functioning within all groups; he calls them the work group and the basic assumption group. The work group is that aspect of group functioning that has to do with the primary task of the group: group goals and mission. The work group is "geared to a task . . . related to reality, [and its] methods are rational. Its characteristics are similar to those attributed by Freud to the ego" (p. 143). A well-functioning work group cooperates in creating a structure designed to facilitate the mission of its members.

The basic assumption group, in contrast, describes the unconscious assumptions of group behavior. Like all unconscious functioning, basic assumption functioning operates outside the awareness of group members, occurs spontaneously, and is present at all times. Bion identified three types of basic assumption groups: dependency, fight/flight, and pairing. In the dependency group assumption, members search for a leader hoping that the leader will omnipotently gratify group members by relieving them of anxiety. In the fight/flight group, members come together in order to fight or run away from a frightening threat. In the pairing group, there is a coupling of members, in the hope of creating something in the future that will magically "save" members.

Ideally, the work group enables stable work and efficiency from its members and keeps basic assumptions from distracting from the work of the group. However, during a crisis of the magnitude of sexual misconduct of a group member, individual members are flooded with affects such as panic, fear, and sadness. The intensity of this affect disrupts the work group's functioning, and basic assumption thinking comes to the forefront. When this happens, the group acts as a closed system that ignores external realities and is preoccupied with unconscious collective dynamics. This is similar to when an individual's ego is overwhelmed and unconscious material rises to the surface and thwarts logical thought. Correspondingly, groups can also lose sight of rational and creative work when the work group is overcome with affect.

Reading Bion helped me understand that when a senior analyst resigns, the work group is disabled under the stress. Noticeable changes in the functioning of the institute, like no further comments after the original email and the whispering voices in hallways, reflect those alterations in the work group.

These alterations felt abandoning and confusing and, I think, caused me to have difficulty thinking freely and logically. Sexual transgressions, particularly by a senior analyst, stimulate primitive anxiety. The ensuing near silence after the announcement creates a whirlwind of powerful, overwhelming, and frightening affects. Without leadership to help members deal with the powerful affects that are stirred up, members are at a loss. The absence of active leadership creates an emotional tsunami within the organization. The trauma is twofold: the violation itself *and* what's stirred up and goes undigested within the group.

At other times when there is a problem, the institute responds by offering perspectives or forums for discussion. With a resignation, there is little or no immediate follow-up. In a rush to discuss with peers what has happened and how such an event could have occurred, rational and organized responses seem impossible. The devolution of the work group's structure disrupts the capacity for constructive thinking within the organization, and individual members lose the structure that helps them keep contact with the group. When sexual misconduct occurs, the process of mutual accommodation is disrupted and has to be renegotiated in light of the new information. In retrospect, I think turning to others was an attempt to re-contact reality and restore healthy thinking; in other words, turning away from the devolving work group and using other smaller structures of trusted friends and colleagues kept basic assumption thinking from coming to the foreground.

In helping me understand why it was hard for me to think rationally during these crises, Bion helped me *to think*. I had temporarily lost my work group, which was my link to reality-focused thinking. As Bion's work helped me to understand what was happening in the work group, I could feel empathy for the group. This empathy increased my interest in moving back toward the group; as opposed to feeling mistrustful, I could feel more engaged.

## The Personal

After receiving a resignation email, I withdraw into myself and small groups to reconstitute. Turning to my analyst, peers and supervisors, I am anxious and overwrought. A sickening accusation has been made. Something deep in me is stirred. It is primitive anxiety, Bion (1961) recognizes, that can "compel individuals to seek allies" (p. 163) to try to become a healthy thinking group again and return to reality. Closer and smaller groups also help me to dilute and assuage my fears. I am afraid the institute could disintegrate and no longer be available to nourish me professionally and personally—that its positive reputation is tarnished, which will hurt me professionally. These smaller groups of friends and mentors reestablish a sense of belonging in case the larger group collapses. Further, these smaller groups help create meaning out of the chaos. Now I understand this better, but back then I was not able to think.

To me, this crisis also means secrets—or what feel like secrets. There is information that would help me to know, but I cannot be told due to legal and privacy protocols. Sex with a patient must be involved, but another side of me wishes maybe not. Whatever happened must be egregious enough to incinerate a reputation and career. Were the victims colleagues, women I've seen around the institute, as is often the case?

I worry if the leadership group is functioning. I imagine its members must be in crisis, too. In many ways, they must feel more disturbed than me. This is a colleague and perhaps a friend, classmate, or collaborator. This must be crushing news to them. Surely, there are some in the group more attached to this person than others. Some may never have liked him. No matter what, there might be disagreement—those who believe the rumors and those who do not. In imagining this, I think they must feel deeply unsettled. In Bion's terms, the work structure is weakened, everyone's anxiety is high, and basic assumptions proliferate. People are in small groups, and there are heated debates grappling with how sex with patients can happen.

I am conflicted about my "need" to know and what I imagine is best for my institute, waiting patiently for the leadership to respond. I am eager for help from the leadership, on the one hand, yet mistrustful of their judgment, on the other. If things like this happen under the watch of senior people, can the same people be trusted to handle the crisis? The leadership is supposed to know more than I do, but it feels dangerous and selfish to ask questions. When I do speak to supervisors and mentors, can they tell me anything? I imagine by talking to them I am putting them in an uncomfortable position. I feel kept out, as if I were not mature enough to know about such things. On the one hand, I am not part of the decision-making group, so my wish to know what they are doing is irrational. On the other hand, I want help, feel demanding of help, but I feel pressure to keep my needs to myself to protect the "adults." I should burden them no further. I should make myself scarce.

Many conversations among my peers are about how an analyst can possibly have sex with a patient; how can an analyst let sex with a patient happen? There are heated debates. I distill the argument into two sides. The first is a model of pathology: there must be something wrong with this person to have violated the code of ethics by defying the implicit and explicit agreement for no sexual contact between our patients and us. There must be a character problem. If someone had a "good-enough" analysis, how could this happen? I feel an intense and abrupt crushing anxiety and sadness as my idealization of psychoanalysis plummets.

The alternate explanation: we are all susceptible. Perhaps any analyst or therapist, no matter how highly trained or analyzed, can make a mistake of this magnitude. If there is a convergence of extreme stressors—loss, illness, divorce, death—everyone becomes vulnerable. No one is immune from a sexual breach. If this theory is true, how do we then protect ourselves, as individuals or as part of the group? Essential questions for me are these: What is the patient's protection? What is our protection as both patients and analysts?

In the end, I am not satisfied with either explanation. In the first theory, a person susceptible to committing a boundary violation is endorsed by the organization. He passed muster but ended up abusing someone. Maybe no one was watching, or no one had the courage to speak up against another group member before the worst happened. No one wanted to spoil the group's harmony. In the other theory, if the conditions are right, then none of us has enough control over ourselves to resist sexually exploiting a patient. We are supposed to be experts on instincts and urges, but ours could be out of control at any time, if circumstances are right. Either way, by not openly and regularly facing the fact of analysts' vulnerabilities, we all deny their existence.

My candidate group is divided along gender lines. More men think that everyone is vulnerable, and more women believe only certain character styles are at risk. I find this difference very interesting, but see no reference to this idea in the literature. I wonder if women are less likely to exploit a patient because of the long history of exploitive acts against women. Perhaps men, who have not been the target of as many exploitive experiences, are more empathic toward someone whose drives have gone awry?

In the end, I need a break from the visceral chill. The adult professional in me wants to know about procedures and protocols. In Bion's terms, I want the work group to do something to make me feel safe. Perhaps this is dependency basic assumption thinking, wishing a leader could help me feel safe. I want relief from this collective anxiety. We know these crises have been with us since the beginning of psychoanalysis, but what have we learned about what to do or why they happen? I long for the organization to resume functioning and assist me in organizing my thinking and bring me back to logic and reality.

## Conclusion

Freud wrote in 1915, "The analyst must never under any circumstances accept or return the tender feelings that are offered to him" (p. 163), and, later, "Treatment must be carried out in abstinence" (p. 165). The psychoanalytic legacy is passed along from one generation to the next, a history of thoughtful, deep clinical work and elegant theory. But our legacy also includes the breaking of promises to our patients and each other. Thus, repercussions of sexual boundary crossings run deep within our psychoanalytic history.

As a candidate and early career analyst, sexual misconduct within my institute impacted my analytic development, damaging my trust in the analytic community, tarnishing my idealistic hopes for a safe and open professional community. De-idealization of psychoanalysis and my institute was painful and caused me to feel lost. Could my institute continue to be at the center of my professional life? Could I still believe in it, endorse it, and teach others about analytic theory and technique?

I think my disenchantment was stimulated early, while my love for analysis was still vulnerable and unsteady. Since I have been able to think, I have realized how fragile my conviction about psychoanalysis was then. Perhaps, further along in my career, I would not have been so dismayed and distrustful. I would have had the experience of knowing analysis—good analysis—continues on despite these tragic missteps. Perhaps for those further along in their careers, the misconduct feels more like a tragedy for their colleague or analysis itself, rather than a threat to their conviction about psychoanalysis. They have long personal relationships with each other and have to stand and watch the tragic loss of a colleague's good standing—or, worse, wish they had done something sooner if they sensed a vulnerability that could have contributed to their colleague's ethical violation. Whether early in one's analytic career or later, sexual misconduct, proven or not, affects our relationship to psychoanalysis by disrupting our trust and altering how the group functions.

Psychoanalysis' history of not dealing openly with the problem of sexual misconduct exacerbates the systemic trauma. At my institute, ghosts are present when we are confronted by these unwanted truths. In the aftermath of a resignation, I often hear comments alluding to how things had been handled in previous cases, particularly certain members being dissatisfied about their outcomes. This is used as an explanation when someone takes a more harsh or rigid perspective. Candidates are usually ignorant of the ghosts that haunt these discussions, and this adds to the trainee's confusion.

The trauma is further exacerbated because the group lacks a language to talk openly about the consequences of a member having sex with a patient. In the absence of an ongoing way of speaking to each other about less disturbing boundary issues, it is all the more difficult to address violations of this magnitude. This adds to the sense that the work group has devolved and cannot be of use to members. An attempt at a response is better than silence. In such a stressed community, the jumbled reaction further traumatizes its members.

Here is the argument for something different: an ongoing and open conversation about the difficult legacy of sexual misconduct in psychoanalysis. I propose—and I have heard others suggest—an ongoing dialogue beginning early in candidate training about the history of sexual exploitation of patients in psychoanalysis. Like sexual harassment training in business and industry, exposing trainees and members to the language of boundary crossings and violations communicates an openness that frees individuals up to address both subtle and significant boundary problems that inevitably come up. Perhaps ongoing conversation and education about sexual misconduct will help keep, in Bion's terms, the work group organized, and thereby keep basic assumptions from interfering with reality-based thinking. This would lessen the stress to members and help keep members engaged in the work group, thinking logically and rationally about what to do.

I am left with the question of how to continue, how to live within my institute's walls. It seems too simple to say that, like in our family, we have to de-idealize our parents, accept them for who they are as people, with all their faults—and mourn our loss of idealization. This acceptance is too easy an abbreviation for what actually happens. When there is sexual misconduct in psychoanalysis, we face a moral problem that involves the deepest of human frailties—the capacity to exploit another human being, even when the explicit task of analysis prohibits the analyst from acting on his desires.

Feeling as if I had lost the work group, the system I had been relying on, I was able to use my colleagues, mentors, analyst, and the clinical work itself to hold myself steady through my worry and anxiety. By using these relationships, I found my way to a more secure psychoanalytic conviction. Writing this chapter also helped, although it was not an easy process. My thoughts have been jumbled and my passions ignited. In remembering how my institute was threatened by sexual misconduct by analysts, I relived the devastation and trauma—for everyone in the analytic community. But, through my confusion during this process, it is the same theory that got psychoanalysts into trouble that has helped me out of it. It offers understanding and a frame for what happened to my institute and me. Reading Bion, thinking analytically about my institute and myself, and writing this chapter takes me full circle, back to my love for psychoanalysis.

The challenge is living with the conflict between the love of analysis and the harm it can do when there is sexual misconduct. I love analysis—it is beautiful, elegant, and poetic. It captures an aliveness about human experience that few other theories or practices capture. Although we may wish to only look at the beauties of the theory and the work at its best, our task as practicing analysts and therapists requires us to take responsibility for all aspects, both the good and the bad. We need to educate our trainees, speak openly when a colleague seems to be at risk, or has a troublingly loose therapeutic frame. Our very human tendency to not think about the taboo is deeply powerful. However, looking at what is difficult is emancipating in its own right, and includes the benefit of developing a language to speak when there is silence. Working to create a climate where all trainees and analysts can openly name subtle and significant boundary crossings will make it easier for us all to speak and question each other when these issues come up. Habituating to discussing this painful and embarrassing topic fights against our trouble identifying when something is wrong. Instead of regressing to Bion's basic assumption thinking, we might be better able to stay within the work group, salvage more of its functioning, and support the victim and ourselves in our analytic work. It is only then that we can have a home where the unspeakable becomes speakable and the beauty is not tarnished by the foul.

## References

Bion, W. R. (1961). *Experiences in groups*. London: Tavistock.
Freud, S. (1915). Observations on transference love. In J. Strachey (Ed. & Trans.), *The complete psychological works of Sigmund Freud* (vol. 12, pp. 159–171). London: Hogarth Press.

# 12

# TRAUMA AS A WAY OF LIFE IN A PSYCHOANALYTIC INSTITUTE

*Charles Levin*

> While we cannot change the history of psychoanalysis, we *can* study it. Family secrets can be brought out into the light of day and examined instead of being reenacted from one generation to the next.
> Gabbard (1999, p. 218; cited in Levine, 2010b, p. 49)

There is a small but cogent literature related to what Kernberg (1986) has provocatively described as "an illness affecting the educational structures of psychoanalytic institutes and societies" (p. 814). This literature addresses "nonfunctional" features in the governance of the psychoanalytic profession, with particular emphasis on the tensions and contradictions of the standard "training system" and some of its variants (e.g., Reeder, 2004). Like the majority of contributors to this literature, Kernberg has identified the authoritarian structures and practices of training institutes and psychoanalytic societies as a major source of the "illness" he diagnoses.

Wider recognition of problems in the training system arose gradually, in piecemeal fashion, then gathered steam concurrently with other literature on the politically more sensitive issue of sexual boundary violations (Gabbard & Lester, 1995), including detailed descriptions of catastrophic circumstances in specific psychoanalytic centers (e.g., Boston: Levine, 2010a; Toronto: Ruskin, 2011). The sounding of the alarm on boundary violations within the profession had a practical impact in the form of increased institutional attention, the development of ethical codes and committees, and important research (Celenza, 2007). Yet with some notable exceptions, especially Dimen (2011), the connection between sexual boundary violations—the "primal crime" (p. 72)—and what Kernberg calls the institutional "illness" of psychoanalysis has not been explored in any great depth. (Levine, 2010b, uses the highly appropriate term "narcissistic boundary violations," but this concept needs further development.)

The emergence of these two important, if still marginal, discourses parallels the rise of a third very significant—and closely related—question for psychoanalysis: the issue of trauma, which has resurfaced dramatically since the publication of the complete archive of the Freud–Fliess correspondence (Masson, 1985). The topic of trauma lay largely dormant within psychoanalysis after Freud's retraction of the seduction theory. As Bohleber (2010) has suggested, the historical trajectory of psychoanalytic ideas about trauma, or lack of them, is indicative of a pervasive "identity crisis."

In the reflections to follow, I wish to explore the underlying connection between these three significant problem areas in the psychoanalytic profession:

1  difficulties in the governance and transmission of psychoanalysis
2  the slipperiness of psychoanalytic ethics
3  the relation of the profession to the psychological conundrum of trauma.

I shall argue that there is a household logic involved. The deadening in psychoanalytic thought of attention to traumatic rupture as a relational phenomenon has allowed the profession, until recently, to continue splitting off and disavowing the trauma of its own institutional life. Everyone connected to the psychoanalytic community suffers from this crippling dissociative process in one way or another, but on the professional side it is the candidates who are affected the most (Wallace, 2007). Their psychological abuse by the training analyst system constitutes the greatest loss to the future of psychoanalysis, with all its varied potential to contribute to human welfare.

My method in presenting this argument will be somewhat unconventional. While attempting to integrate the relevant literature as much as possible, I will focus intensively on a particular case—namely, my own career trajectory within the psychoanalytic profession in a culturally unique location, the bilingual French-English psychoanalytic culture of Montreal in North America.

It would not be an exaggeration to say that my analytic career began in childhood. It continued through a series of traumatic experiences, including: the rupture in adolescence, and repair in early adulthood, of my relationship with my father, who was a psychoanalyst; the split between the English and French psychoanalytic groups in 1967; my father's premature death and the commencement of my own psychoanalytic training in the mid-1980s, when I was in my early thirties; my early career and eventual decision to become a training analyst; and the traumatic sequelae of that decision. In the course of my narrative, I will touch in a personal way on a variety of interrelated factors that are difficult to synthesize in theory: the role of personality and contingency in the choice of an analytic career; the reactionary identifications that are often bundled into the decision to become an analyst (and to go on being an analyst); and the emotional and existential dilemmas entailed by psychoanalytic practice and identity—tensions between freedom and servitude, surrender and submission (Ghent, 1990), life and death.

To go on being a psychoanalyst, one must be willing to undertake and endure the constant questioning, if not scrambling, of one's own basic orientational dimensions in time, space, personal intimacy, and social connection. To become a psychoanalyst involves a significant personal risk, with serious emotional consequences. But we do not take very good care of ourselves as a group. The tragic failure of our profession is that we have tended to institutionalize defensive denial of traumatic rupture through a form of collective projective identification. It is as if we are in constant "fear of breakdown" (Winnicott, 1974); the disaster has already happened, but we anxiously reimagine it as the future of psychoanalysis—the "future of a disillusion" (Scarfone, 2000)—namely, the next generation of analysts, the training process and its victims. In envy of their naïveté and idealism about psychoanalysis, we displace onto our candidates not only the misery of our own training experience, but also the anguish of struggling, day after day, with our unconscious hatred of psychoanalysis itself and the transference (Mauger & Monette, 1999).

## Preliminary Reflections on the Concept of Institutional Illness

In his diagnosis of institutional illness, Kernberg (1986) emphasizes two factors: In addition to the structural and functional problems mentioned earlier, he proposes the idea of "radioactive fallout" from the psychoanalytic process itself. He points out that there is a problem unique to psychoanalysis, which lies in:

> [T]he nature of the product handled in psychoanalytic institutes, namely, *the uncovering of the unconscious*, in the context of the institutional boundaries of the psychoanalytic institute, and the particular effects of this operation on candidates and training analysts alike ... [O]ne might say that *the therapeutic process of psychoanalysis liberates radioactive products* and the dispersal of this radioactive fallout, which ordinarily occurs in psychoanalytic treatment carried out in an open social setting, is interfered with by the constraining and amplifying effects of the closed environment of psychoanalytic institutions.
>
> (p. 814; emphasis added)

My approach will put a slightly different spin on this important issue. In contrast to Kernberg's formulation, which I take as broadly representative, I would like to question the implication that the institutional problem peculiar to psychoanalysis can be traced to the radiating effects of the candidate's analysis, or the candidate's transference. No one disputes that analysis is a highly unusual procedure for any social group to contain, especially when combined with the "closed environment of psychoanalytic institutions." But Kernberg's metaphor of toxic radiation fallout suggests a questionable logic of quarantine, of segregation and mutual insulation. While cordoning off the candidate's analysis makes some sense in terms of protecting candidates from the threat of institute power and politics, as Kernberg intended, it also plays into a tendency within the profession to view candidates as anomalous creatures whose status is peculiar and unresolved (Wallace, 2007).

I shall argue that the illness Kernberg and others have identified is rooted not in the general fact that every analyst undergoes personal or training analysis, but rather in the persistence of a certain kind of transference toward the candidate. Especially through the vested authority of institutes, the psychoanalytic community tends to collude with a paranoid attitude toward candidates and young graduates. In my closing discussion, I will suggest that this unfortunate aspect of the traditional ethos of the analytic profession is rooted in a proprietary ideology that can be traced back to Freud's original "inner circle" and the earliest formalizations of training procedures. In this fantasy, or training ideology, the applicant for psychoanalytic training is viewed as a questionable claimant to the grand psychoanalytic legacy. This view is supported by a discourse in which there is an implicit false equation between the concept of "analyzability," or "having been analyzed," and the judgment whether someone is behaving in a manner appropriate for the analytic profession. When candidates create a disturbance, or members question conventions, it is more or less automatically assumed that they have not been sufficiently analyzed. If there is conflict in the group (community), this is attributed to incomplete analysis and unresolved transference. These habits of explanation seriously distort the social reality of the field, but they are like junk food for analysts—easy to swallow and pass around. They provide a convenient way of evading the possibility that the group itself might have an "illness" that precedes anybody's particular analysis.

One of the liabilities of psychoanalytic discussions is the tendency, still prevalent, to rely on a hypostatized model of the individual unconscious. This encourages us to locate the "radioactive products" in the "unconscious" of the candidate. The implication is that these "products" are being "liberated" and "dispersed" for the first time by the training analysis. Although not entirely inaccurate, this way of looking at the problem has the disadvantage of minimizing the ongoing element of trauma in psychoanalytic life, and of closing off or evading the question of its unconscious and enigmatic transmission—its "secret history" (Faimberg, 1988)—from one generation of analysts to the next.

Our current approach to this problem also tends, in my view, to reproduce without questioning the cultural misrecognitions of a self-serving perspective on psychosexual development—the version of Oedipus that begins on the road to Thebes, skipping over the paranoid infanticidal crisis in which a child is mutilated and abandoned for dead by the parents. In contrast to the institutionalized bias of the psychoanalytic version of Oedipus, we need to consider the possibility that the "radioactive products" identified by Kernberg do not originate in the mythic Oedipal child, or in her training analysis, but rather in what is predicted and fantasized, in a paranoid way by the analytic community, about her future behavior. I am referring to the perpetuation of a patriarchal system that, at best, sublimates its murderous desire to destroy the candidate's creativity (Kernberg, 1996).

The following "case history" provides material for discussion of these issues. My aim in telling this story is to not criticize any individual, or to provide a historical record of real events, but rather to sketch my impressions of a group atmosphere and its key components, and how they are detrimental to psychoanalytic education. The purpose of my narrative is to contribute to our ongoing self-examination concerning matters of governance, ethics, training, and community life. My story is not an indictment of any of the individuals involved, except perhaps myself. It is an attempt to portray the "institutional illness" in which I have played a part. I try to achieve this by evoking two kinds of complex psychosocial process: the installation of paranoid forms of relating as the norm in the psychoanalytic group; and the way in which common, malignant dynamics are favored by authoritarian institutional structures, notably the training analyst system, resulting in massive collective trauma, rupture, and dissociation.

## A Psychoanalytic Lifeworld

The relevance of the circumstances described below for other analytic communities will have to be judged by them. What follows are situations that developed in the particular context of Canadian psychoanalysis, which was heavily conditioned not only by American, but also British and French, psychoanalytic traditions of theory, practice, and organizational style. The relative independence of the Canadian Psychoanalytic Society (CPS) from the American Psychoanalytic Association (APsaA) made it possible for someone like me, with no clinical background, to be accepted for analytic training in the mid-1980s. Although the CPS still greatly over-favored applicants with medical degrees, even to the disadvantage of registered psychologists, it did not feel bound by the IPA agreement to tolerate a medical monopoly on psychoanalysis in the US. This monopoly was finally broken in 1989 (Appel, 2004) with the out-of-court settlement of an antitrust suit brought against the APsaA and the IPA. However, the fact that the CPS had been marginally more liberal in its admission policies, thus avoiding any serious legal challenges, had one very damaging consequence: The Canadian Psychoanalytic Society was never seriously forced to reexamine its institutional structures, or the conservative nature of its training programs, which remained essentially as they had been in the United States prior to the 1989 settlement. In the United States, the controversy around the medicalization of psychoanalysis opened up a lively and creative period of democratic reform in many parts of the country. In Canada, however, apart from getting rid of the practice of "reporting analysis," the mid-century status quo of the so-called "golden years" remained largely unchallenged in Canada.

The Canadian Institute of Psychoanalysis (CIP) is a national organization consisting exclusively of training analysts, with quasi-autonomous branches in all major population centers. The details of the training program requirements and curriculum in each branch are determined at the local level, in broad conformity with the Berlin (Eitingon) model. Among other things, the Berlin model stipulates that all training analyses, and all supervised "control" cases, must be conducted at a minimum rate of four times a week. Moreover, the analysis of the candidate will be recognized by the institute only if it has been conducted by a member of the CIP, in other words, a "training analyst."

In Montreal, however, there are not one but two IPA-affiliated CPS branches, one English speaking, and the other French. The French-speaking institute, although housed under the same roof in Montreal (also the headquarters of the National Society and Institute), operates according to a different set of IPA rules, one that prevails primarily in France. This "French model" of psychoanalytic training stipulates a minimum of three times a week and recognizes analysis with non-training analysts, thus allowing candidates to remain with their original analysts during their training.

The coexistence of the English and French societies and institutes has constituted, in my experience, one of the major saving graces of psychoanalysis in Canada. The two linguistic groups have been forced by their differences and conflicts to find ways to get along with one another institutionally, in spite of their radical differences. To the extent that the two linguistic groups have succeeded in sharing ideological and social space, this cross-fertilization has fostered creativity in each group. More specifically, for the English group in Montreal, the overlapping but contrasting legitimacy of the French group has provided a desperately needed safety valve, and also a needed container for the paranoia of the English group.

English-speaking psychoanalytic institutions in Montreal are in many ways a reflection of the decline of Anglo-American cultural dominance in that city. In the late 1960s, during what is known as the "Quiet Revolution" in the province of Quebec, French analysts, many of whom were trained in France, asserted their independence from the predominantly American model of the CPS. A few years later, with the election of a "separatist" provincial government in 1976, hundreds of thousands of English-speaking Montrealers emigrated westward, primarily to Toronto, where the younger offshoot of the original, Montreal-based CPS was growing rapidly. There was a kind of Anglo "brain drain," which decimated the medical community, and left English-speaking psychoanalysis in Montreal in a state of paranoid insecurity at the professional level. While the medical school at McGill University retained its national and international prestige, the political and economic climate became increasingly unfavorable to psychiatric residents, who might otherwise have stayed and considered psychoanalytic training.

The English-speaking training institute in Montreal nevertheless retained unusual political and economic power within the CPS and the CIP. Since this institute was the direct descendant of the founding group in Canadian psychoanalysis, it had acquired substantial financial holdings, and was incorporated in a way that gave its members, a small group of training analysts, absolute legal autonomy to conduct themselves as they wished, completely insulated from the governance of the Psychoanalytic Society. The institute did not shrink from the full exercise of this absolute power, and resisted every attempt at institutional reform. During the early 1990s, for example, officers of the Society discovered that the Institute was not bothering to take advantage of higher interest rates on its holdings; it was also alleged that revenue sharing between the two groups was inequitable. At first, it seemed that the Society might have gained the upper hand, but the outcome of the scandal was discouraging for the membership at large. The Society's advice about investment placements was followed, and there were a few adjustments in the way revenues were distributed between the Institute and the Society, but the basic challenge to the institute's junta-like power was quashed. The individuals who did the work of exposing the financial problems were vilified and marginalized in various ways. The institute remained safely ensconced behind its legal stonewall, smugly self-satisfied and supreme.

When I eventually became a training analyst, the institute was a remnant of what it once had been. Several major independent figures had retired or died. As I sat for the first time around the boardroom table with this august group, I realized with confusion and horror that nearly every single individual at the table had been analyzed by one man. Dr. Fish, as I shall call him, was, of course, himself sitting at the table. It was he who had, during my training years, conducted the second of my three analyses. Of the individuals who comprised the institute, ruling as the gatekeepers of the entire psychoanalytic community, only one had not been in analysis with him (apart from himself). She had transferred to our institute from another city, making her the only active woman training analyst in English Montreal at that time.

I was struck by another possibility, which had been the subject of rumor: some of the training analysts sitting around the table might still be in treatment with Dr. Fish. The way that some of them watched with rapt attention as he delivered his rambling perorations seemed to confirm this. They had been with him before I started with him, and they had continued with him many years after we had concluded. In addition to this, so far as I knew, I was one of only very few of his former analysands sitting around the table who had had any other experience of personal analysis. One colleague had previously been in analysis with Dr. Bienveillant, which we had discovered at his funeral in the late 1980s.

Dr. Bienveillant, my first analyst, was affiliated with the neighboring French-speaking institute. He was for me a caring, sensitive, and creative man who helped me enormously in my twenties and early thirties, when I was in danger of not having much of a livable life. Years later, before I became a training analyst, I had a third experience of analysis that was ultimately more satisfying. But my early, pre-training experience with Dr. Bienveillant has remained precious to me, perhaps because it occurred at such a crucial time in my life. I learned more from him about the value of psychoanalysis than I did from all my official training, though I was lucky enough to have three excellent supervisors.

Unfortunately, it turned out that Dr. Bienveillant had some personal problems, which were disruptive of my analysis with him and my own development. In his mid-forties, after I had been working with him for a few years, he suffered and survived life-threatening cancer, and married a former patient (a psychoanalyst who had been a candidate) following a messy divorce. He died 10 years later. During the period of his painful decline, which was filled with a great deal of manic creativity, but also increasing professional ostracism, my analysis with him devolved from the couch to a once-weekly face-to-face meeting, probably heading toward hiatus or termination. At this point, we were essentially discussing my wish to become a psychoanalyst. Tragically, as I was taking my first steps toward training, my beloved father suddenly died. Dr. Bienveillant then called me to an urgent meeting and told me that he wished to terminate the treatment with me. He said that I no longer needed him as an analyst and that now we were colleagues. More shocking, he told me that he had originally agreed to see me (although my finances were limited) as a favor to my father, who had treated him during a period of crisis, when he had begun to feel isolated and misunderstood in the French analytic community.

A year or so later, when I began with Dr. Fish, I was preparing my application to the institute. I went to Dr. Fish on recommendations that were partly a misunderstanding. He was the institute director at the time, and when people had told me that I should "see" him, what they had meant was that I should have a meeting with him as director. I had thought they meant that I should go into analysis with him. I was very naïve at the time.

Once we began, I realized quickly that I had made a terrible mistake. Dr. Fish may have been an effective analyst for others—I do not entirely doubt this, but he was unsuitable for me. One of the first things he told me was that he did not tolerate politically "unreasonable" people on his couch, because they tend to be unanalyzable. The example he gave me was of a woman who was involved in the anti-nuclear-weapons movement. When she insisted on this, they got into an argument, and he kicked her out of analysis. Dr. Fish espoused an ethic of aggressive "honesty" similar to the one ascribed to Dr. Schiffer in Toronto by Masson (1990).

Early in the analysis, on the first day of the week, and just before getting on the couch, as I entered the room, I said, "I hope you had a pleasant weekend." Dr. Fish immediately stopped me in my tracks, and in a withering tone of reproach, he stated that he would not tolerate my addressing him in a familiar tone. He underlined this in very forceful terms: "If you think that I will put up with . . ." and so on. I was humiliated, and never did have a chance to explore the unconscious meaning of my no doubt problematic greeting.

Analysis with Dr. Fish was a continuously embarrassing process, during which I believe that I was dissociated and chronically depersonalized. We were in constant disagreement, and I spent much of the time trying to cope with his open and direct criticism. I longed for an analyst who would just give me an interpretation. Occasionally he did, which was like bathing in soft, warm water. But for the most part, he wanted to interact with me in this feisty way, forcing his political opinions on me, gossiping about other analysts and candidates, and trying to convert me to his philosophy of life. He told me that the father of the primal horde is the ideal of masculinity—such a man has no Oedipus complex, no castration anxiety, no fear of rivals, and can have any woman he wants. Meanwhile, he mercilessly criticized the woman I loved (on the grounds that she was older than me and already had children). Even though I soon learned to refrain from taking his bait, he remained determined to persuade me, among other things, that the prime minister was a "card-carrying communist," and that apartheid in South Africa was a necessary and beneficial thing. When I won the candidate essay prize, which happened to be named after my father, he responded by telling me that he had been on the jury and that he had ranked my paper last out of the eight submitted papers. He took up the session explaining the scoring procedure for ranking the papers and criticizing the other jury members. In response to my protest that I was feeling hurt by him, he replied that I should not feel this way, since he had not known at the time that I was the author.

If Dr. Fish was aggressive with me, perhaps it was because he disliked me. He was often critical of the way I walked and dressed, or how I spoke in the candidate seminar. His apparently negative attitude toward me might also have had to do with his feelings about my deceased father. My fantasy now is that when I came to him for training analysis, Dr. Fish thought he had just caught a very big fish indeed, and rubbed his hands in glee at the prospect of getting the dirt on my father. Whether this was indeed the case, I treated his potential interest as insurance that I would eventually be accepted for training. (I had no clinical background whatsoever, so this was a concern for me.) In any event, his view of my father was confusing and sometimes shocking. He did express a certain respect, but he also mocked him, particularly with the charge of pedantry, as when my father had corrected him at a training committee meeting about a quotation from Freud's *The Ego and the Id*. My father had apparently said: "It is the *character* of the ego, *not the ego as such*, which is a precipitate of abandoned object cathexes." In response to material I was relating about my father, Dr. Fish would often retell this story. He would feign hurt feelings (as if to sympathize with my own hurt feelings in relation to my father's sometimes very harsh treatment of me).

I saw Dr. Fish four times a week for a total of five years. It was a grueling process. Why did I not consider this choice more carefully at the outset? Describing a similar situation, Masson (1990) remarked that, in those days, "trying to find things out about one's training analyst seemed to be actively discouraged. To do so is considered a kind of lèse-majesté" (p. 22). Be that as it may, I am still unable to resolve the mystery of why I stayed. The dynamic around my father was certainly one of the factors that kept me in the analysis. It was not just Dr. Fish who was seeking the dirt on my father, but me as well. Among other things, I used Dr. Fish as an authoritative guide through the labyrinth of my superego, not so much to analyze it as to find ways to get around or through its unsoftened tangle of briars. This had a certain freeing effect with respect to my "internal father," but it also helped me to rationalize my own self-serving tendencies, fostering a penchant for cynicism that I only began to recognize clearly during my third analysis years later.

So I graduated and continued my career as if nothing untoward had happened. The analysts of my generation and those that followed were bright, open-minded, and little concerned with prestige or convention. The trend that we now witness today was already beginning 25 years ago: people were no longer becoming analysts because they thought it was a good career move, as many had in previous decades; they did the training, so expensive and arduous, for the crazy reason that they *loved* psychoanalysis—they found it exciting, truthful, and meaningful for their own lives. We wanted to share this wonderful gift that we had received, and we could not understand why the Institute and our senior colleagues in the Society kept slapping us down.

One important contingency in my career had to do with the formation, by a group of analysts, of a private, nonprofit, low-fee psychotherapy center called the Argyle Institute of Mental Health. The Argyle quickly built itself up into a major teaching center and training program, with associates moving their private practices into the rented building. As soon as I graduated, the Argyle became a lifeline for me, providing me with teaching and supervising opportunities that I would not otherwise have been able to enjoy as an analyst. Predictably, however, the Psychoanalytic Institute issued an edict forbidding its own members to participate in this rival organization. This threat followed the Argyle's initiative to hold a series of conferences with major guest analysts from Britain. In consequence, many analysts withdrew from the new organization. The Argyle continued to thrive, however, and eventually became an important source of candidates for analytic training when the Institute's traditional feeding channels dried up. Contrariwise, many of the brightest young analysts shifted their energies away from the Psychoanalytic Society and Institute, where they felt unwanted, and devoted their talent and time to building the Argyle, where they did not have to ask for permission to be creative. What had been a golden opportunity to expand the psychoanalytic culture and to deepen its links with the community was effectively scuttled.

Through all this, we carried on fearlessly (or dissociatively?)—forming study groups, developing extension programs and film series for the Psychoanalytic Society, and generally trying to raise spirits and initiate spontaneity in what was already a chronically deflated and demoralized professional community. I became the chair of the "scientific committee," which planned the monthly round of clinical papers and guest speakers. This responsibility was expanded to planning the national meetings, where we tried to liven things up; concurrently, I was elected president of the Society for two terms. We did everything we could to break the stranglehold of the Institute, holding town hall meetings, passing motions, negotiating—all to no avail.

We were dealing with a culture of entrenched and exclusive power, a legally incorporated body whose members were elected for life and were answerable to no one but themselves. New graduates entering the Society tended to fall into a black hole. Candidates were dissatisfied with the training seminars, which were often poorly thought through, disconnected, and flat. There was a shortlist of ordinary members who were eligible to teach candidates, but they were rarely called on. Perhaps most telling of all was the fact that no one with the spirit of openness that we were feeling was coming forward to become a training analyst. Neither the Society nor the Institute was willing to give the other a good feed. As the luminaries of the old guard began to fade, and founding members such as Clifford Scott passed away, the institute itself began to reflect the starvation it had imposed on the Society.

I decided to become a training analyst. I had completed my third personal analysis and was feeling that I could help to open things up from the inside of the inner circle. I thought that if I could just get myself on the curriculum committee, there was plenty of potential for renovation. But, in making this calculation, my thinking was confused by denial. Although I knew it consciously, I dissociated the fact that I had already compromised and degraded myself considerably in order to do what I felt was needed in order to become an analyst. Now I wanted to be a training analyst! Looking back, I can see that I was living in a professional version of what Primo Levi (1988) called the "gray zone":

> The harsher the oppression, the more widespread among the oppressed is the willingness, with all its infinite nuances and motivations, to collaborate: terror, ideological seduction, servile

imitation of the victor, myopic desire for any power whatsoever, even though ridiculously circumscribed in space and time, cowardice, and, finally, lucid calculation aimed at eluding the imposed . . . order.

(p. 43)

I remember a poignant moment when Ethel Person had come to speak to our group and was horrified to discover the extent of the institute's control over professional life. She spoke about democratic reform and the need to struggle against elitist tendencies in the culture. She was right. But I remember nevertheless finding her argument too easy and wanting to push her further. "Isn't there something peculiar (perhaps even perverse) about psychoanalysis?" I asked, "Something that requires a certain 'sequestering' from the demand for democratic 'transparency' and common sense?" The irony of this argument is that in my heart I wanted to protect psychoanalysis from the institute itself, which I imagined (in my own elitist way) was filled with hacks who parodied psychoanalysis or did not even pretend to do it. I was going to join the institute to protect psychoanalysis from the institute itself—a project doomed to fail.

Up to this point, one can see in my conduct and state of mind a pattern that resembles what Marxists used to call, with some justification (although the terms have fallen into disuse), "false consciousness" and "reification" (Lukács, 1971). Over the span of my career, from candidacy to training analyst, I committed all the sins of arrogance, narrow-mindedness, and elitism that I thought I opposed, and I fed right into the toxic institutional dynamic that prevailed when I arrived on the scene. In addition to the difficulties of my personality, my insecurity, and my identifications with various kinds of corrupt and problematic authority, I was ambitious and competitive. Since I had no professional fallback position within mental health, I *needed* psychoanalysis to be something smart and credible that I could identify with, and which I could try to become, or at least to represent, if not embody. I believed in it far too ardently, even after my shattering experience with Dr. Fish.

In my new career as a training analyst, I never managed to get on the curriculum committee, was for a long time excluded from giving continuous case seminars, and was at first assigned very little teaching. I had to fight for every scrap I could get. But members of the mental health community liked me; they came to me for psychoanalysis, and they came for supervision. After a few years had passed, I found myself in a rather comfortable position, with several candidates in analysis, French and English, and several in supervision. In the new cohort, there were more than a handful of candidates, all women, no MDs. One-third of them were on my couch, and some in supervision. They had had a very good first year of training, bonding together as a group, and were just beginning their second year of training. Everything seemed to be swimming along, and then something uncanny and dreadful occurred.

Dr. Fish had been assigned to conduct the first seminar of the second year. According to reports, he arrived in a surly mood, summarized the assigned readings for 10 minutes, then stated that he was essentially finished for the evening. He said he assumed that the candidates had not done the readings, and, in any case, he was not interested in what they had to say. But if they had any questions, he would try to answer them.

The candidates were frozen with terror. They had no idea what was happening, or why it was happening, but they felt that they were under assault. Some nervous discussion followed, but Dr. Fish was unremitting in his expression of what they felt was hostile disdain.

The next morning, on my couch, my analysands were in a state of traumatic shock. But they were also angry. They said that they were not going to submit themselves to this kind of sadistic treatment again. Little did they know.

At first, all the candidates had decided to complain. Independently, some of them made the decision to skip the next week's seminar with Dr. Fish. A letter was produced, but this protest was compromised by fear and differences of affiliation. Effective retribution was swift and brutal. The candidates were threatened with expulsion—or, at least, this was what they were given to understand.

In an institute meeting that followed the incident, Dr. Fish coolly outlined how he saw the consequences if any candidate missed his seminar the following week. He stated that in his long career he had never witnessed anything like this. The level of insubordination was unprecedented, and these candidates were in any case a worthless group, the least qualified he had ever seen. In medical school, they would have been expelled. Of course, none of them had a medical degree; they were just middle-aged women with strange ideas. It was also stated at the meeting that the candidates were trying to organize a boycott of Dr. Fish, and that this was unacceptable behavior for an analyst or prospective analyst. It was agreed to take the situation in hand: the candidates would be warned, and they were expected to apologize and recognize the wrongness of their behavior.

There was nervous silence around the table, punctuated by a few grunts and murmurs of assent. In a state of high anxiety, I argued that "boycott" was a trumped-up charge and that these candidates were frightened, confused, and not at all united. I said that we needed to consult with them independently about why they had become so upset by Dr. Fish's seminar before taking any disciplinary action. I was not completely isolated on the committee, but it was difficult to get a real discussion going. My voice was compromised by the fact that I had two of these candidates in analysis. Perhaps it was felt that I should not have spoken, that I was biased, or that I should even have left the room. I know now that some believed that I had orchestrated the candidates' reaction to Dr. Fish. In any event, the fact that I spoke up for them, based on my knowledge of what I had heard from the couch after the event, was considered unethical.

However its policy may have been conceived in the mind of the institute, in my opinion, a campaign of intimidation began. Candidates were phoned at their homes and interrogated. They became divided among themselves, and the once pleasant atmosphere of the seminar (even when the seminar content left something to be desired) descended into full-blown paranoia. Dr. Fish's allies on the training committee argued that the problem was "splitting"—there was a split within the institute (i.e., disagreement) and the candidates were somehow picking this up, and reflecting it through their misgivings about Dr. Fish. This way of framing the situation fed directly off the "radioactive fallout" theory of institutional illness. There was, I am sad to say, little recognition of the agony of the candidates themselves—no concern that they were being systematically traumatized by the institute for no other reason than the fact that they had, in a disorganized and confused way, objected to the contemptuous manner in which they felt they had been treated. In this regard, however, I believe that Dr. Fish's presumption of superiority, already well-known in the community, was only a symptom of the institutional malaise. The candidates had already received the same message of haughty contempt from others, although primarily as a de-dramatized social signal, a weirdness in the way they were being addressed. It just happened that, in this first seminar of their second year, the hostile content of the institutional message had suddenly become clear to the candidates.

I could have warned my analysands not to protest, and I still fret over my decision not to coach them in the way Dr. Fish regularly did during my analysis with him. Do this, he would say, it will put you in good favor; do not do that, it will get you into trouble. Instead, I took the candidates' perception of the situation at face value, and did not discourage them from assuming the consequences, however painful, of their willingness to see the social reality for what it was, not to pretend it away. The candidates had come face to face with something very unjust and they were struggling to name it. The alternative to letting this painful process unfold would have been to rationalize institutional abuse through simulated neutrality, or outright denial.

While this was going on, I had other analysands who were planning to apply for training with the next cohort. I agonized over the question whether I should warn them—perhaps dissuade them from applying for psychoanalytic training? Their lives might be ruined, I worried to myself, and I began to feel a deep sense of guilt. I was letting these enthusiastic young clinicians, who had fallen in love with analysis, walk innocently into a professional lion's den, a gingerbread house equipped with a holocaustal stove.

In addition to guilt, I have never experienced such intense feelings of shame as I have during those periods when disputes between the Institute and the candidates were at their height. Beleaguered, frightened, demoralized, and disenchanted analysands and supervisees would drag themselves into my office, often in a state of misery and despair. It is painful to stand by and observe the swift and brutal destruction of optimistic spirits: the disappointment, the dashing of hope, the destruction of inspiration. I was forced to witness this corrosive process day after day, week after week, month after month, as that horrifying year dragged on, to be followed by another with the next cohort. I now understood that I was paying the personal price for my abject submission during the period of my training many years before, when I was too cowardly to change analysts before I had graduated. I had fed the monster, and my fear of losing my petty little status as a "real" analyst, as someone with conferred authority and social status, who was more than just a teacher but a healer and an expert on human nature—all this contributed not just to the maintenance, but to the re-creation of a narcissistic monster, the fantastic and destructive lies that the Institute had become. And I was a part of it. I had willingly joined that group, selling my soul for a mess of professional potage.

## Discussion

There is no end to a story like this. The hope in beginning to tell it is that someone may extract some wisdom. But on what basis? In any narrative, a character like Dr. Fish is a construction, a figment of the writer's excited imagination. The writer himself is really just another character in the story, more carefully constructed perhaps, but still an unreliable narrator, with a voice no more dependable in principle than the other characters in the story.

It may be, for example, that over the years since my training analysis, I have unconsciously used the memory of my negative experience with Dr. Fish as a way of hanging onto an idealized image of him (and of psychoanalysis) as invulnerable in a way that I knew my father was not. What I could not see at the time was that I was also a burden on Dr. Fish, and that behind his haughty exterior, he was probably quite vulnerable to my transference and its "radioactive fallout." He seemed to need to hide this fact about himself—but then I needed him to hide it, too.

After my analysis with Dr. Fish, and in the course of my own work as analyst, I encountered in myself an identification with him that I struggled to dispel. I would sometimes find myself speaking to patients in a certain knowing manner that reminded me of him. When he used to speak in this way to me, he was usually providing a rationalization by means of which I could exculpate myself, perhaps to lift the pressure off himself as well. When I would find myself speaking in this way to my patients, I would have a vivid sense of how his authoritative tone was neither convincing nor truly reassuring for me at the time. Then I would wonder how my patient felt, hearing the same kind of thing from me. These episodes always involved a feeling of being overwhelmed, or not knowing how to think about what was going on between me and the patient.

Perhaps it was the same for Dr. Fish? In fact, he told me a fair bit, in his debonair way, about his early life: it involved flight from an oppressor. I wish I could have recognized at the time that this was perhaps his way of trying to connect with the traumatized side of me.

My argument that the institutional illness of psychoanalysis is a transgenerational (rather than merely intergenerational) issue may be overdetermined by the fact that my father was an analyst, further complicated by his unexpected death while I was on the cusp of training. I suspect that I remain in unconscious identification with an important part of my father that he repudiated—his evident dislike of authority and his suspicion of "politics." I knew my father to be extremely uncomfortable with any subversive element, and I have lived what I now believe to have been his projection of this into me with great internal distress.

It is also relevant that my father could be cruel to my rather helpless mother—and cruel to me when I tried as a child to defend her. No doubt my ambivalent relationship with psychoanalytic authority is overdetermined by this feature of my own psychic history as well.

In addition, the fact that my father did not live to see me become an analyst surely obfuscated my awareness of our potential rivalry within the field, and may also have encouraged me to idealize psychoanalysis in a highly narcissistic way. It was only gradually that I became aware of my own unconscious delusion that psychoanalytic knowledge was a property to be "owned" and shared with only a select few, through an imaginary birthright. It is hard to exaggerate how toxic this idea really is in our profession and how it cuts us off from the life around us. The problem it posed for me was not that my sense of entitlement through my IPA training made me lazy—on the contrary, my anxious sense of the preciousness and precariousness of psychoanalysis made me defensive and intemperate about the wide variations of style and substance within the profession. This, in turn, led me to identify with the elitist training ideology, even as I opposed the passive-aggressive authority of the Institute I would eventually join.

Although my father would sometimes shake his head when he spoke of the conflicts within the psychoanalytic society, I had no real idea how tension filled the psychoanalytic community was until I began my training. As a candidate and young graduate, I was completely bewildered by the intimidating atmosphere at scientific meetings, and I put these feelings down to my own neurotic insecurity (partly true). Because the situation in our group was so frustrating and so chronic, I resorted to massive dissociation in order to continue my new career and bolster my sense of belonging to a supportive professional environment. Apart from a few generous colleagues who continued to sponsor hope, there was, at least in the early going, very little support—especially for an analyst who had no other mental health affiliation. As the social prestige of psychoanalysis rapidly declined in the closing decades of the twentieth century, the institute hunkered down behind a veil of indifference, while ordinary members like myself were expected to sink or swim. There were many in my cohort who quietly retreated or dropped out, though they were passionate about psychoanalysis. I probably would have done the same if I had had anywhere else to go.

Usually the intergenerational aspect of the institutional illness of psychoanalysis is attributed to the passing on of an idealizing identification—ultimately with either Freud or one of his rivals, but more specifically one's own analyst, and his or her allegiances. It is correctly pointed out that this pattern of inherited and unexamined emotional affiliation quickly leads to conflict within the group, and schismatic processes. But this does not account for the psychic deadness of the psychoanalytic milieu in which I found myself. I think something else beyond attachment to idealized personalities can be passed on unknowingly between the psychoanalytic generations, something much more corrosive. For the sake of simplicity, I shall ascribe this broadly to the trauma of becoming a psychoanalyst, and the professional ordeal of continuing to be one.

In the training analyst system, the candidate's analyst is always going to be somebody who has been traumatized in precisely this way; when we as aspiring analysts identify with our analyst, we inevitably internalize her secret history. We take in something of which we can have no understanding, rather as if we have swallowed a container whose contents have not been identified, even by the transmitter, our analyst. Thus, each successive generation of trained analysts becomes like a still more complicated Russian doll, full of nested, unprocessed trauma. The candidate's analyst will have been traumatized as a candidate, and also by her analyst, who was in her turn traumatized. And this analyst, having to cope with the ongoing trauma of appurtenance to the group, will also be traumatized by us and what we come to represent about the painful undigested past that she relives, consciously and unconsciously, as she sits behind the couch trying to analyze us.

Every candidate represents the potential healing of the traumatic ruptures in psychoanalytic history, but she also represents the possibility of a new rupture in the imaginary family line, a rupture of the collective fantasy of ownership and inheritance of psychoanalysis. The candidate cannot help but disappoint all those who came before her, and she soon understands the risk that this may become her primary role in their eyes. Because she cannot possibly make the collective trauma of the psychoanalytic community go away, no matter how good a girl she is, she will feel doomed, unless she takes evasive action, to become a scapegoat, the representative of a threat both to the institutional authorities and the community they dominate. Perhaps it is for this reason that psychoanalysis seems to go out of its way to make the training process so miserable and arduous. One might describe the latter as the psychic equivalent of boot camp, but its purpose is only superficially to make candidates "tougher," like good psychoanalytic soldiers. Its real function may be to relieve the burden on the community of its own secret knowledge of disillusionment. If it is inevitable that the candidate will be disappointed by the analytic community, then why not get this over with, and make the candidate carry the shame of it at the same time?

It is traumatic to be in the position of someone who is expected to banish the ghosts of the past, without knowing who or what they are, and without any forum for discussion of these painful aspects of psychoanalytic life and history. In such a Hamlet-like position, how does one tell the difference between a hawk and handsaw? Yet the tradition in many psychoanalytic communities has been to place the candidate precisely in this position—the position of a child in relation to the narcissism of parents who are profoundly shaken and guilty about who they are. I am theorizing this syndrome in the now familiar terms of generalized seduction (Laplanche, 1999), the telescoping of generations (Faimberg, 1988), and other formulations of the idea of an alien or enigmatic psychic introject (Ferenczi, 1933). With reference to psychoanalytic training, Cabré (2011) has suggested we revive an evocative neologism from Ferenczi's (1955) last notebook entry—"intropression" (p. 279). Although I have described the transmission and transplantation of the enigmatic message in terms of my personal experience, the message I am trying to interpret does not originate in any real personality I have known. It is passed on through the gaps and hidden recesses in the psychic life of the other, emanating from his or her other. Psychic obscurities of this order cannot be resolved exclusively in private psychoanalysis; they need to be addressed at the collective, cultural level of understanding, the level on which their denial is ritually enacted. In this sense, the trauma of the candidate is not created by individual psychoanalysts—it is repeated and passed on through the compromised functioning of the group.

Yet there is still a form of willful cruelty in this aspect of generational transmission, a cruelty that is systematically disavowed by training authorities and dissociated by the witnesses in the community who have also been through this painful process. Psychoanalysis is haunted by what Gerson (2009) has aptly described as the "dead third." Perhaps it is not a coincidence that if you run a PEP title search on the word *cruelty*, you will turn up seven items (only three of which are serious clinical studies) in the entire electronic archive.

How does one go on being an analyst, or becoming one, after the traumatic rupture of one's faith in the profession? The answer is often to forestall the experience of the trauma by identifying with psychoanalytic authority—even if one believes one is challenging it, as I did—and to soldier on. The interconnection between the analyst's identification with authority and occupational trauma is pervasive in psychoanalytic practice. This is partly due to the fact that a significant part of what is traditionally called "resistance" in psychoanalysis actually consists of a profound fear of questioning internalized authorities on whom we once depended. For this reason, both the analyst and the patient are in the same position with respect to the traumatic enforcement of unconscious allegiances.

I noticed this in the transference as I was beginning to recognize and relinquish my own defensive attachment to the analyst's presumed authority and knowledge. Certain patients seeking a similar solution to their traumatic history easily picked this up, and tried to get me to be less egalitarian, less democratic, less *uncertain* of the professional healer's status and power in society. I came to feel that my patients and I were struggling with a deep-seated dominance-submission dynamic. The latter may or may not have a biological foundation, but in either case, I now believe that the psychoanalytic process can only be conducted in painful cultural tension with it. Coming to this realization has been very important for me in my practice, helping to untangle me from the need to be in the right with my patients. This has, in turn, helped them to free themselves from their own need to identify with an arbitrary authority.

One of the ongoing traumas of being an analyst is that one is implicitly expected to "represent" a corrupt or abusive authority. To the extent that the analyst can do this comfortably, and in good conscience, the patient can learn to question her own "submissive transformation of narcissism" (Giesbrecht & Levin, 2012)—and discover that her survival does not ultimately rest on this kind of dependent subordination. Before I could get to such a place in my own way of working, however, I first had to dismantle my unconscious fantasy that I had inherited a private preserve of analytic authority; then I had to learn to live with the fact that my faith and conviction in the creative richness of the internal world was not necessarily redemptive for others.

Several important practical and theoretical questions raised in this chapter will have to be answered elsewhere. I shall conclude with a general reflection on my own experience. It is true that conflict in psychoanalytic groups is very destructive, but it may not be the root problem that our profession faces. In an oppressive system, conflict should not be dismissed as a mere question of splitting and projection, attributed in a facile manner to transference attachments, failure to contain the "radiation," and incomplete analysis. It may be a way of refusing the murder of passionate love. One of the great merits of Kernberg's (1986, 1996, 2012) ground-breaking interventions on the question of institutional illness in psychoanalysis is that he was not sidetracked by the problem of conflict, which enabled him to successfully identify the core issue of psychic deadness in the group and hatred of creativity on the part of vested authority. Conflict in psychoanalytic groups may be a way of resisting the self-serving strategy of an elite to stifle the vital energies in the community. I have argued that this strategy perpetuates a dissociative professional style designed to insulate a defensively constructed psychoanalytic identity from attention to the trauma that produced it. That kind of mentality can induce analysts to become very cold fish indeed, especially when they get into impervious positions of power. I believe these facets of institutional illness also underlie the problem of sexual boundary violations in analysis and, more importantly, the difficulty we have as a group discussing our collective complicity in this tragic betrayal of the psychoanalytic spirit.

## References

Appel, P. (2004). The New York State psychoanalytic license: An historical perspective. In A. Casement (Ed.), *Who owns psychoanalysis?* (pp. 157–176 ). London: Karnac.

Bohleber, W. (2010). *Destructiveness, intersubjectivity, and trauma: The identity crisis of psychoanalysis.* London: Karnac.

Cabré, L. G. M. (2011). From introjection to intropression: Evolution of a theoretical concept and its consequences for psychoanalytic technique. *American Journal of Psychoanalysis, 71,* 321–328.

Celenza, A. (2007). *Sexual boundary violations: Therapeutic, academic, and supervisory contexts.* Lanham, MD: Jason Aronson, Inc.

Dimen, M. (2011). Lapsus linguae, or a slip of the tongue? A sexual violation in an analytic treatment and its personal and theoretical aftermath. *Contemporary Psychoanalysis, 47,* 35–79.

Faimberg, H. (1988). The telescoping of generations: Genealogy of certain identifications. *Contemporary Psychoanalysis, 24,* 99–117.

Ferenczi, S. (1933). The confusion of tongues between adults and children. *Contemporary Psychoanalysis, 24,* 196–206.

Ferenczi, S. (1955). *Final contributions to the problems and methods of psychoanalysis.* London: Hogarth Press.

Gabbard, G. (1999). Boundary violations in the psychoanalytic training system. *Journal of Applied Psychoanalytic Studies, 1,* 207–221.

Gabbard, G. O., & Lester, E. P. (1995). *Boundaries and boundary violations in psychoanalysis.* New York: Basic Books.

Gerson, S. (2009). When the third is dead: Memory, mourning, and witnessing in the aftermath of the Holocaust. *International Journal of Psychoanalysis, 90,* 1341–1357.

Ghent, E. (1990). Masochism, submission, surrender: Masochism as perversion of surrender. *Contemporary Psychoanalysis, 26,* 108–135.

Giesbrecht, H., & Levin, C. (2012). *Art in the offertorium: Narcissism, psychoanalysis, and cultural metaphysics.* New York: Rhodopi.

Kernberg, O. (1986). Institutional problems of psychoanalytic education. *Journal of the American Psychoanalytic Association, 34,* 799–834.

Kernberg, O. (1996). Thirty methods to destroy the creativity of psychoanalytic candidates. *International Journal of Psychoanalysis, 77,* 1031–1040.

Kernberg, O. (2012). Suicide prevention for psychoanalytic institutes and societies. *Journal of the American Psychoanalytic Association, 60,* 707–719.

Laplanche, J. (1999). *Essays on otherness.* London: Routledge.

Levi, P. (1988). *The drowned and the saved.* New York: Vintage.

Levine, H. (2010a). Sexual boundary violations: A psychoanalytic perspective. *British Journal of Psychotherapy, 26*(1), 50–63.

Levine, H. (2010b). The sins of the fathers: Freud, narcissistic boundary violations, and their effects on the politics of psychoanalysis. *International Forum of Psychoanalysis, 19*, 43–50.

Lukács, G. (1971). *History and class consciousness: Studies in Marxist dialectics* (Trans. R. Livingston). Cambridge, MA: MIT Press.

Masson, J. M. (Ed.) (1985). *The complete letters of Sigmund Freud to Wilhelm Fliess, 1887–1904.* Cambridge, MA: Harvard University Press.

Masson, J. M. (1990). *Final analysis: The making and unmaking of a psychoanalyst.* Reading, MA: Addison-Wesley.

Mauger, J., & Monette, L. (1999). Pure culture. *Bulletin de la Société Psychanalytique de Paris, 55,* 8–77.

Reeder, J. (2004). *Hate and love in psychoanalytical institutions: The dilemma of a profession.* New York: Other Press.

Ruskin, R. (2011). Sexual boundary violations in a senior training analyst: Impact on the individual and psychoanalytic society. *Canadian Journal of Psychoanalysis, 19,* 87–106.

Scarfone, D. (Ed.) (2000). *L'Avenir d'une désillusion.* Paris: Presses Univérsitaires de France.

Wallace, E. M. (2007). Losing a training analyst for ethical violations: A candidate's perspective. *International Journal of Psychoanalysis, 88,* 1275–1288

Winnicott, D. W. (1974). Fear of breakdown. *International Review of Psychoanalysis, 1,* 103–107.

# Part IV

# ENDPAPER

# 13

# SAYING GOODBYE

## Traumatic Reverberations in the Subjective Sense of Time[1]

*Dianne Elise*

It is indeed a significant risk to enter analytic treatment, to open oneself to a relationship, an ever-present dialogue, with one's analyst. This unique partnership has the potential to engage our hearts and minds, our psyches, at the deepest levels—more so, potentially, than any relationship since early childhood. The depth of attachment and psychic involvement also renders one vulnerable to great loss. This chapter addresses the painful circumstance of the analyst's death in the midst of an analysis. That loss may be the literal death of the analyst or the symbolic death brought about by an ethical violation. One way or another, the trusted, "good" analyst has "disappeared." This rupture has profound implications for the analysand's subjective experience of time and for termination. With a full termination phase foreclosed, something must be done about time.

In contending with death and mortality—fatal and fateful losses—one is made acutely aware of the peculiar relationship we each have with temporality—the multifaceted quality of our complex, ambivalent relationship to the exigencies of time. Trouble with time shows itself most especially in our difficulties with the emotional pain of saying goodbye. In living, we are required to say many goodbyes: to people we have loved, to lost hopes, to our former selves. This effort of mourning takes time and requires personal creation: through extended night and day dreaming, one crafts a lamentation to what has been lost. An elegy, Ogden (2000) writes,

> [M]ust capture in its own voice, not the voice that has been lost, but a voice brought to life in the experiencing of that loss . . . there can be a sense that the new voice has somehow been there all along in the old ones, as a child is somehow an imminence in his ancestors and is brought to life both through their lives and through their deaths.
>
> (pp. 86–87)

This chapter is about the creative use of time inherent in the capacity to dream and to imagine that induces ghosts to become ancestors.

## Death

### *The Voice That is Silenced*

In analytic treatment, the termination phase creates an expanse of time—real and psychic—to say goodbye. A full termination phase holds open much more time than patients initially comprehend; surprised, they query: "What will we talk about for all that time?!" Patients, like most people, hope to collapse the time to say goodbye. We commonly see people waiting until the last minute at the airport security gate, for instance, before expressing tearful exchanges from which they can then quickly flee. But premature, sudden death gives us no time at all to say goodbye. Deutsch (2011) describes what this painful reality meant for her when her analyst died unexpectedly.

In her moving portrayal of the aftermath of her analyst's untimely death, Deutsch describes the loss, and then the finding anew, of her analytic voice—a voice developed through many hours of shared conversation with her analyst. In losing her analyst, Deutsch found that her own self, her voice, had gone missing, the sound of one hand clapping echoing a bereft silence. Through a series of dreams after her analyst's death, Deutsch works hard to recover from the shock of sudden loss, and to recover her shared dialogue with her lost analyst within the context of a new analytic relationship. Dream images develop and shift, creating time to say goodbye; dreams also foreshadow changes in the new analysis. Deutsch's analytic voice, so abruptly silenced, slowly regains its strength—a tenuous process that needed the containment provided by the new analyst.

It is said that "time heals." It is linear time that is referred to—the pages of the calendar dictating our steady, and unsteady, march forward without the person we have loved and lost. But Deutsch's experience elucidates the healing potential of a transitional use of omnipotence in the creation of psychic timing—in being able to spend our time as we wish, where we want and with whom we want, especially when that person has died without warning.[2] In this grievous situation, we do not want to *spend* time so much as to *extend* time, to create it, reverse it. Reality-based, chronological time is not what we wish for, but, instead, the malleability of psychic, nonlinear time. Omnipotently, we walk off the calendar page on a trajectory of our own making. Dreams are uniquely helpful in this quest to "mess with" time.

In reading Deutsch's (2011) paper, I thought of how devastated I would have been if my analyst had died (noting to myself that I had picked him especially *not* to die, in his being more youthful than the other referral I had been given). I began to think explicitly about the issue of time itself, and about the role of dreaming, when faced with overwhelming loss. My thoughts turned to my own dreams that began soon after my father's death, dreams whose theme persisted almost unchanged for many years.

As in Deutsch's experience with her analyst, my father died young, suddenly, and unexpectedly; there was absolutely no time to say goodbye. We humans never want to permanently part from those we love, but when death comes prematurely and without warning, eviscerating time, it is traumatic. I was 22. For the next 17 years, I had many dreams about my father; he was never dead; in many places, but never dead. Initially, and throughout many years, I dreamt that the notion that he was dead was a mistake and that really he had been "at the office" all along. These dreams coexisted with and outlasted my conscious experience of intense mourning that gradually abated over two to three years to a quieter sense of loss and sadness.

It took me many, many years to comprehend that all death is not like sudden, premature death; the element of time is central. The deceased did not live out the full time of their life; otherwise, their advancing age would be a real-life equivalent of an analytic termination phase with time to say goodbye. Our loved one was robbed of time and so are we—not only of time to be living out life together, but also of time to say goodbye, which takes a lot of time. We say that a person "died before his or her time." We have great expectations regarding time. Deutsch's loss of her analyst emphasizes that dreams persist, insist, consist of our absolute need to have time to say goodbye. In her dream life, Deutsch creates time with her lost analyst that was not there in reality; she reverses time, expands time, stretches it out to be more of what she needed. She cheats with time in the face of being cheated by it. In dreaming, Deutsch creates a world—psychic reality—where time is on her side.

We all recall the line from the Rolling Stones' hopeful ballad, "time, time, time, it's on my side, yes it is." This is the song we all wish to sing. Mick Jagger's optimistic insistence that a lost love will indeed come back is conveyed not only by repetition in the lyrics, but by the unhurried melody as well. But, as another music classic reminds us—unfortunately, and terribly painfully— "Time has come today." The Chambers Brothers' unforgettable, staccato, reverberating, and repeated bellow, "Time!" captured the stark reality of time's limits, and was, as a Vietnam war protest, intended to create the impact of dropping bombs hitting the ground and exploding. The realization hits that time is up. When reality is traumatic, we are not ready for time to come today; instead, we must go back to yesterday in order to create a tomorrow that we can live with. Three years, 230 dreams, Deutsch tells us—*this is time*, the time needed and created when someone has suddenly dropped out of sight.[3]

Winnicott (1953) encouraged a "respect for illusory experience" (p. 90) where an initial need for magical omnipotent control becomes part of a growing ability to accept reality:

> It is assumed here that the task of reality-acceptance is never completed, that no human being is free from the strain of relating inner and outer reality, and that relief from this strain is provided by an intermediate area of experience which is not challenged ... [an area] between primary creativity and objective perception based on reality testing.
>
> (pp. 95, 96)

Transitional phenomena constitute a normal aspect of development and contribute throughout life to the intense experiencing that belongs to creativity. This intermediate area of experience is integral to our ability to dream and to play with time in order to create a psychic space with potential.

Winnicott (1953) emphasized that in the area of transitional phenomena we are not to ask, "Did you conceive of this or was it presented to you from without?" (p. 95). This ambiguity—between personal creation and the reality presented to us—infuses our relationship with temporality. To whom does time belong? Do we just have to take it as we find it? Or can we mess with it, mash it up, stretch it as though playing an accordion—out, in, up, down, faster, slower—insisting, "I won't take time as I find it; it's mine to do with as I wish!" The omnipotence of certain psychic phenomena can facilitate healthy development (Winnicott, 1971). Psychic omnipotence also has the potential to create space for healing from traumatic loss. In this context, the use of omnipotence is temporary, in the service of psychic movement rather than stasis (manic denial), and fosters mourning rather than avoidance of grief.

When my father died, he was young and so was I. Of course, at 22 I felt that I was quite adult and that, at 47, he was almost elderly. One knows better now how young the young truly are. At present, my mother is 88. Even though she may live several more years, I have already started my goodbyes to her privately in my own mind (and she to me?). With her advancing age, I have lots of time—like an analytic termination—to think about my eventual loss of her: to imagine, cry, pause, reflect, return, repeat. Time is not cheating me, thus far, of my goodbye to her. Although time could still be cut short, that would be nothing like the loss of my father, just as Deutsch's loss of her analyst is nothing like a planned termination. Traumatically, time was not on our side.

### *Keeping Time: The Containing Function of the Analyst*

We frequently say to children, "Time to say goodbye!" meaning, "Time's up; say goodbye." Deutsch's time with her analyst was up, but she could not say goodbye; she needed more time. And in the context of her relationship with her new analyst, more time was created. The new analyst was like a drumbeat, "keeping time" while the rest of the music of Deutsch's dream life unfolded. Deutsch's 230 dreams speak to the enormity of her loss and to the massive effort at retrieval and transformation. With both analysts available in her mind, "real" time and created—*co-created*—time overlap and coexist. In permitting both analysts to be present in her internal world at the same time, "a rearrangement of memory" (Deutsch, this volume) changes the future. An "analytic third" (Ogden, 2004) was necessary. Deutsch's new analyst showed up too soon in a way, an unwanted yet needed intruder. In contrast, I waited for my analyst for many years. Although tardy, he also made available a needed third.

Since my analysis, I no longer dream that my father returns, that he is not really dead. This significant shift in a previously longstanding dreamscape took some years after termination for me to fully register as an ongoing, stable change. At some point during my analysis, I am not sure when, such dreams of my father started to abate, opening up space for my dreaming to move forward. In the relationship with my analyst, a paternal figure was brought to life and kept safely alive for as long as I needed. As Deutsch emphasizes, it is not time for gradual *detachment* that is needed; one needs a relationship of *attachment* within which to bend time to one's own will. This attachment is to both the lost object and to the newfound object. I did not "give up" my father for my analyst; my analyst's presence helped me absorb, in deeper layers of my psyche, the true nature of my father's absence. I could then let my father's death be part of my relationship to him, rather than a concrete fact my rational intellect had complied with while my inner self insisted, "Oh no, that's not true." Such an inner journey, made possible by the analytic relationship, can thaw time frozen by traumatic loss. In my eventually terminating and leaving my analytic father, he is someone to whom I have had the opportunity to say, "fare *well*." He is someone who cannot drop dead on me, because I was able to have the time with him that I needed, and only then to go off into my life with the comforting knowledge that he is indeed still "at the office."

Deutsch was pressed by painful circumstances into meeting a new analyst too soon. I waited 17 years for my analyst to "show up," but both Deutsch and I made use of the new object relation to play with time and to mourn a loss. Dreaming mattered, creating change, and then being changed. In the fluidity of her dreams, moving "forward into the future and then back-tracking,"[4] Deutsch takes her time to terminate with her lost analyst. The new analyst holds the space within which this process can take place. As Deutsch notes, Freud's (1917) theory on mourning focuses on what is occurring in one mind about two people: the self and the deceased. However, it is apparent that mourning is greatly facilitated by a third person, whether this person shows up very soon or very much later. Attachment to a new object creates a space for transformative dreaming, and is not merely a substitution of the new object for the one lost: "Telling one's analyst a dream is a bid for aliveness" (Parsons, 2009, p. 40). Hopefully, clinicians do not lose sight of our responsibility to keep time as each patient sings her plaintive songs of mourning.

## *Dreaming, Development, and Time*

Parsons (2009) identifies the complex relationship between temporality and dreaming:

> In dreaming, the time-governed structures of everyday life, by which people live but by which they also defend themselves, are laid open without possibility of control, to unstructured timelessness. To tell a dream in the analytic situation is more than narration. It is to expose one's dreaming, and this is to place oneself where time and timelessness collide.
>
> (p. 38)

When an analysand can dream a lost analyst to a new analyst, she can take both analysts with her on her life's journey—a journey that itself inevitably comes to its own ending for each of us. As Green (2009) expresses, "Thanks to the activity of dreaming, life becomes bearable by conserving in us a portion of hope in the form of illusions to which our being owes the capacity to bear the inevitable disillusionments to come" (p. 18).

Sadly, Deutsch was confronted with the shocking reality that her dead analyst was not coming back to the office, and that she herself would not go there ever again either. At first, true dreaming was not possible, only "swirling colors" like a kaleidoscope gone mad: "Immediately after my analyst's death, my dreams became inchoate, raw emotion in a sea of swirling colors. I would wake from these dreams disrupted and disconsolate" (Deutsch, this volume). Traumatic disruption to the internal object world blots out any dream narrative that would rest on a relationship to temporality where past, present, and future can be taken for granted.

Green (2009) refers to such disorganizations of temporality—where factors such as massive bereavements impede integration or even elude representation—as that of an exploded time ("*temps éclaté*"; p. 17).[5] This experience of extensive temporal collapse—the obliteration of time as anything that can be meaningfully registered—is the catastrophic aspect that the Chambers Brothers' antiwar song captured, an incursion of the Real in Lacanian terms.

With losses less massively overwhelming to the psyche, attempts are made to defend ourselves: Singing, "time, time, time; it's on my side, yes, it is," blatant bravado expresses itself in the manic denial of any vulnerability to the passing of time or to loss. This maneuver can be contrasted with the depressive position of yet another classic song, "Unchained melody," by the Righteous Brothers. Here, the power of time is attested to—"and time can do so much"—in the experience of it going by slowly, "a long, lonely time" as, uncertain and in need, one hungers for the touch[6] of the beloved. The poignant lyrics, along with their heart-wrenching melody, give palpable expression to need, hope, and humility in the face of time and potential loss.

Depressive position capacities—tolerating separations, the ability to wait with hope, and, eventually, the ability to mourn—are built up over time, and rest on a relationship to temporality that takes shape initially in the rhythms of the baby's body in relation to the maternal body (Bornholdt, 2009). The maternal container is essential in our ability to live with, and in, time. Bornholdt (2009) emphasizes that temporality and the structuring of the depressive position evolve together and regulate one another: "Temporality is like an underground fountain whose water constantly flows throughout development and the psychoanalytical process" (p. 110). Human development is inseparable from our development in relation to time, and our capacity to cope with time is always vulnerable to regression in the face of trauma. As Smith (2009) notes, "The fear of death, the effort to be its master, to preserve life and defy mortality, is the most fundamental instinct we possess, and it affects all our thoughts about time and its treatment" (p. xxi). Hopefully, manic denial can give way to the sad acknowledgment that time passes, and so do we. For adults troubled by time, analysis offers a space for mourning losses and for moving forward into the rhythm of time (see Levine, 2009).

In the last line of her paper, taken from her final dream where she now passes by the Renaissance art galleries, Deutsch (this volume) asserts: "Why do I have to spend my time here?" She is on her way toward the modern art wing. Having experienced a rebirth, a renewal of life, after the labor of mourning; she can now live in the present, "modern" moment. As Deutsch so poignantly describes:

> I orchestrate my analyst's death by crafting a death whose timing is now under my control and for which I have planned. By redoing her death, I can say goodbye to her. To accompany me into the future, I orchestrate a companion, a new internal object.

When confronted by the death of one's analyst, this sorrowful task of grieving is certainly challenging. Unfortunately, mourning becomes infinitely more difficult when the analyst has "died" as a good object: Ethical violations generate the presence of a bad object that obstructs the grieving process. However creative one might be, mourning is initially overtaken by melancholia.

## Betrayal and Symbolic Death

It is particularly evident, as many of the chapters in this volume attest, that the absence of a hoped for termination phase—as the somewhat obscured outcome of an ethical violation—is pernicious in its impact and reverberations. In these ruptured treatments, usually some, even many, sessions focus on the need to end prematurely, but that discussion is definitely not a *good* goodbye. One is forced to construct one's own termination not from a deceased good object, but from an alive, bad object—a haunting, persecutory presence. The sudden "death" of the former good object must be mourned while contending with the intrusiveness of a "new" bad object that not only has taken over and destroyed the treatment trajectory, but that also gets in the way of a symbolic goodbye to the lost good analyst. Through a generational transmission of trauma (Faimberg, 2005b), the egregious outcome of an ethical violation results in the former analyst becoming a ghost—not at rest or in peace—in the mind of the analysand. The clinician–analysand is robbed of a crucial ancestor, and may come to feel that *only* ghosts haunt her professional identity. The parental generation collapses; along with it goes the foundation of the clinician-analysand's professional, as well as personal, well-being.

When one registers the import of a full termination to an analysis, one can more deeply understand how its absence contributes to the fallout of a breach (see Burka, 2008). The actual breach understandably draws the focus, shadowing the reality that a true termination is foreclosed. One sees complicated bereavement rather than a productive process of mourning—something that *may* hopefully be fashioned by the patient at some *much later* point. In betrayal, mourning may be delayed in time far into the future—a crucial difference when confronted with the symbolic death of a good object versus a literal death of the good analyst. But that delay is only one aspect of how time figures into betrayal and deception: The vicissitudes of time enter the picture in significant, and quite complex, ways.

### *When Your Past is no Longer Your Past*

I want to call attention to the sense of mental confusion that can result from the discovery of a deception regarding events that have been taking place over time. In being deceived for some time, a lived reality turns out to *not* be true. Dissolved in seconds, lived truth turns out to be a fiction, replaced with a bad dream that *is* true. In one stunning moment of registering truth, one realizes that one has been deceived over a substantial period of time. This devastating knowledge attends the realization of a reality that one had not been aware of, but that is true and that has been happening over some time as one discovers that your past is no longer your past.

The fact that ethical violations have usually been occurring for some time leads, on discovery, to a need to rewrite one's analytic history. In being cheated of the truth, something one has lived—one's analysis—has no longer taken place; how can that be so? This unraveling of history—a retroactive reconfiguring (see Eickhoff, 2006; Faimberg, 2005a, 2005b; Perelberg, 2006, 2008)— is profoundly disturbing to one's sense of reality testing, and leads, often, to crippling doubt about the ability to determine what is true. This assault on truth

(Elise, 2012) can be as, or even more, disruptive than the actual violation: one does not solely lose trust in the analyst, but in one's own mind, in one's hold not only on the object, but also on reality.

I see in betrayal a subjective experience of temporality where meaning travels backward and suffuses one's object relational past, creating a *new history* that is now personally registered (although not "remembered") as immensely painful. A complex analytic literature focuses on "tricks with time" at play in, and plaguing, personal subjectivity (Birksted-Breen, 2003; Eickhoff, 2006; Faimberg, 2005a, 2005b; Glocer Fiorini & Canestri, 2009; Green, 2002, 2008; Loewald, 1972; Perelberg, 2008, 2009; Pine, 2006; Sodre, 2005; Thoma & Cheshire, 1991; Winnicott, 1974). Each of these conceptualizations addresses the nonlinearity of time in psychic life—a bidirectionality such that in various circumstances past meaning can be reconfigured, retranscribed, by retrospective attribution.

With deception, the *truth* is the traumatic event, and does reconfigure one's personal history, rather than necessarily referring back to any previously registered, concrete event(s). The analysand may have experienced the analysis, when it was in progress, as beneficial—a basically good relationship. This earlier life, where one had been innocent of the knowledge that any painful "event" is taking place, now needs to be completely restructured. *Deception constitutes the foreclosure of the possibility of registering* prior events as problematic. Truth becomes the trauma in that it refers back to an absence of any earlier event that would have undone the deception. Deception constitutes a non-event-based trauma—something that *did not occur* in the individual's *experienced* history, an "absent event"—where the revelation of the deception and the betrayal is the event that is traumatic. This painful realization of truth, in the immediate moment, sends further pain flooding back into the past, thus spoiling far more than the present experience and future prospects.

Questions of how to proceed in responding to a suspected betrayal generate strong feelings of anxiety and self-doubt. Determining truth against a series of logical dismissals rests on trust in one's "intuition"—an emotional conviction such that one is not dissuaded by clever denials. The sudden realization of a reality previously unknown, unregistered, creates a sense of reality dissolving; the boundaries of time can seem to dissolve as one hovers in an endless moment—a sense of time "standing still." With a felt sense of being dislocated in time and space, one may temporarily lose hold of the coordinates of one's being. An assault on truth has the capacity to disrupt our minds, our going on being; this experience can be quite destabilizing.

Prolonged over time, an anxious preoccupation compels a need to reconstruct *past* reality. One cannot go forward until the past is revisited and brought into alignment with what has actually been the case. Efforts to go back in time, approximating the duration of the betrayal, focus on intensive, fact-finding searches that are excruciatingly painful, yet continue to have a sense of vital urgency. The entire period of time absorbed in this effort is one of great anxiety and mistrust likely blanketing all object relationships, including with a new analyst. One seems to have stepped "off the page" that everyone else is on in order to pursue a quest for which others may not understand the crucial need. Eventual restoration is preceded by a grueling period of intrapsychic chaos. Confidence in one's mind, the normal sequence of time, and the reality of one's personal history—all can come into question. It is imperative to regain a grasp on the past, in order to restore confidence in a personal sense of reality testing.

In this process, what may hold fast for an extended period, as a continued source of anxiety and "paranoia," is a fear of being betrayed again due to not being able to discern falseness. This fear of the future, based on a past betrayal, shadows the present. Since a betrayed analysand has likely not suspected the first time, what would or could she rely on to tell her if anything similar were to occur? Undermined trust in one's mind in relationship to one's objects has far-reaching consequences, requiring the exceedingly difficult, complex task of rebuilding *trust in the self*—specifically, trust in one's mind, one's capacity to differentiate truth from fiction, to detect deceit.

### *Tracing the Past, Dreaming a Future*

In coping with traumatic losses, both symbolic and real, complexity mounts in a layering of demanding psychic tasks: Mourning the lost loved analyst, one's past as one knew it, one's former self, and one's lost future; overcoming melancholic submission to a persecutory object; risking new relationships—to others and to oneself—in order to contend with the pain of betrayal and to reconcile with the truth. Time must be dreamt into a web that can hold these intricate psychic maneuvers.

In the film *Imagining Argentina* (Hampton, 2003), the protagonist Carlos has prescient, waking dreams about the fates of lost loved ones who have (been) "disappeared," and with whom no goodbye has been possible. In providing a context in which to say goodbye, his dreams offer some closure to those who cannot move forward until they have looked back and found the truth of what has occurred: "People disappeared . . . they told us we must never look back, but we have to look back." Although painful, this process stands in stark contrast to the fate of those bereaved left in limbo, marching continuously around the plaza with only a flat image of their missing person on a placard.

There is actual death in these disappearances, but also symbolic death through tyranny and betrayal, as most of the missing have been taken away by corrupted political powers that should have been in place to protect the people. Instead, loved ones have been abducted, likely murdered, maybe imprisoned, leaving only a desperate hope that they are in hiding and will at some point return. The film emphasizes that dreaming and imagination constitute acts of freedom that can be neither stolen nor controlled, and that elegiac narratives about those who have been lost form a bridge to both the past and the hoped for future: "That's why your stories are so important . . . go on telling your stories," a friend tells Carlos.

The "art of mourning," Ogden (2000) states, centrally involves:

> [A] demand that we make on ourselves to create something—whether it be a memory, a dream, a story, a poem, a response to a poem—that begins to meet, to be equal to, the full complexity of our relationship to what has been lost and to the experience of loss itself. Paradoxically, in this process, we are enlivened.
>
> (p. 65)

Similarly, Kristeva (1989) writes that an actual or imaginary loss can summon up aesthetic activity that overcomes melancholy "while keeping its trace" (p. 128). As "a means of countervailing the loss of other and of meaning [creative work is] a means more powerful than any other . . . ['an essential recourse'] for it fills the same psychic need to confront separation, emptiness, death" (pp. 129–130). Carlos dreams a shared goodbye to the dead for many mourners, and in this way the truth is kept alive and the future a possibility.

## Saying Goodbye and Looking Back: Termination and Post-Termination Phases of Treatment

The process of writing this chapter has been an emotional journey. Looking back through the years, in compassionate resonance with others' experiences of traumatic loss, has brought a tender sympathy for my young, bereaved self—a perspective only possible through the lens of passing time and my own aging. Many feelings, known to me, resurfaced with surprising intensity. My gratitude to my analyst for living, and my appreciation for all that he gave me in his presence. My long quiescent grief at the loss of my father, accessed once again through empathic identification. And the sadness of what we all have to go through in contending with the erratic, unruly nature of time—impervious to our sufferings. All this has brought home to me in a deeper way—more than any of the many courses and papers on the subject of termination that I have been exposed to—the powerful emotional reverberations of the termination process,[7] as well as the significant detriment to the patient (and likely to the analyst as well) when aspects of this process are foreclosed.

Clinicians themselves often have a very complicated relationship to the termination phase of treatment: for one, our narcissistic vulnerabilities can lead to a diminishment in our own minds of our role in the patient's life. This erasure can join with the patient's defenses against saying a full, and deeply felt, goodbye. It is well-known that newer clinicians especially, not fully registering how profoundly significant they have been to the patient, tend to then underestimate the import of the termination process. In training, entire courses are given on what it is exactly that is supposed to take place. What may be less readily apparent is the degree to which individual clinicians may defend against a full goodbye with each patient, due to their own anxieties about grieving. The analyst's character defenses against loss, finitude, mortality may parallel the patient's wish to ward off emotional pain, and the analytic couple may collude in a goodbye that is less than powerful.

Not having the chance to say goodbye, such as is quite often overtly the case in loss of the analyst through death, illness, ethical violations, and other untoward circumstances, underscores in a most painful manner the distinctive value of the termination process—likely the singular time when a person can truly take the time to say goodbye, whether she wants to or not. Less obvious is the lost opportunity when termination is diluted by the analyst's avoidance. The analyst's participation is crucial in ensuring that this process of parting unfolds to its fullest extent, allowing for mortality to weave its way through the tapestry of termination. The goodbyes of life, the necessary and unnecessary, fated and ill-fated losses, have relevance, of course, for all of our clinical work, but gain urgency in termination (see Orgel, 2000). The analyst's unique role in this process is not only to aid the patient in grieving past losses, as well as the loss of the analytic relationship itself, but to give each patient an opportunity, not eagerly sought out, but invaluable, to "practice" with future losses, including that of one's own life.

I would now like to consider a bit further that ambiguous period of time that *follows* termination: an analytic "afterlife." It was not until some time after the termination of my analysis that I could be aware of the ongoing shift in my dreams of my dead father. This aspect of delay illustrates that the positive effects of analytic work are often not felt, fully registered, until many years after termination. Although I noted this change in my dreams to myself, I had never discussed it with my analyst (or anyone else) until writing this chapter. This alteration of my psyche had not yet taken full shape within my analysis, and I did not go back to my analyst at any point in the intervening 15 years to report this change. In a recent communication with my analyst, after my sending him an earlier draft of this chapter, I was surprised to find that he had felt concerned that he had not helped me enough with my father's death. I relate this exchange to the reader to underscore how often it is likely the case that the full impact (hopefully positive) of analytic work is not known to the patient until well after the termination, and that such change may *never* be known to (and only hoped for by) the analyst.

Furthermore, even though some years after my analysis, I was aware that my dreams of my father had shifted from what they had been for 17 years—and this felt very significant to me—all of what this meant for me was not entirely evident with the immediacy that it is now having written this chapter. Analytic changes registered post-treatment can easily be lost in the haze of passing time and busy lives, and may not emerge with clarity, possibly ever, or except in a fortuitous unfolding of events. This time lag is an interesting and curious aspect of our work that many chapters in this volume illuminate: the value of looking back over time.

Looking back, and continuing to make further meaning of past experiences, tends to be undervalued in our culture. We are a "forward-looking" society; "dwelling on the past" is discouraged. Grief, most especially, is typically expected to be cordoned off into a time-limited process—"take a week or two off" (cry at home), "look on the bright side," "get back into the swing of things," and so on, all function to say, "don't remind us that anything bad has happened to you or to anyone else." Resistance to acknowledgment of loss leads to a poverty of extended communal mourning in our culture, with little time at various later points to revisit loss. Cultural discomfort takes its shape in particular familial configurations as time passes: avoidance of speaking of the deceased, or only in brief, happy recollections, the subject quickly switched. Rarely do we sit with any group of people—one's family, friends, professional group—to revisit the *evolving* meanings of earlier losses that only become apparent over significant passage of years.

I think this contextual lack may be an aspect of why television shows on the anniversaries of famous deceased persons are so attentively watched, even though it may be painful. These programs constitute a rare chance to put a loss in perspective as subsequent decades unfold. But this time-lapse communal reflection is rarely done regarding personal losses; neither is it shared with people with whom one feels an emotional connection. Instead, focusing on a celebrity or national figure is easier—one step removed; everyone watches a two-dimensional screen on electronic equipment in their separate homes, often not even commenting to any other person who might happen to be sitting there as well. The result of this avoidance of personal retrospection is that we often fail to identify what an earlier experience means to us as the time of our life unfolds. This obscuring of slowly unfolding meaning can occur in relation to one's analysis as well. Moreover, when analysands do reflect on their post-analytic experience, the analyst's knowledge of such is usually quite curtailed.

Analysis is a strange situation where the analyst has to say goodbye to the patient before the full impact of the analytic work can be known by either member of the pair. The patient will ultimately have at least the possibility of accessing such an impact. The analyst goes on faith. Ideally, time has been taken to carefully say goodbye, but time continues to unfold the analytic process beyond the knowledge of the analyst. Here, time seems almost personified—a wise and kindly wizard (Gandalf?) who can see far further into the future than the mere mortals of the analytic dyad. This curious working of time has the analyst hoping that time will guide the patient toward a destination only pointed to at the time of the termination. Thus, in addition to termination being a rather unique event centering on the process of saying goodbye, it is evident that post-termination is an even stranger process in which we rely on time itself to take the analytic process further in its desired direction.

Too often, an analysand is forced to create a termination phase after losing the analyst due to the sudden termination of the analyst's life or, alternatively, to a "disappearance" in an ethical violation. But even in the best of circumstances, every patient will hopefully continue, whether in or outside of their conscious awareness, the analytic work after the formal termination of their analytic relationship (see Craige, 2002). In human development, parents hope that what they have given to their child at one stage will continue to have positive reverberations at later points. Unlike parents, clinicians typically do not actually witness later stages to ascertain that further growth has indeed unfolded (see Schachter et al., 1997). Continued growth is a future hoped for, but not necessarily ever known to have actually taken place. As patients go forward in time without us, we participate symbolically in a future unseen by us. This is immortality.

Clinicians are trained to think in terms of beginning, middle, and end phases of treatment. Classes are taught identifying the various anticipated elements of each phase. We do not as clearly delineate a post-termination phase. Yet, we recognize that the time needed to fully actualize therapeutic change usually surpasses the boundaries of the "in person" relationship. Psychoanalytic time is idiosyncratically crafted by each patient in order to continue needed psychic work that, possibly, can take place *only after* the goodbye. Those next months and years constitute a therapeutic phase in its own right—the post-termination phase of analysis (Craige, 2002)—a particular process that the patient is actually deprived of in circumstances in which the clinician does not ensure that a termination actually takes place. Saying goodbye is an experience that is necessary, valuable, and instructive, and likely always to be an ongoing process that rarely arrives at any definitive end. Life itself is a process of saying goodbye that takes time, the ongoing time of our lives. Time/life is always passing, and what passes—living, dying—we bid goodbye. Such is the tempo of our lives carrying us along in its inexorable rhythms.

## Conclusion: Time and Psychic Growth

Paraphrasing a line from the film, *The Curious Case of Benjamin Button* (Fincher, 2008): "While life must be lived forward, it can only be understood backward." I think that this observation may especially apply to one's analysis. A successful analysis is never over even after it is terminated. If successful, the work has led to the development of capacity of mind that will itself continue the analytic process—ongoing, alive, evolving—leading to further change in oneself and in relationship with one's analyst in the internalized dialogue that continues for a lifetime. This is what we are hoping for with our patients, and, most likely, our own experience in analysis influences what we have in mind for those with whom we work.

In a clarification regarding Freud's assertion of the timelessness of the unconscious, Hanly (2009) underscores that, although unconscious processes do not proceed in accord with linear time, unconscious contents can be modified by time and are not at all immune to change. Most certainly, the contents of the unconscious can be changed by the analytic process. We see the continuous, evolving nature of dream life where object loss and the passing of time can come to be represented. When healing can take place, past experiences that have been traumatic, and thus frozen in time, "can take their place in the temporal sequence of the individual's life" (p. 31).

Creative license with time, a period of bending time to meet one's internal needs, can allow one to move into the future in an alive way. A paradoxical relation exists in that ignoring, for the time being, the reality limits of time can actually allow one to gain the psychic momentum necessary to re-establish a healthy relationship to the ongoing passing of time. Healthy psychic omnipotence allows for us to play fast and loose with time. In the beauty of such improvisation, time has the potential to become music to our ears.

## Notes

1 Portions of this chapter have previously been published in Elise, D. (2011). Time to say goodbye: On time, trauma, and termination. *Psychoanalytic Inquiry*, *31*, 591–600. Reprinted with permission.
2 Clinicians tend to think of omnipotence in its pathological manifestation as a stopgap tactic aimed at foreclosing any experience of grief. Alternatively, I here employ Winnicott's thinking to conceptualize a transitional use of omnipotence that can facilitate mourning.
3 As Burka (2008) poignantly describes, also utilizing dream self-analysis, this "dropping out of sight" can encompass the loss inherent in an ethical violation.
4 See Green (2009) regarding "the bidirectional tendency of the psyche, which is well-illustrated by dreams" (p. 4).
5 See Elise (2012) for an extended clinical example of the subjective experience of exploded time.
6 It is interesting to note that the exquisitely painful longing for physical embrace is precluded with both the dead and with one's analyst.
7 Wrye (2012), like many, finds the label *termination* unfortunate: "This is the beginning of 'real life' after analysis, better described by words like threshold, transition, embarkation, launching, imparting, or birth" (p. 65).

## References

Birksted-Breen, D. (2003). Time and the après-coup. *International Journal of Psychoanalysis*, *84*, 1501–1515.
Bornholdt, I. (2009). The impact of the time experience on the psychoanalysis of children and adolescents. In L. Glocer Fiorini & J. Canestri (Eds.), *The experience of time: Psychoanalytic perspectives* (pp. 97–116). London: Karnac.

Burka, J. B. (2008). Psychic fallout from breach of confidentiality: A patient/analyst's perspective. *Contemporary Psychoanalysis, 44*, 177–198.

Craige, H. (2002). Mourning analysis: The post-termination phase. *Journal of the American Psychoanalytic Association, 50*, 507–550.

Deutsch, R. (2011). A voice lost, a voice found: After the death of the analyst. *Psychoanalytic Inquiry, 31*, 526–535.

Eickhoff, F. W. (2006) On *Nachträglichkeit*: The modernity of an old concept. *International Journal of Psychoanalysis, 87*, 1453–1469.

Elise, D. (2012). The danger in deception: Oedipal betrayal and the assault on Truth. *Journal of the American Psychoanalytic Association, 6*, 679–705.

Faimberg, H. (2005a). Après-coup. *International Journal of Psychoanalysis, 86*, 1–6.

Faimberg, H. (2005b). *The telescoping of generations: Listening to the narcissistic links between generations*. London: Routledge.

Fincher, D. (Dir.) (2008). *The curious case of Benjamin Button*. USA: Paramount.

Freud, S. (1917). Mourning and melancholia. In J. Strachey (Ed. & Trans.), *The standard edition of the complete psychological works of Sigmund Freud* (vol. 14, pp. 243–258). London: Hogarth Press.

Glocer Fiorini, L., & Canestri, J. (Eds.) (2009). *The experience of time: Psychoanalytic perspectives*. London: Karnac.

Green, A. (2002). *Time in psychoanalysis: Some contradictory aspects*. London: Free Associations Books.

Green, A. (2008). Freud's concept of temporality: Differences with current ideas. *International Journal of Psychoanalysis, 89*, 1029–1039.

Green, A. (2009). From the ignorance of time to the murder of time. From the murder of time to the misrecognition of temporality in psychoanalysis. In L. Glocer Fiorini & J. Canestri (Eds.), *The experience of time: Psychoanalytic perspectives* (pp. 1–19). London: Karnac.

Hampton, C. (2003). *Imagining Argentina*. USA: Arenas Entertainment.

Hanly, C. (2009). A problem with Freud's idea of the timelessness of the unconscious. In L. Glocer Fiorini & J. Canestri (Eds.), *The experience of time: Psychoanalytic perspectives* (pp. 21–34). London: Karnac.

Kristeva, J. (1989). *Black sun: Depression and melancholia*. New York: Columbia University Press.

Levine, H. (2009). Time and timelessness: Inscription and representation. *Journal of the American Psychoanalytic Association, 57*, 333–355.

Loewald, H. W. (1972). The experience of time. *Psychoanalytic Study of the Child, 27*, 401–410.

Ogden, T. (2000). Borges and the art of mourning. *Psychoanalytic Dialogues, 10*, 65–88.

Ogden, T. (2004). The analytic third: Implications for psychoanalytic theory and technique. *Psychoanalytic Quarterly, 73*, 167–195.

Orgel, S. (2000). Letting go: Some thoughts about termination. *Journal of the American Psychoanalytic Association, 48*, 719–738.

Parsons, M. (2009). Why did Orpheus look back? In L. Glocer Fiorini & J. Canestri (Eds.), *The experience of time: Psychoanalytic perspectives* (pp. 35–43). London: Karnac.

Perelberg, R. J. (2006). The controversial discussions and après-coup. *International Journal of Psychoanalysis, 87,* 1199–1220.

Perelberg, R. J. (2008). *Time, space and phantasy.* London: Karnac.

Perelberg, R. J. (2009). The first narrative, or in search of the dead father. In L. Glocer Fiorini & J. Canestri (Eds.), *The experience of time: Psychoanalytic perspectives* (pp. 133–153). London: Karnac.

Pine, S. (2006). Time and history in psychoanalysis. *International Journal of Psychoanalysis, 87,* 251–254.

Schachter, J., Martin, G. C., Gundle, M. J., & O'Neil, M. K. (1997). Clinical experience with psychoanalytic post-termination meetings. *International Journal of Psychoanalysis, 78,* 1183–1198.

Smith, H. (2009). Foreword: The past is present, isn't it? In L. Glocer Fiorini & J. Canestri (Eds.), *The experience of time: Psychoanalytic perspectives* (pp. xv–xxii). London: Karnac.

Sodre, I. (2005). "As I was walking down the stair, I saw a concept which wasn't there . . ." Or, *après coup*: A missing concept? *International Journal of Psychoanalysis, 86,* 7–10.

Thoma, H., & Cheshire, N. (1991). Freud's *Nachträglichkeit* and Strachey's "Deferred action": Trauma, constructions and the direction of causality. *International Review of Psychoanalysis, 18,* 407–427.

Winnicott, D. W. (1953). Transitional objects and transitional phenomena: A study of the first not me possession. *International Journal of Psychoanalysis, 34,* 89–97.

Winnicott, D. W. (1971). *Playing and reality.* London: Tavistock.

Winnicott, D. W. (1974). Fear of breakdown. *International Review of Psychoanalysis, 1,* 103–107.

Wrye, H. (2012). *Pulling up stakes: Stepping into freedom.* Los Angeles: Rare Bird Books.

# INDEX

abandonment 1, 4, 37, 42, 51, 81, 83; fear of 14, 23, 88
abusive relationships 63, 129
acoustic envelope 16
affect 1, 15, 16, 20, 22, 61, 115, 116, 118, 169
affect states 14
aggression 15, 17, 21–2, 27, 28, 106–7, 113, 184
Alexander the Great 93
aliveness 20, 25, 58–9, 174, 201, 211
analyst, second (following analyst death) 79–89
analyst death 3–4, 6, 32–3, 35–7, 40–1, 49–50, 58, 61–4, 79, 83–5, 87–8, 114, 116, 117, 120, 199, 204, 205–6, 208–10, 212
analytic dyad *see* analytic relationship
analytic identity 74–6, 105, 107, 114
analytic relationship 1–5, 15–16, 32, 34, 38, 41–3, 85, 113, 114, 117–18, 199, 202, 203, 210; and abandonment 1, 4–5; and betrayal 1, 4–5, 38, 98, 103–4, 109–10, 113, 119, 126, 129, 130, 133, 138, 204–6; collaborative 2, 36; containment in 2, 17, 198; and language 116; and opposing pairs 2; repair of 2; rupture of 2–5, 18, 64, 110, 112, 116; safety in 2; social construction in 15; support in 2
analytic third 201
anger 2, 21, 23, 27, 53, 62, 63, 68, 69, 86, 100, 103, 105, 109, 111, 117, 121, 129, 156
attachment 2, 24, 33, 39, 40, 62, 69, 114, 119, 140, 141, 165, 192, 194, 199, 203

bandwidth 16–17, 21
Baranger, Madeleine 19–20
Baranger, Willy 19–20
basic assumption groups 100, 155, 169–74
bereavement 14, 15, 18, 27, 28–9, 35, 40, 51, 69, 87, 202, 207
betrayal 14, 123, 133, 139, 206; and analytic relationship 1, 4–5, 38, 98, 103–4, 109–10, 113, 119, 126, 129, 130, 133, 138, 204–6
Bion, Wilfred 17, 20, 21, 100, 155, 164–5, 168–74
blind spots 16, 99, 102
Bloom, Amy 120
boundary violations 4, 14, 28, 101, 103, 104–6, 110–11, 114, 119–23, 131–4, 138, 141, 149, 155–6; collateral damage of 104, 105, 106, 109, 110; narcissistic 176; responses to 94, 109, 134, 165; sexual 7, 29, 93, 98, 102, 109–12, 122, 127–30, 141, 142, 149–52, 154, 160, 163–74, 176, 195 *see also* ethical violations
bridging analyst/function 35, 85, 115
bright spots 16, 22

cancer 64, 66, 80, 84, 183
candidate–analyst relationship 94, 123, 192
Chambers Brothers, the 199, 202
child–parent relationships 1, 14, 49, 51, 61–2, 88
clinical dyad *see* analytic relationship
closeness 82, 118, 131; fear of 14
co-construction 15
communication 27, 53, 57, 63, 85, 104, 116, 154, 160, 161; social

216

# INDEX

155, 156, 160; unconscious 14–17, 158
confidentiality 2, 96, 97–8, 107, 133–6, 147, 152, 154–8; breaches of 110, 126, 127, 129, 141
containment 17, 18, 29, 100, 101, 203
contempt 27, 86, 128, 129, 131, 189
countertransference 14, 15, 20, 21, 63, 82, 83, 88, 107, 115, 118, 148, 153; fractured 110, 120
creativity 2, 59, 83, 121, 169, 180, 181, 183, 186, 194, 198, 200, 203, 207, 211
cruelty 193
*Curious Case of Benjamin Button, The* 210

"dead mother" complex 14–15, 58, 62
deadness 20, 53, 58, 192, 194
death 4, 13, 15, 17–18, 22, 23, 28, 29, 34–5, 55, 58, 61–2, 66–7, 112–14, 171, 178, 199–203, 210, 212; of an analyst 3–4, 6, 32–3, 35–7, 40–1, 49–50, 58, 61–4, 79, 83–5, 87–8, 114, 116, 117, 120, 199, 204, 205, 208–10, 212; big 25; little 25; of a parent 49, 63; sudden 3, 4, 6, 13, 34–7, 42, 69, 109, 112, 183, 200; symbolic 199, 206, 208 *see also* suicide
death anxiety 130
*Death of a Salesman* 122
de-idealization 107, 110, 119, 123, 127, 130, 152, 154, 172, 174
denial 49, 57, 61, 64, 67, 74, 81, 88, 99, 112, 132, 151, 153, 178, 186, 189, 193, 205; manic 200, 202, 203
dependency groups 169
depression 49, 61, 68, 85
depressive position 28, 202–3
detachment 39–40, 118, 201; and mourning 40
dialogue 14, 16, 29, 33, 43, 116, 121, 122, 141, 150, 155, 173, 199, 200; internal 137, 141, 210
disclosure 14, 20, 99
dis-identification 106, 107, 109–10, 119, 127, 130
dissociation 17, 18, 25, 29, 51, 57, 59, 69, 177, 180, 184, 186, 191, 194
divorce 18, 171, 183
dreams 23–4, 32, 36–8, 40–3, 54–60, 63, 69, 112–13, 127, 130, 199–204, 208–10, 213

early care 1
ego 63, 130, 169, 185
elegy 199
empathic attunement 2
enactments 14, 24, 149, 150, 157, 193
envy 22, 153, 178
epigenetic model 75, 76
Erikson, Erik 66, 75, 76
ethical dilemmas 128, 131, 141
ethical violations 3, 4, 6–7, 93, 98, 104–5, 109, 111, 113, 117, 119, 126, 129, 131, 133–7, 139, 142, 149–51, 153, 155–61, 164, 173, 203, 204–5, 208, 210, 211n3; history of 148–9; silencing after 7, 134, 147–8, 150–2, 154–61 *see also* boundary violations
ethics committees 93–4, 97–9, 103, 128, 132–7, 139–40, 151, 154, 156, 176
exquisite corpse, fantasy of 22

fantasy 17, 20, 22, 82, 86, 98, 107, 114, 118, 120, 148, 151, 158, 159, 160, 166, 168, 179, 184, 192, 194
Ferenczi, Sándor 16, 20, 21, 105, 148, 193
field theory 19
fight–flight groups 100, 155, 169
Fliess, Wilhelm 177
Freud, Sigmund 15, 21, 38, 40, 63, 148, 158, 169, 172, 177, 179, 185, 192, 203, 213

Gestalt theory 19
ghosts 20, 62, 173, 200, 204
going-on-being 1, 3, 13
grief 4, 6, 25, 61, 75, 77, 98, 100, 103–4, 109–10, 112–13, 120, 121, 200, 207, 209, 211n2
grieving 23, 66, 70, 85, 113, 128, 203, 208
group contagion 101
group dynamics 95, 100, 102, 147, 155
group functioning 100, 102, 165, 168–9
growth 77, 113, 149, 165, 167, 210; personal 69, 77, 165; professional 69, 77, 165; psychic 130, 210–11
guilt 15, 23, 28, 42, 52, 56, 62, 64, 69, 71, 81, 105, 106, 120, 121, 131, 132, 158, 189

hate 2, 17, 18, 28, 100, 114, 118, 130, 131
holding environments 4, 100
holding in mind 17, 18–19

217

# INDEX

human development 203, 210
human spirit 123

idealization 114, 122, 148; of analyst 54, 97, 98, 104, 105, 113, 127, 152–3, 174, 190; of the institute 154; of psychoanalysis 164–5, 190
identification 19, 40, 63, 74, 97, 119, 167; projective 63; reactionary 177
illness 28, 34–6, 57, 62, 63, 71, 80, 120, 171, 183, 210; denial of 64; institutional 7, 176, 178, 180, 189, 191, 192, 195; terminal 50, 52, 62, 64, 66, 80, 84
*Imagining Argentina* 208–9
incest 158, 160, 166
incest taboo 151, 166–7
intergenerational transmission 23, 62, 102, 191, 192, 193
internalization 32, 39, 42, 109, 118, 119–20, 149, 192, 193, 212
intersubjectivity 2, 15, 32
*In Treatment* 154
intropression 193

Jung, C. G. 148

Kennedy, John F., assassination of 1
Khan, Masud 148, 149
Klein, Melanie 96, 101, 148
Kleinians 148

Lacan, Jacques 202
language 34, 38, 116
Levi, Primo 186–7
Lewin, Kurt 19
libido 39–40
life stage model 66, 75
Little Red Riding Hood, tale of 153
loss 3, 4, 6, 7, 14, 18, 20, 21, 34, 35, 39, 40, 113, 114, 115, 117, 120–1, 123, 158, 171, 199, 201, 202, 209–11; catastrophic 89, 117; of connectedness 2; early 15, 28, 51–2, 62; experiences of 14; of language 3; of love 14; of meaning 14; of a therapist 49, 58, 81, 88–9, 114–15, 117, 119, 210; traumatic 35, 36, 41, 58, 81, 82, 123, 202, 203, 208, 209 *see also* analyst death

love 19, 21, 28, 85, 114, 115, 118, 119, 121, 123, 130, 131; analytic 118; loss of 14

Marxists 187
masochism 107
meaning 1, 3, 16, 17, 21, 25, 26, 38, 66, 70, 72, 74, 77, 103, 116, 130, 136, 142, 163, 170, 184, 185, 204, 207, 211; loss of 14, 209; personal 5–6; symbolic 116
melancholia 39, 42, 205
memory 42, 59, 190, 203, 209
mental health 68
microbial model 101, 102, 110, 158, 160
Miller, Arthur 122
Monroe, Marilyn 66
moral complexity 127, 134, 136, 138, 141
moral development 129, 131–2, 137
moral enormity 134
moral pluralism 127, 138–9, 141
mourning 6, 14, 15, 17–18, 21, 23–25, 27, 33, 36, 39, 42, 61–2, 82, 85, 104, 114, 174, 203, 208, 213n2; and the analyst 13, 36, 77; art of 209; and detachment 40; and melancholia 39, 42, 205; romance of 22; unassimilable 15

narcissism 16, 121, 193, 194, 209
Newtown (Sandy Hook Elementary School massacre) 1
"nuclear fallout" metaphor 7, 109, 110, 122

objects 14, 17, 20, 27, 32, 39–40, 63, 107, 201; bad 101, 119, 120, 140, 206, 207; external 89; good 14, 101, 133, 206; infantile 118; internal 89, 119, 133, 205; persecutory 68, 206, 208; primary 89; splitting of 101
Oedipal dynamics 166, 180
Oedipus 179–80
Oklahoma City Federal building bombing 1
omnipotence 23, 24, 26, 149, 158, 159, 160, 169, 200–202, 213

pain 35, 57, 61, 64, 71, 119, 199, 207, 208

# INDEX

pairing groups 169
Palos, Elma 148
paranoid-schizoid position 96, 101, 132
parent–child relationships 14, 49, 51, 61–2, 88
parent–infant interactions 1, 61, 116, 205
Pearl Harbor 1
Person, Ethel 187
phenomenology 19
Philoctetes 13
Plath, Sylvia 66
postmodernism 132
posttraumatic stress 114
professional identity 74–6
projection 19, 66–7, 101, 103, 110, 191, 194
projective identification 63; collective 178
psyche, the 14, 28, 114, 142, 199, 203, 204, 210, 213n4; gaps in 14, 62
psychic omnipotence 202, 213
psychoanalysis 1–2, 13, 16, 50, 66, 74, 79–80, 85, 87, 93, 96–7, 108, 110, 113–14, 117, 118, 123, 128, 130, 132, 139, 148, 164–5, 172–4, 176–8, 185, 187, 190–4, 203, 211–12; Canadian 177, 180–2; communities of 79, 123, 149, 177, 180–1, 193; de-idealization of 172; ethics in 177, 180; faith in 7, 127, 165, 193; future of 178; governance of 176, 177, 180; hatred of 123, 178; history of 2, 148, 151, 166, 172–3, 176–7, 179, 192–3; idealization of 164, 171, 191; loss in 18; medicalization of 181; mourning in 18; mutual 105; post-termination phase of 211–12; public image of 110, 128, 191; resistance in 27, 28, 193–4; spirit of 195; termination of 7, 82–3, 89, 103–4, 107, 110–12, 115, 117, 118–20, 201, 202, 203, 205, 209–12, 213n7; and timelessness 114–15, 118, 204, 213; transmission of 177; and trauma 177 *see also* analytic identity; analytic relationship
psychoanalytic institutes 4, 7, 93–105, 109–12, 121–3, 127, 130, 132–3, 135, 138, 139–40, 147, 150–3, 155–8, 161, 163–74, 176, 178–83, 185–9, 191; culture of 134, 169, 187; group process in 155, 161; idealization of 154, 166; power structures at 149, 160, 182
psychoanalytic writing 3
psychosexual development 179–80
psychosocial crises 75
psychotherapy 49–62, 66, 69, 73, 74, 75, 77, 84, 107, 165, 185
*psychose blanche* 15, 26
purge mentality 9

"radioactive fallout" metaphor 178–9, 189, 190, 194
Real, the 204
reality testing 202, 206, 208
reverie 14, 16, 26
Righteous Brothers, the 204
Rolling Stones, the 199
rumor 4–5, 7, 32, 132, 134, 155, 164, 171, 182
rupture(s) 1–5, 18–19, 69, 112, 116, 118, 165, 180, 199; literature on 3–4; types of 5; traumatic 1–3, 6–7, 118, 177, 178, 192, 193

sadism 26
*Saving Private Ryan* 115
saying goodbye 7, 199–203, 205–6, 208–10, 212
seduction theory 177
self 15, 166; and loss 40; loss of 51; and other 15; sense of 1, 3–4
self-blame 71
self-care 16–17
self-harm 74
self-states 1, 114; destabilization of 1
separation anxiety 88
Sexton, Anne 66
shame 2, 6, 15, 49, 53, 56, 57, 59–60, 64, 67, 69, 71, 75, 76, 106, 110, 158, 189, 193
social fabric 1, 139
Social Intuitionist Model 140
Spielrein, Sabina 148
splitting 1, 22, 97, 101, 103, 131, 132, 153, 177, 189, 194
subjectivity 6, 114, 135; analyst's 14, 19; ruptured 6, 19
suicidality 51, 71, 73–4
suicide 66, 72; of a patient 3, 6, 18, 34, 66–77

superego 69, 71, 185
symbolic thinking 130, 138

Tausk, Victor 66
temporality 7, 20, 114–15, 202, 204–5, 207
thirdness 28, 203; dead 193
time 7, 199–204, 206–11, 213; external 7; internal 7; psychic 114–15, 200, 207; psychoanalytic 212
training (of) analysts 7, 67–8, 74–5, 76, 84, 93–5, 97, 100, 101–4, 115, 121–2, 131, 149–53, 157–9, 163, 165–8, 176, 177, 180–93, 210
transference 15, 20, 21, 23, 32, 35, 57, 59, 63, 85, 87, 88, 106, 114, 117, 118, 148, 166, 178–9, 194; erotic 105, 107, 153; fractured 110, 120; hostile 107; idealizing 113; negative 81, 86, 103, 113, 119; parental 61; positive 166, 167
transitional phenomena 202
trauma(s) 1, 7, 50, 57, 62, 63–4, 66, 76, 81, 93, 101, 116, 128, 138, 158, 174, 177, 191, 192, 206; early 14, 82; collective 93, 123, 149, 180; environmental 1; group 122, 170; history of 4–5; idealizing 97; metabolization of 3, 5, 122; institutional 7; organizational 7, 123; processing of 13; and psychoanalysis 177; separation 61; systemic 173; thinking about 3; unconscious registration of 14; writing about 129–30
traumatic events 1, 2, 158, 165, 207
"truthiness" 140

unconscious 4, 20, 25, 34, 69, 130, 140, 164–5, 178, 179, 213

value systems 139–40
voice 4, 6, 34–5, 41, 42–3, 117, 161, 199; analytic 117; authorial 4, 43; dream 36, 42

West, Ellen 66
Winnicott, D. W. 1, 3, 100, 149, 178, 201–202, 213n2
withdrawal 49, 55, 61, 75
witnessing 17, 18, 21, 23, 136–7, 141
work groups 100, 155, 159, 168–70, 172, 173–4
World Trade Center 1
writer–reader relationship 6